MW01252924

John Maynard Keynes

John Maynard Keynes

Free Trader or Protectionist?

Joseph R. Cammarosano

LEXINGTON BOOKS
Lanham • Boulder • New York • Toronto • Plymouth, UK

Published by Lexington Books
A wholly owned subsidary of Rowman & Littlefield
4501 Forbes Boulevard, Suite 200, Lanham, Maryland 20706
www.rowman.com

10 Thornbury Road, Plymouth PL6 7PP, United Kingdom

British Library Cataloguing in Publication Information Available

Library of Congress Cataloging-in-Publication Data

Cammarosano, Joseph R.
John Maynard Keynes : free trader or protectionist? / Joseph R. Cammarosano.
pages cm
Includes bibliographical references and index.
ISBN 978-0-7391-8951-1 (cloth : alk. paper) -- ISBN 978-0-7391-8952-8 (electronic)
1. Keynes, John Maynard, 1883-1946. 2. Keynesian economics. 3. Free trade. 4. Protectionism. I. Title.
HB99.7.C34 2014
330.15'6--dc23
2013037878

Printed in the United States of America

To my children, Gene, Nancy, and Joseph

Contents

Acknowledgments

This book is the outcome of a research proposal suggested to me many years ago by my friend and mentor, the late Charles M. Walsh. The question he posed was related to the commercial policy views of John Maynard Keynes: Was he a free trader or a protectionist? Over the years, I have not chanced upon a satisfactory answer to Professor Walsh's query and so I decided to publish the results of my own research on the subject. Hopefully, I have finally answered Charlie's question.

In all aspects of life, one does not go it alone. Assistance comes from all quarters; some directly and some indirectly; some sooner and some later, and that has been my experience as well. I have benefited greatly from the help I have received from colleagues in higher education and in the public sector as well. But my greatest debt is to Fordham University. My association with it and the Jesuits extends well beyond the year of my retirement. Indeed, were it not for its president, the Rev. Joseph M. McShane, S. J. who encouraged me not to set aside the chalk and eraser, but to continue to teach as an adjunct professor and to remain active in the field, this work would not have seen the light of day. For his warm encouragement and kind support I am profoundly grateful.

For the rest, I would like to express my appreciation to the staff of Lexington Books, especially Joseph Parry, Scott Lutsky, and Meaghan White. Notwithstanding the tight deadlines they imposed upon me, they were extremely generous with their assistance and extremely proficient in shepherding this publication from start to finish. I also want to thank Robert Swanson for indexing the book, Marc Anderson of the Cambridge University Press who guided me through the labyrinth of copyright law, and the Royal Economic Society for permission to quote Keynes' work.

Introduction

Over the course of his life, John M. Keynes often abandoned ideas he had previously developed and at times assumed positions that were diametrically opposed to his earlier thought. This inconsistency, if it can be called that, is nowhere more evident than in his thinking in the field of international economics, where he alternated between free trade and protectionism.[1]

From the early years of his career, during which he first served as a teaching fellow at Cambridge and later as a member of the Indian Commission on Currency and Finance, to the early post–World War I period Keynes subscribed to views consistent with those of free traders in the classical tradition. After that time, his attitude toward the efficacy of free trade started to change in sympathy, no doubt, with Great Britain's declining economic fortunes. Keynes's gradual change of views during the twenties culminated in an open break with the tenets of free trade in the spring of 1931 when he came out in favor of protection for Great Britain. Following the British Treasury's abandonment of the gold standard in September, 1931, Keynes modified somewhat his views respecting the need for the protection of British industry.[2] His feeling was that the advantage to be gained by British manufacturers from a devalued pound now made the need for restricted trade much less urgent. In fact, under these circumstances restricted trade would be disadvantageous for Great Britain, since she could gain more from a liberal than from a restricted commercial policy. Nonetheless, his new position on this issue did not reinstate him as a free trader, for during the remainder of the 1930s he largely espoused a policy of national autarky.[3] It was not until he began to work on his Clearing Union Proposals in late 1941 that Keynes gave any indication of moderating his views on the question of free trade and international cooperation.[4] But despite this change of attitude, it is questionable whether Keynes did completely revert to the free trade doctrine of the classical School or whether his altered position still left him outside the pale of orthodoxy.

In view of the variable and uncertain character of Keynes's thinking on this question of free versus restricted trade, it is difficult to find agreement as to what his ultimate position was on this issue. For example, Professor Lawrence R. Klein believes that Keynes's break with classical thinking on free trade was of short duration. He maintains that although Keynes broke with the free traders in 1931, he "made a complete turn-about on the question of free trade" in 1933 with his publication of *The Means to Prosperity*, wherein he suggests a simultaneous expansion of trade through the abolition of trade restrictions.[5] Professor Seymour Harris is also of the conviction that Keynes's break with free trade was short-lived. He contends that Keynes broke with the protectionists following Great Britain's abandonment of the gold standard and the attending devaluation of the pound sterling in September of 1931.[6]

There is another body of professional opinion that feels that although Keynes did return to the free trade camp, he did not do so until a much later date. Professor Alvin H. Hansen, one of the foremost Keynesians in this country, contends that Keynes had a change of heart respecting free trade sometime toward the end of 1941.[7] Others, among whom may be numbered Professor Roy F. Harrod, claim that Keynes reverted to a position of free trade only toward the close of his life.[8]

There is a third school of thought that maintains that Keynes was never able to resolve the conflict between free trade and protectionism. This is the view of A. E. Robinson, one of Keynes's students at Cambridge and later coeditor of the *Economic Journal*.[9] The *London Economist*, long an advocate of free trade, similarly questions whether Keynes effectively resolved this issue. In its estimate, Keynes, through the greater part of his career, had tried to insulate the domestic economy from the disturbances of the outer world, and yet, as chief architect of the Bretton Woods System, accepted many provisions from the Americans that contradicted his earlier position. His untimely death, reported the *London Economist*, "caught him in one of his major inconsistencies" and deprived him of the opportunity to resolve his difficulty one way or another.[10]

A review of this and other conflicting evidence leaves the student of the New Economics without a satisfactory explanation of Keynes's ultimate position on this important question of free versus restricted foreign trade. Left unanswered by the commentaries on Keynes's contributions to international economics are such questions as whether Keynes, in modifying his protectionist position of the late 1920s and 1930s, did, in fact, revert unequivocally to the principles of free trade toward the end of his life or whether he failed to completely close the breach. In addition, what effect did the *General Theory of Employment, Interest and Money*, his work at Bretton Woods, and his efforts on behalf of the Anglo-American Loan have on his attitude toward commercial policy?

The contention of this work is that after he abandoned the tenets of classical free trade in the early 1930s, Keynes never again returned to them, as such. Instead, he subscribed to those principles of international trade and finance, developed by him from the *Tract on Monetary Reform* to the *General Theory of Employment, Interest and Money*, which placed internal economic considerations above those of a purely external character.

Perhaps one of the reasons why there has been so much confusion in interpreting Keynes's commercial policy views is that attempts to resolve this question have been based largely on whether he favored or was opposed to tariffs. This, though, is not a proper criterion. If this were, indeed, the norm for judging Keynes's attitude toward commercial policy, he would, of necessity, have to be classified as a free trader, for he openly favored tariffs only a few months in 1931.

The fact that Keynes may not have consistently favored the imposition of tariffs does not of itself make him a member of the classical free trade school, since many of the objectives that can be realized through this medium can be obtained just as effectively through other protective devices such as regulation of foreign investment, exchange control, quotas, manipulation of foreign exchange rates, exhortations to buy at home, and similar measures.

The real issue is far more subtle than whether Keynes favored the imposition of tariff barriers on the flow of international trade. The problem relates not so much to Keynes's attitude toward tariff restrictions as it does to the broader question of whether his economic philosophy was oriented toward national or international considerations. Only by first resolving this question will it be possible to determine whether Keynes was, in the final analysis, an orthodox free trader or something less than that.

An important first clue to this question may be gained by examining Keynes's attitude toward the so called automatic international monetary adjustments. The difficulty confronting Keynes in the international sphere was not unlike the one he had to face in the domestic sector. There the question for him was whether the most intimate relations of our economic system should be left to the operation of automatic forces or whether they should be subjected to some form of conscious guidance and control. An examination of any of Keynes's major works, be it *Indian Currency and Finance* or the *General Theory of Employment, Interest and Money*, reveals unmistakably that he was in favor of the latter course of action. According to A. L. Rowse, the famed British historian, Keynes was "no more sympathetic to the old orthodoxy that prevailed in external economic policy than to that which obtained in internal policy."[11]

By contrast, the free traders of the classical and neo-classical schools of economic thought were more inclined to leave the adjustments required for the maintenance or restoration of external equilibrium to so-called automatic forces such as gold flows and fluctuations in domestic prices and incomes. Unfortunately, equilibrium through these means often had to be achieved through deflation and widespread unemployment at home. This, in Keynes's judgment, was much too high a price for any nation to pay.

Keynes rejected reliance on the working of automatic forces for the maintenance of equilibrium in a nation's international balance of payments, because they often interfered with the promotion of domestic economic objectives. In fact, they often depended for their effectiveness on the disruption of domestic economic well-being. In place of these automatic devices, Keynes recommended the employment of measures that would consciously bring about the necessary correction in the external sector while exerting only a minimal impact on the internal sector of the economy. Thus, in place of an automatic international gold standard of the type that prevailed prior to World War I, Keynes would substitute a managed gold standard; instead of inflating and deflating the currency and credit system in accordance with the requirements of the gold flows, he would establish an autonomous monetary policy geared to the internal needs of the economy, and in place of a fixed foreign exchange rate and a fluctuating domestic price level, he favored a variable exchange rate and a stable domestic price level.

Another consideration that helps to establish Keynes's primary concern with domestic problems and thus further distinguishes him from the more internationally minded economists of the classical school was his preoccupation with the problem of unemployment.

In Keynes's view, a condition of full employment is the exception rather than the rule, for the economy has a tendency to equilibrate at a level of less than full employment. Because of the economy's tendency to settle at a level less than full employment, Keynes sought measures to raise the level of consumption and particularly the volume of investment in order to sustain aggregate demand at a high level. To realize these objectives he was not averse to pursuing policies that would subordinate external considerations to those of a purely domestic character.

The classicists and their followers, on the other hand, started with the assumption that full employment already exists; hence, their principal concern was with the optimum allocation and most efficient use of economic resources. Their thinking was largely structured in terms of the opportunity cost analysis that naturally presages the validity of the comparative cost argument. In the classical system, free and untrammeled international trade is the logical answer to the quest for the optimum allocation and maximum efficiency of the productive factors. Thus, by virtue of the objectives that they sought, the classical economists were naturally inclined toward a system of free trade.

Of course, Keynes was keenly aware of the advantages to be derived from a system of multilateral free trade when combined with the full utilization of manpower and resources. Under an ideal condition of full employment and free trade among nations, real wages and other factor returns would be maximized, since labor and capital productivity would everywhere be at their highest levels. In circumstances such as these, each country would produce those items in which it enjoyed the greatest comparative advantage and exchange them with other countries for commodities in which they, in turn, enjoyed the highest comparative advantages of free trade, as the following passage appearing in his chapter on Mercantilism in the *General Theory of Employment, Interest and Money* will attest:

> If nations can learn to provide themselves with full employment by their domestic policy, there need be no important economic forces calculated to set the interest of one country against that of its neighbors.
>
> International trade would cease to be what it is, namely, a desperate expedient to maintain employment at home by forcing sales on foreign markets and restricting purchases, which, if successful, will merely shift the problem of unemployment to the neighbor which is worsted in the struggle, but a willing and unimpeded exchange of goods and services in conditions of mutual advantage. [12]

If the self-restorative powers of the modern economy are sufficiently strong to guarantee a reasonably high level of employment and income, surely the arguments in favor of free trade cannot be refuted. However, if the international specialization of labor is carried on between economies that are experiencing less than full employment of their manpower and resources, then it is not necessarily true that these nations will be better off in pursuing policies aimed at increasing productivity and expanding trade, for what is gained through the international division of labor may be more than offset by the displacement of workers in the home market. [13] A second argument that may be advanced against the free trade doctrine in conditions of depressed activity is that a liberal commercial policy and efforts to promote full employment—for example, an easy monetary policy—may in such circumstance be incompatible. [14] Thus, just as the classicists' assumption of full employment caused Keynes to differ with them on matters of theory and domestic economic policy, it was this same postulate that caused him to take exception with their doctrine of free trade.

Essentially, the problem for all economists is to seek domestic measures that do not restrain international cooperation and policies that do not frustrate the attainment of full employment at home. [15] Ideally, each country should enjoy simultaneously the high productivity of labor and capital from free trade and the maximum output and employment from the full utilization of its productive capacity. [16] Unfortunately, it is not always possible for a nation to realize both of these advantages concurrently, because of the conflict that often emerges between its membership in an open free trade system and its promotion of full employment policies. Professor Gottfried Haberler describes this difficulty in the following terms:

> One of the most challenging tasks of rational economic policy and one of the most intriguing and controversial problems to economic science is how to avoid or eliminate conflicts between domestic prosperity and maximum gain from international trade and international division of labor. Maximization of national output and income depends on both full employment of resources at home and full utilization of the opportunities of international trade.
>
> Conflicts between the two conditions in the sphere of monetary and fiscal policy are quite frequent, because measures appropriate for maintaining full employment are not always conductive to promoting stability of foreign exchange and of international trade and vice versa. These conflicts are rarely, if ever, irreconcilable, but there is no simple formula or easy automatic device which would permit satisfactory conciliation in every single case. [17]

The difference between Keynes and the classical free traders came down to this: should a conflict develop between the promotion of full employment and the furtherance of foreign trade, Keynes would support the former objective, whereas for the classical economists the possibility of such a conflict was not a serious consideration, since they started with the premise that full employment already existed. Unlike the classicists, who were concerned with the development of principles applicable to an open or world economic system, Keynes, during much of his career, was engrossed with the formulation of principles for a closed economic system.[18] Owing to his deep concern with the problem of unemployment, Keynes was more inclined to placing the needs of the domestic economy above purely external considerations. Add to this the fact that he was primarily a Briton who was keenly aware of his country's post–World War I needs, and one has the essential reasons why Keynes could not be classified as a free trader in the tradition of the classical school.

The fact that Keynes was at all times and above all else a Briton had a very significant impact on his foreign trade views. Although he was intensely concerned with the inter-war problems as they affected the community of nations, he was particularly concerned with the way in which they influenced Great Britain.[19] Keynes's writings were always concerned with the formulation of policies to meet the changing status of English economic life.[20] His theories were fundamentally the product of the post–World War I depressions, especially the long period of deflation in Great Britain during the 1920s and the worldwide depression of the 1930s that was in a way superimposed on the continuing British depression.[21]

In tracing the development of Keynes's thought during this period, it is well to bear in mind that the Great Britain that emerged from World War I was a seriously weakened nation. British foreign trade and investment were decreasing in importance. London was steadily losing her international supremacy. Taxes were heavy. British industry was plagued by obsolescence. The formerly well-disciplined English laborers were now well organized; British costs relative to the rest of the world were high. Tastes and technology were rapidly changing. Many of Britain's old customers were now able to produce goods, for example, textiles, formerly produced by her. In addition to these ominous developments, Great Britain had to face in her foreign markets the increasing competition of the United States, which was rapidly becoming the dominant world power in wealth and productive capacity.[22]

Professor Schumpeter aptly summarizes the British post–World War I situation when he says:

> She (Great Britain) had not emerged from the war of the Napoleonic era. She had emerged impoverished; she had lost many of her opportunities for the moment and some of them for good. Not only this, but her social fabric had been weakened and had become rigid. Her taxes and wage rates were incompatible with vigorous development, yet there was nothing that could be done about it.[23]

Keynes was conscious of these new conditions. He was especially aware of the impact these changes had on Britain's external affairs. His desire to cope with these changes forced him to alter his position, in consequence of which he was accused of inconsistency. However, one should not make the mistake of identifying Keynes's practical inconsistency, if such it should be called, with an inconsistency of the Keynesian mind.[24]

That Keynes was inconsistent in certain areas of thought cannot be denied, but this was only because the views of Keynes the economist reflected those of Keynes the administrator, the adviser, the business man, the statesman, and the diplomat,[25] and if ideas previously developed by him were unable to stand the test of practicability, he was quick to discard them and set to thinking along different channels. Keynes was essentially practical and when convinced that the best solution to a problem was unattainable, he was willing to seek another. He had no vested interest in his own past thoughts and never permitted them to impede further intellectual progress.[26]

For some, consistency involves pressing the same solution through thick and thin just because it is the best solution. Whether there is any hope of its being adopted does not enter into their calculations. To these people, going over to a less satisfactory, though more practical solution, seems to constitute an inconsistency. But as far as Keynes was concerned, "no one ever better demonstrated that a foolish consistency is the hobgoblin of little minds."[27]

Notwithstanding Keynes's alleged inconsistency in the realm of ideas, he was completely consistent when it came to advancing the best interests of his country. That Keynes's economic thinking was always colored by British considerations may be evidenced by the following excerpt of an article written by the Canadian economist, W. A. Mackintosh:

> The most steadfast of his roots was his passionate belief in and concern for England. This is often not explicit in his writings but is imbedded in the fabric and is an essential clue to the pattern. From the *Economic Consequences of the Peace* to his last article in the *Economic Journal*, whether he was concerned with the dismemberment of Europe, the flexibility of the exchange rates, the relation between investment and income or buffer stocks of food and raw materials, the pattern of his problem was English. [28]

The essentially British character of Keynes's thinking may be further corroborated by Schumpeter's revealing testimony.

> It cannot be emphasized too strongly that Keynes's advice was in the first instance always English advice, born of English problems even where addressed to other nations. Barring some of his artistic tastes, he was surprisingly insular, even in philosophy, but nowhere so much as in economics. And he was fervently patriotic of a patriotism which was indeed quite untinged by vulgarity but was so genuine as to be subconscious and therefore all the more powerful to impart a bias to his thought and to exclude full understanding of foreign viewpoints, conditions, interests, and especially creeds. Like the old free traders, he always exalted what was at any moment truth and wisdom for England into truth and wisdom for all times and places. [29]

Our task in the chapters that follow will be to survey Keynes's writings on international economics from his earliest pronouncements on the gold standard before the outbreak of World War I to his final contributions to the Bretton Woods Agreements and to the negotiations attending the Anglo-American Loan during and shortly after World War II. In doing so, we shall try to demonstrate that Keynes was primarily concerned with the attainment of domestic well being—high levels of employment and stable prices—and because of the high priority he assigned to this objective could not accept unequivocally and without qualification the traditional tenets of free trade. It all depended on whether or not the home economy was at full employment. Trade policy for him became the handmaiden of full employment.

This book is organized into four parts. Part I consists of a review and appraisal of Keynes's opposition to the operation of the traditional international gold standard. In this section, we shall attempt to show that the reason Keynes was opposed to this standard is that in order to restore balance in a nation's foreign accounts it often necessitated adjustments in the internal sector that worked at cross purposes with the promotion of full employment and stable prices. But as was noted earlier, Keynes was not disposed to having purely external considerations supersede or interfere with the pursuit of domestic policies aimed at achieving high employment and stable prices; hence, his opposition to the orthodox gold standard. Part II outlines Keynes's views on the question of free trade versus protection from the very beginning of his professional career to the early 1930s. Part III deals with Keynes's foreign trade convictions as expressed during the period of his *General Theory of Employment, Interest and Money*. The fourth and concluding section examines Keynes's foreign trade position during World War II when he was largely preoccupied with the formulation of his Clearing Union Proposal, work at Bretton Woods, and with the negotiations for the Anglo-American Loan. This section also provides a concluding chapter evaluating Keynes's ultimate position on the issue of free versus restricted trade, a question that continues to be a major preoccupation of nations in our time.

NOTES

1. R. Hinshaw, "Keynesian Commercial Policy," in *The New Economics*, ed. S. Harris (New York: Alfred A. Knopf, 1947), 315.

2. J. M. Keynes, "Proposals for a Revenue Tariff," *The New Statesman and Nation* 1, no. 2 (March 7, 1931): 53–54.

3. J. M. Keynes, "National Self-Sufficiency I," *The New Statesman and Nation* 6, no. 124 (July 8, 1933): 65–67.

4. R. F. Harrod, *The Life of John Maynard Keynes* (New York: Harcourt, Brace, 1951), 525–26.

5. L. R. Klein, *The Keynesian Revolution* (New York: Macmillan, 1947), 41–42.

6. S. Harris, "International Economic Relations," *The New Economics*, ed. S. Harris (New York: Alfred Knopf, 1947), 245.

7. A. H. Hansen, *A Guide to Keynes* (New York: McGraw-Hill, 1954), 225–27.

8. Harrod, *The Life of John Maynard Keynes*, 469–70, 531, and 609–10.

9. A. E. Robinson, "John M. Keynes," *Economic Journal* 57, no. 225 (March 1947): 46.

10. "John M. Keynes," the *London Economist* 155, no. 5492 (April 87, 1946): 658.

11. J. M. Keynes, the *General Theory of Employment, Interest and Money* (New York: Harcourt, Brace, 1935), 382–83.

12. N. S. Buchanan, *International Investment and Domestic Welfare* (New York: Henry Holt, 1945), 150. Also, see D. Dillard, *The Economics of John M. Keynes* (New York, Prentice-Hall, 1948), 283.

13. J. E. Meade, *Public Works in Their International Aspect* (London: The New Fabian Research Bureau, 1933), 17–20.

14. J. B. Condliffe, "Exchange Stabilization and International Trade," *The Review of Economic Statistics* 26, no. 4 (November 1944): 166.

15. T. Scitovszky, "Trade of Nations—A Review," *Journal of Political Economy* 55, no. 5 (October 1947): 475.

16. G. Haberler, "Comments on National Central Banking and the International Economy," n.d., p. 82.

17. J. H. Williams, *Postwar Monetary Plans* (Oxford: Basil Blackwell, 1949), 160.

18. J. H. Williams, "An Appraisal of Keynesian Economics," *American Economic Review* 38, no. 2 (May 1948): 275.

19. B. Banerji, *A Guide to the Study of Keynesian Economics* (Calcutta: N. N. Dey, 1951), 62.

20. C. B. Hoover, "Keynes and the Economic System," *The Journal of Political Economy* 56, no. 5 (October 1948).

21. G. A. Elliott, "The Significance of the *General Theory of Employment, Interest and Money*," *Canadian Journal of Economics and Political Science* 13, no. 3 (August 1947): 372.

22. J. A. Schumpeter, *Ten Great Economists from Marx to Keynes* (New York: Oxford University. Press, 1981), 724.

23. J. A. Schumpeter, *Ten Great Economists from Marx to Keynes* (New York: Oxford University Press, 1951), 274.

24. Harrod, *The Life of John Maynard Keynes*, 470.

25. "The Law and the Prophet," the *London Economist* 155, no. 5492 (November 27, 1948): 879.

26. "John M. Keynes," the *London Economist*, 658.

27. Harrod, *The Life of John Maynard Keynes*, 469.

28. W. A. Mackintosh, "Keynes as a Public Servant," *Canadian Journal of Economics and Political Science* 13, no. 3 (August 1947): 380.

29. Schumpeter, *Ten Great Economists from Marx to Keynes*, 274.

The Priority of Internal over External Considerations as evidenced by Keynes's Opposition to the Pre–World War I International Gold Standard

Part I deals with Keynes's early and long held view that nations, particularly Great Britain, should be free to pursue their own best economic interests and not be fettered by considerations of an external character such as trade imbalances, the movement of speculative capital, and the lack of foreign exchange flexibility. Although Keynes's priority of domestic over external economic matters was not immediately evidenced by his views on foreign trade policy, as such, it was much more discernible in his attitude toward the traditional international gold standard

To place its currency arrangements on the international gold standard meant that a country would have to surrender much of its autonomy in monetary policy and be forced to adopt policies—for example, the need to reduce costs, prices, the level of employment, and income—that were not promotive of its own best domestic interests. Membership in an international gold standard system meant that all members would have to maintain the same level of relative prices and the same rate of interest, even if domestic conditions required otherwise. In effect, a nation would have to move in lock step with all other members on the same standard.

In the next three chapters, Keynes's reasons will be developed for his opposition to the standard. Keynes felt that gold should not be allowed to circulate from hand to hand, but should instead be held as a reserve by the monetary authority to be used for balance of payment requirements. Given a larger reserve, a nation would have a longer period of time to place its affairs in order and thereby forestall the need for more immediate remedial action. Other reasons for his opposition to the standard included the fixity of exchange rates, the loss of control over a country's rate of interest, the adjustment of trade imbalances through deflationary measures, and the unwanted transmission of fluctuations from one country to another.

Also noteworthy was his opposition to Britain's return in 1925 to the international gold standard, which had been suspended during the war, at the pound's pre-war parity. Keynes felt that in order to justify such an overvaluation, Britain would have to undergo a serious reduction of costs, prices, and the level of employment. Although such a return to sterling's pre-war value may have been beneficial to London's international financial standing, Keynes felt that it would have imposed much too high a price on the general economy. For that reason, very notably, he took exception with Mr. Winston Churchill, the then Lord of the Exchequer, for prematurely returning the pound to its pre-war standing in his *The Economic Consequences of Mr. Churchill*.

In time, it was this same concern and the priority of internal over external needs in monetary matters that caused Keynes in the late 1920s and early 1930s to part company with the tenets of orthodox free trade.

Chapter One

Keynes's Attack on the International Gold Standard

Keynes's attitude toward the international gold standard provides an important first clue to his economic philosophy. His views on the gold standard indicate, even at the outset of his career, the priority he assigned to domestic over international considerations and his preference for the conscious management of our economic affairs. Keynes was opposed to leaving international monetary arrangements to the blind operation of so called free or automatic forces, because they often relegated domestic considerations to a subordinate position. In their place he suggested a policy of monetary management. Keynes's concern for domestic economic well-being and his preference for conscious management of our economic affairs later became evident in his thinking on the issue of free versus restricted foreign trade and reached a climax in his the *General Theory of Employment, Interest and Money* (*General Theory*), wherein he favored monetary and fiscal policies purposely designed for the attainment of full employment.

Basically, Keynes took exception with the international gold standard, because it tended to circumscribe a nation's autonomy in dealing with its own domestic problems and because it often transmitted disturbances from other countries to the home economy in the form of unstable currency and credit, price fluctuations, and unemployment.

A review of Keynes's early pre-World War I writings reveals that his rejection of the gold coin standard, especially for debtor countries such as India, and his recommendation of a managed gold exchange standard in its place were largely rooted in his belief that each nation should enjoy as a high a degree of independence as possible over its monetary affairs. Keynes's preference for monetary management is further evidenced in his pronouncements immediately after World War I when he urged nations to forego attempts to return to a monetary system wherein gold coin freely circulated and to institute, instead, a gold bullion standard—a system wherein local currency could be exchanged for gold only on a limited basis. During the 1920s, Keynes continued his fight against the traditional gold standard on grounds that such a monetary system did not always permit the central monetary authority to pursue money and credit policies suited to its internal needs, but instead compelled it to implement policies that conformed to the average behavior of all the other nations in the system.

In addition to causing a nation to surrender discretion over its own economic requirements, Keynes pointed out that the gold standard often left a nation vulnerable to wide fluctuations in its price level and volume of employment. This, too, was a recurrent theme in his writings of the 1920s and was especially evident in his opposition to Great Britain's return to the gold standard at the pre-war parity of exchange in 1925.

In this and in the next chapter, Keynes's opposition to the pre–World War I gold standard will be more fully explored, following which a brief account will be given of the type of monetary system Keynes thought the nations of the world, particularly Great Britain, should have implemented in the period after World War I. As these issues are developed, the reader will become increasingly aware of Keynes's belief that each nation should have the right to economic self-determination, especially in monetary matters, and of his preference for the management of our economic affairs over their determination by so called automatic or free market forces. Subsequently, it will be shown that it was this same high priority that Keynes attached to the right of each nation to exercise mastery over its own economy and to pursue policies consistent with the promotion of its best economic interests that caused him to condition his views on the unequivocal acceptance of international free trade.

One of the earliest objections raised by Keynes against the international gold standard is that it circumscribed the ability of nations, especially the financially weaker ones, to cope with gold flows and the attending disruption of their exchange rates.

In his first major work, *Indian Currency and Finance*,[1] Keynes noted that while the gold coin standard, that is, one in which gold coin circulates freely within the home economy and is freely convertible into domestic paper currency as well as into foreign exchange, worked reasonably well in a creditor country such as Great Britain, it did not function equally well in a debtor nation such as India. Keynes's contention was that variations in the bank rate, on which the gold standard depends for the maintenance of equilibrium in a nation's foreign accounts, were not equally effective in a debtor as in a creditor country. In a creditor country, an increase in the bank rate may be quite effective in restoring balance in its foreign accounts, since this will serve to reduce the volume of its short term foreign loans and thus help to redress the imbalance. In a debtor country, on the other hand, the solution is not quite so simple. It is already a borrower in the international market and its attempt to increase further its indebtedness cannot always be accomplished with facility and with the necessary speed.

Keynes believed that debtor nations that did not have highly developed nor self-supporting money markets should forego attempts to place their currency arrangements on a gold coin basis and institute, instead, a gold exchange standard[2] of the type that had been gradually evolving in India.[3] Such a standard, he believed, would permit them greater latitude over their internal money and credit systems.

Keynes likened the principle underlying this type standard to that of ordinary commercial banking. He pointed out that just as individuals have learned that it is cheaper and safer to keep their funds on deposit in the local bank, so, too, some nations have recognized that it is cheaper and safer to keep a part of their banks' cash reserves on deposit in a foreign money center.

The difference between the orthodox gold coin and the gold exchange standards rests in the partial suspension under the latter type standard of free payments in gold. Briefly, the essentials of the gold exchange standard, as described by Keynes, are the utilization of a non-gold medium of circulation at home, an unwillingness to exchange that local currency for gold, but a willingness to sell foreign exchange for payment in local currency at a specified rate, and the use of foreign credits with which to accomplish this. With regard to the local medium of exchange, Keynes pointed out that so long as it can be converted into gold for payments of international indebtedness at an approximately fixed ratio, it makes little difference whether or not gold actually circulates internally.[4] Citing India as an illustration, the gold exchange standard would work something like this in practice: the government of India would redeem the local currency, rupees, in bills payable in an international currency, gold, at a foreign center such as London, rather than to redeem it outright locally. The government of India would also assume responsibility for providing local currency in exchange for international currency; hence, it would have to maintain two types of reserve, one for each purpose.

To sum up in Keynes's own terms, a gold exchange standard obtains,

> when gold does not circulate in a country to an appreciable extent, when the local currency is not necessarily redeemable in gold, but when the Government or Central Bank makes arrangements for the provision of foreign remittances in gold at a fixed maximum rate in terms of the local currency, the reserves necessary to provide these remittances being kept to a considerable extent abroad.[5]

Keynes favored a gold exchange standard for India, because he thought that such an arrangement would accord greater stability to the Indian currency and price systems.[6] It should be noted that during that time India served as the sink for the world's excess gold supply, thus giving the western nations a cushion against inflationary price movements. But while this diversion of the precious metal to India and to other parts of Asia may have been beneficial to the nations of the western world, it led to considerable price fluctuations and undesirable currency speculation for India. To cope with these excesses, Keynes thought that the government of India should have at its disposal a more substantial gold reserve.

The gold exchange standard, by substituting a cheaper domestic medium of exchange for gold, Keynes noted, would make possible a release of the yellow metal to the monetary authority.[7] Reinforced with these centralized gold reserves, the authority would be in a stronger position to meet extraordinary foreign monetary drains, and thus be in a better position to safeguard its exchange rate and to combat price and currency gyrations. By contrast, the government's ability to deal with such crises under the gold coin standard was very seriously limited, for the amount of gold at its disposal in such circumstances was but a fraction of the total amount of gold in circulation. Moreover, it was virtually impossible for the monetary authority to withdraw from circulation the amount of gold required to deal with such an emergency, since "gold in the pockets of the people [is] not in the least available at a time of crisis or to meet a foreign drain."[8]

For these reasons Keynes considered internal gold circulation much too burdensome for the economy of a country such as India. Although he recognized the value of gold as an international medium of exchange, Keynes questioned whether the domestic economy should be saddled with this expense solely because of certain advantages accruing from the standard to the conduct of foreign commerce. A gold exchange standard, on the other hand, by effecting economies in the use of gold, would permit nations not possessing large stocks of it to enjoy the international advantages of a gold standard without at the same time having to suffer the internal disruptions often attending it.

In sum, Keynes's preference for a gold exchange standard over a gold coin standard reflects his conviction, evident even at this early date of his career, that each nation should be free to exercise control over its own monetary and economic affairs and should not leave them to the insensitive operation of impersonal market forces, especially to external ones. In the period following World War I, Keynes crystallized further his objections to the international gold standard and gave additional expression to his preference for monetary management. In a major article written for the *Manchester Guardian Commercial Supplements on Reconstruction in Europe*[9] in the spring of 1922, Keynes voiced a strong protest to the restoration of the pre-war gold coin standard.

At the conclusion of hostilities, Europe was in a state of political convulsion and economic disrepair. Production had virtually ground to a halt and trade between nations was practically non-existent. Because of the highly specialized character of European production and its dependence on international trade, Keynes recognized the importance of restoring the normal channels of trade. To this end he recommended the early restoration of the gold standard. Such a standard with its fixed system of exchange rates is promotive of trade, because it eliminates much of the risk attending the international exchange of goods and services. Stable foreign exchange rates help to eliminate risk by enabling those who deal in foreign transactions to know how much they will have to pay and how much they will receive in terms of their own currency. Moreover, a return to the gold standard, reasoned Keynes, would promote "a tremendous revival not only of trade and production but also of international credit and the movement of capital to those areas where needed most."[10]

Although Keynes favored restoration of the gold standard at the earliest possible date, he emphasized that he was not recommending a return to the gold coin standard of the pre–World War I era. Rather his preference was for the implementation of a gold bullion standard. Actually Keynes's objective was the same now as it was when he recommended a gold exchange standard for India in 1913, namely, to maximize the monetary authority's gold reserves by minimizing the amount of the yellow metal in circulation. By concentrating the gold stock in the coffers of the central bank or other monetary authority, each nation would be in a more favorable position to deal with gold flows and thus exercise greater control over any monetary disturbances it might experience.

Keynes felt that in the post-war economic setting the nations of Europe would need all the gold they could muster to combat fluctuations in their rates of exchange. Strategically, they would be in a better position to ward off an exchange crisis, if they could keep their reserves mobilized for immediate use than if they were to have gold dissipated in the pockets or hoards of the public.

Specifically, the standard urged by Keynes required the banks of each country to exchange legal tender for gold; however, they would not mint this metal nor permit it to circulate as legal tender. Gold would be available on demand in exchange for notes at a fixed ratio; however, the gold so obtained would be used exclusively for international transactions. To restrict the use of gold in this manner, Keynes suggested that notes be exchanged for gold bullion only in large amounts, for example, £50,000 or more.[11]

By withdrawing gold from circulation and by increasing correspondingly the amount of the precious metal in the vaults of the central bank, the gold bullion standard would enable nations better to cope with external disturbances. For example, an increased gold reserve would better equip national

monetary authorities to withstand an outflow of gold. Given this added reserve strength, they would be under much less pressure to initiate credit and
budget policies that, while stemming the outflow, might cause serious disruptions in internal prices and employment. Thus, if the gold bullion standard
were substituted for the gold coin standard and a conscious effort were made
to gear reserve requirements to the needs of international trade and finance, a
nation could more effectively combat temporary exchange disturbances and
external imbalances without having to transmit their harmful effects to the
internal sector.

Keynes regarded the utilization of gold reserves for warding off foreign
exchange disturbances and for sheltering the domestic economy from outward disruptions so important that he also suggested that the Bank of England determine its gold reserve requirements in accordance with the needs of
its international balance of payments, rather than with respect to the note
issue. He observed that the Bank of England's gold reserve was needed to
meet fluctuations in the nation's international account, which depended part-
ly on the balance of trade, but principally on its extensive international banking and investment business. In these circumstances, it is not reasonable, he
argued, to fix the amount of gold required for international purposes by
reference to the volume of notes in circulation, since in practice there is very
little direct connection between the two. [12] In short, the proper level of a
nation's gold reserves should be geared to the maximum probable strain that
a temporary disequilibrium in the balance of payments will exert on the
economy. The proper function of a gold reserve is not to enable a country to
meet the gold claims against its currency liabilities, but to satisfy the deficits
it incurs in its international balance of payments. By better enabling a nation
to deal with its external imbalances, a larger gold reserve would permit the
national monetary authority to gear its monetary policies to the needs of the
home economy, as noted in Keynes's comment on this point:

> Therefore, if the Bank of England had this volume of gold reserve available for
> foreign trade considerations, then at any moment the expansion of production
> and employment at home would not have to be interfered with by irrelevant
> considerations arising out of our international banking business. In this way
> the threat of enforcing a contraction of credit injurious to home industry would
> be greatly reduced. [13]

Compare the monetary mechanism advanced by Keynes to that prevailing
under the old gold coin standard. Under that system most nations' discretion
over their own monetary affairs was greatly circumscribed. Because of their
limited gold reserves, caused in part by free coinage and circulation, nations,
especially debtors, were often unable to manage their monetary affairs to
promote their internal economic well-being. In fact, matters were just the

other way around, for nations had to subordinate their domestic economic requirements to those of their monetary standard.

Thus, Keynes was opposed to the traditional gold coin standard because it dissipated a nation's gold resources and thereby weakened its capacity to deal with its monetary disturbances. Keynes was more favorably disposed toward a gold exchange or a gold bullion standard, since these systems made possible an economy in the use and a centralization of gold reserves that in a time of crisis could be employed to combat exchange fluctuations and other external disturbances. Whether Keynes was diagnosing the pre-war economic problems of India or those of the war-weary nations of Europe, characteristically, his prescription emphasized monetary management and national self-determination. Although he was cognizant of the advantages associated with an international monetary system like that of the pre-1914 era, he was even more conscious of the havoc and disorder visited by such a standard on the internal sector of the economy. Fundamentally, it was his desire to shield the home economy from these disturbances that caused Keynes to reject the so called automatic gold coin standard and to urge in its place a modified version that would permit each nation greater latitude over its monetary affairs.

The fact that the gold coin standard wasted gold reserves in the hands of the public and thereby limited the monetary authority's ability to defend its exchange rate was only one facet of Keynes's opposition to it. A more fundamental objection was that the orthodox gold standard did not permit nations to pursue monetary policies attuned to their own internal needs.

The reason why the gold standard did not permit autonomous action in monetary matters is that in practice it tended to establish a uniform currency standard throughout the world without regard to particular national needs.[14] In an international gold standard system, the primary duty of each central bank is to keep gold movements to a minimum through manipulation of the interest rate. But by so regulating its credit policy in a way that gold will flow neither into nor out of its vaults, the central bank surrenders its right to independent action. In these circumstances, a country finds itself pursuing money and credit policies that may not be consistent with its own domestic needs and, instead, may be more closely related to the average behavior of all other central banks. For example, if the more powerful central banks are pursuing a restrictive monetary policy, then the other monetary authorities will have to implement a similar policy whether their internal circumstances warrant it or not. Even a small and temporary divergence between their local interest rates and those obtaining in other countries may upset their external balance.[15] For as interest rates are raised in the more powerful financial centers, gold will start to flow there in quest of the higher interest returns. To halt this gold outflow, the central banks pursuing more moderate monetary policies would have to raise their bank rates to conform with those of countries following restrictive monetary policies. In this way, the behavior of each central bank will be made to conform with the average behavior of all the other banks in the system.

Although this common behavior pattern serves to minimize the transfer of funds between countries and helps to promote equilibrium in each nation's balance of payments, these objectives cannot always be achieved without damage to a nation's monetary autonomy.[16] This was especially true of Great Britain in the period after World War I. In this regard, Keynes observed that if Great Britain were to return to the gold standard at that time, she would have to surrender her economic independence to the United States. The gold standard, he contended, is simply a device for tying up the economy of a weaker nation with that of stronger countries.[17] Since the Federal Reserve Banks were in control of the major share of the world's gold supply at that time, Keynes feared that monetary policy in Great Britain would be placed largely at the mercy of decisions made by the Federal Reserve Board of the United States. Regulation of the British price level and the handling of the credit cycle, he thought, would have to be surrendered to the Federal Reserve Board. Even if the most intimate and cordial cooperation were to exist between the Board and the Bank of England, the preponderance of power would still belong to the former, Keynes argued. The Board could disregard the interests of the Bank, but if the Bank disregarded the Board, it would leave itself open to be flooded with or depleted of gold, depending on the needs of the Board.[18]

Keynes was opposed to gearing Great Britain's monetary policy to the average behavior of all other central banks, which in the post–World War I era was largely influenced by the policies of the Federal Reserve Banks. In his judgment, the primary function of monetary and credit policy was to service the domestic, not the external, needs of the economy.[19] The economic situation prevailing in Great Britain in the early 1920s made the retention of national monetary autonomy all the more critical. Keynes pointed out that with Britain's industries in their then struggling condition and employment at a low level, it was imperative that Great Britain retain control of its internal credit system. The nation was not in a position to withstand the shocks and storms often visited upon it by the gold standard. Keynes felt that Britain would make a serious mistake to expose itself to these disturbances merely for the convenience of a fixed rate of exchange with the dollar. Adoption of the gold standard, he said, would mean losing control of the credit system, which Britain might have used more profitably for the mitigation of the curses of unemployment and trade instability.[20]

Basically, the trouble with the international gold standard system was that its members had to set their bank rates in accordance with their balance of payments requirements rather than in keeping with their domestic needs and objectives. According to Keynes,

With an international currency system, such as gold, the primary duty of a Central Bank is to preserve 'external' equilibrium. Internal equilibrium must take its chances or, rather, the internal situation must be forced sooner or later into equilibrium with the external situation.[21]

The bank rate mechanism has two separate sets of consequences. One is its effect on the international flow of capital, as noted earlier, and the second is its effect on the internal credit situation.[22] Although this instrument is quite effective in maintaining or in helping to restore external equilibrium, its utilization in this capacity takes away from the monetary authority the liberty to employ it to achieve full employment, stable prices, and other domestic objectives.

To cite the case of a country experiencing a trade deficit, the proper policy for it under the orthodox gold standard would be to raise the bank rate. By raising its structure of interest rates, that country would induce an influx of foreign capital while at the same time slowing down the outflow of its own capital abroad. In the internal sector, meanwhile, such an increase in the rate of interest would bring about a contraction of credit and a decline in capital spending. This, in turn, would lead to a reduction of employment and income. As unemployment became sufficiently widespread, employers would force a general reduction in wages, which would help to accelerate the decline in prices initiated by the curtailment of credit and spending. When costs and prices were thus sufficiently reduced, the goods and services of the country experiencing the readjustment would again become competitive in world markets. This would stimulate exports and contract imports, thereby helping to correct the adverse trade balance. The reversal of the capital flows, together with the adjustment of the trade balance, would check the outflow of gold and equilibrium would be thus restored.[23]

If these tendencies were sufficiently strong, the balancing of the foreign account could be quickly achieved and the parity of the exchange safeguarded. But though the bank rate mechanism would restore equilibrium in the external sector, it might do so at the expense of price stability and domestic employment and income. To state the argument in Keynes's own words,

> The instrument of Bank Rate and Credit Contraction can only be successful as a. means of remedying a fundamental international maladjustment, so far as it diminishes employment and, if the unemployment thus caused is sufficiently intense and prolonged, eventually forces a reduction of money wages.[24]

Actually, the greater the success realized by the monetary authority in raising the interest rate to achieve external equilibrium, the less successful is it likely to be in promoting full employment and stable prices, since these objectives may require a lowering of interest rates. Under the gold standard, the attainment of external equilibrium and full employment may at times be mutually exclusive. For a central bank that has membership in such a system must surrender its monetary autonomy and right to independent action. [25]

In the pre–World War I era, there was no conflict between external and internal monetary policy requirements so far as Great Britain was concerned. For during that time the strength of the Bank of England was so great that it succeeded in making the average behavior of all the central banks conform to the best domestic interests of Great Britain. Writing about this period in his *Treatise on Money*, Keynes pointed out that "during the latter half of the nineteenth century the influence of London was so predominant that the Bank of England could almost have claimed to be the conductor of the international orchestra."[26] By modifying the terms on which she was prepared to lend, Great Britain could, to a large extent, determine the credit conditions prevailing elsewhere. The fact that she was willing to vary the volume of her gold reserves, while other central banks were unwilling to vary theirs, also gave her a considerable degree of control over credit terms throughout the world.

However, Great Britain's economic and financial status of the 1920s was markedly different from that of the pre-war period. No longer could the Bank of England prescribe an international money policy consistent with the best domestic interests of Great Britain. In the altered conditions of the post-war world, the maintenance of a single monetary standard failed to take cognizance of the varied and divergent policies that were now required to promote Great Britain's domestic well-being as well as that of other nations.

Keynes was opposed to the surrender by the Bank of England of its independence in directing the credit system toward the realization of domestic objectives such as price stability, high levels of investment, and full employment. In his estimate, the bank rate should be manipulated solely for the promotion of domestic well-being and not to neutralize financial developments in other countries. But under the international gold standard, the bank rate had to be tied to external considerations. Each central bank had to keep in step with the policies of every other central bank, regardless of whether its own domestic circumstances warranted such action or not. And because nations having membership in such a system were obliged to relinquish control over their internal economic affairs, Keynes broke with the traditional gold standard.

Although Keynes recognized the advantages of foreign exchange stability as provided by a system of fixed exchange rates (note, for example, his recommendation immediately after World War I for a gold bullion standard with fixed exchange rates to facilitate trade among the nations of Europe), he pointed out that at times it is difficult to achieve simultaneously a stable exchange rate and a steady internal price level. The reason for this is that the value of a nation's exchange rate depends largely on the relationship between the internal and external price levels; hence, unless both price levels remain stable, the exchange rate will vary. But such stability of both price levels is unusual, for while a nation may succeed in stabilizing its own price level, it is not too likely that it can similarly influence the external price level.

Therefore, if the external price level fluctuates, as it often does, the economy is faced with two courses of action. It may keep its internal price level the same and vary its exchange rate or it may alter its internal price level and keep its exchange rate constant. Given the existence of external price fluctuations, each nation is obliged to choose between a stable internal price level and a constant rate of exchange.

The choice will largely be determined by the relative importance of foreign trade and investment in each country's economy; however, even in those countries where the volume of trade is of sizable import, Keynes felt that the stability of prices is of greater domestic benefit, because it avoids the evils of both inflation and deflation.[27] Although both types of stability are desirable, he concluded that "there does seem to be in almost every case a presumption in favour of the stability of prices, if only it can be achieved."[28]

Prior to World War I, gold served the double function of providing the nations of the world a stable exchange rate and a stable internal price level. But even during that period the gold standard owed its success more to its ability to achieve a stable price level than to its capacity to attain a stable exchange rate. According to Keynes, the convenience of traders and the primitive passion for the solid metal might not have been adequate to preserve the dynasty of gold, if it had not been for another, half-accidental circumstance; namely, that for many years past gold had afforded not only a stable exchange but, on the whole, a stable price level as well. As a matter of fact, the choice between stable exchanges and stable prices had not presented itself as an acute dilemma.

Under the pre-war monetary arrangements, the internal price level adjusted itself to the external value of a nation's currency; however, the required adjustments were minor in character and so were not too disruptive of internal price stability.[29] Another significant factor was that during the pre–World War I period, and particularly during the nineteenth century, the expansion of gold output kept pace with the expansion in general production.

Although the gold standard succeeded in providing moderate price stability in the pre-war period, owing to the relatively minor adjustments that had to be made between a nation's internal price level and that prevailing internationally, Keynes did not believe that it would be equally effective in the post-war economic environment. In the new economic setting, Keynes doubted whether the gold standard could cope with the large and sudden divergences between a nation's internal price level and that prevailing abroad.[30] The reason why such wide disparities were occurring between internal and external price levels is that the domestic price levels were no longer being geared to the value of fixed exchange rates, as was the case prior to the war. In the post-war setting, monetary and credit policies were, instead, being related to internal price requirements.[31] Insofar as these credit policies varied between countries, disparities naturally emerged between their respective price levels.

Keynes contended that while it was theoretically possible for the pre-war gold system to insure fixed exchange rates, it was likely to break down in practice, because it could not effect fast enough the necessary price adjustments. The pre-war process of adjustment was slow and insensitive and might take months to work itself out. But in the post-war world a nation's gold reserve might be completely depleted before the corrective forces had completed their work. Moreover, the degree of inflation or deflation required to bring the two price levels into balance with one another might be of such magnitude as to impose intolerable strains on the economy.[32] The price a nation had to pay to restore balance between its own price level and that prevailing in the external sector—in order to stabilize its exchange rate—was especially heavy when deflation was in order. In these instances, the cost to the home economy was often general contraction and widespread unemployment.

Another reason why the gold standard could not operate effectively in the post-war period is that internal price and cost structures were becoming increasingly rigid owing to the action of trade unions and cartels. Yet, the gold standard could not restore equilibrium between external and internal prices unless home prices could be readily adjusted downward. Therefore, if the gold standard was to operate under such rigid price and cost conditions, it would either force the brunt of the correction on the internal sector in the form of business losses and unemployment or completely break down. If an adjustment had to be made between internal and external price levels, Keynes preferred that the correction be made in the external sector. Writing in the *Tract on Monetary Reform*, he concluded that,

> when stability of the internal price level and stability of the external exchanges are incompatible, the former is generally preferable; and that on occasions when the dilemma is acute, the preservation of the former at the expense of the latter is, fortunately perhaps, the line of least resistance.[33]

In place of fixed exchange rates, Keynes favored a system of fluctuating exchange rates such as emerged in the absence of the gold standard in the immediate post-war period. Under a fluctuating exchange rate system, adjustments between a nation's internal price level and that obtaining abroad could be achieved instantaneously and without need of inflating or deflating the currency as was the case under the gold flow mechanism.

In a system of fluctuating exchange rates, the brunt of the adjustment between national and external price levels falls on the rate of exchange. An illustration will help bear this out. If at the prevailing exchange rate the amount of sterling offered in the market exceeds the available supply of dollars, because of lower prices obtaining in the United States, there is no way of procuring the added dollars except by paying a higher price for them. At this new level of exchange, more sterling must be surrendered for the same amount of sterling as received heretofore, or too, fewer dollars need be surrendered for the same amount of sterling. As a result of the new rate of exchange between sterling and dollars, the relative prices of commodities entering into British and American trade—for example, cotton, copper, and wheat—will adjust themselves to the new exchange within the hour.[34] At this point, the formerly lower American prices will appear higher to British importers because of the higher cost of American dollars. On the other hand, British prices will now appear cheaper to the American importers because of the lower cost of sterling.

In this way, the British and American price levels are brought into balance with one another without recourse to either inflationary or deflationary credit policies. The implementation of these policies can be avoided or at least postponed, since the variation of the exchange rate did not of itself trip off a gold flow from Great Britain to the United States. Clearly, the advantage of a system of fluctuating rates over a system of fixed exchange rates is that adjustments under the former mechanism are effected immediately and without need to upset domestic prices through an inflation or deflation of the currency. Equilibrium may be restored in the external sector through a mere modification of the exchange rate. In this way, the stability of prices, output, and employment in the home economy may be preserved.[35]

The one disadvantage of a fluctuating system of exchange rates, according to Keynes, is that it is extremely sensitive. As a result, relative prices may be altered by any purely transitory development. But despite this shortcoming, Keynes believed that when fluctuations are large and sudden, a quick reaction as is provided by a system of flexible exchange rates is needed for the maintenance or restoration of equilibrium. A system of fixed exchange rates was much too insensitive and could not react quickly enough to the wide price gyrations of the post-war period. For this reason Keynes considered a fluctuating exchange rate indispensable in the volatile economic climate of the post-war world.

In addition to its superiority as a device for restoring balance in a nation's foreign accounts, Keynes claimed a number of other advantages for a system of fluctuating exchange rates. First, a variable exchange rate makes possible a high degree of national monetary autonomy. In such a system, the interest rate need not be used for keeping the internal price level in line with the parity of the exchange. There is no need to adjust internal credit policy to the exchange rate; rather, the adjustment is made the other way around. The exchange rate must adapt itself to whatever credit policy is required at home. Thus freed from the need to conform its credit policy to external requirements, the monetary authority is at liberty to gear its credit policy to the internal needs of the economy.

By contrast, a system of fixed exchange rates does not accord the national monetary authority the same degree of freedom in the management of its credit, since all members of the system must keep in step with one another or experience the disequilibrating effects of the gold flows. For example, if a particular central bank is pursuing a policy of monetary ease in keeping with its domestic needs, while no similar effort is being made elsewhere, it will be subjected to a drain of monetary reserves. To check this outflow, the bank will have to raise its interest rate structure to conform with that obtaining in other countries. But in doing so, it terminates its program of monetary expansion, the requirements of the domestic economy notwithstanding. Thus, a nation on the gold standard was often obliged to surrender control over its own economic best interests. It was this loss of national monetary autonomy that explains why Keynes, who was so intent on employing monetary policy for the promotion of domestic economic welfare, should be so opposed to the gold standard and its rigid exchange rates.

Another advantage of a fluctuating over a fixed exchange rate is that it better protects the home economy from disturbances originating in the foreign sector.[36] A fluctuating exchange rate is more effective in helping the monetary authority to insulate a country against external cyclical disturbances and undesirable price movements. This consideration was one of the more compelling reasons why Keynes urged Great Britain to abandon the traditional gold standard and to substitute in its place a monetary system with flexible exchange rates.[37]

In the pre-war gold standard system, the currencies of all member countries were placed on a common basis. Because of the fixed exchange rates, all national price levels had to be in approximate balance with one another. Changes in the price level of one country were transmitted to other countries. Consequently, the inflation and deflation that occurred at different stages of the business cycle, particularly that of a stronger nation, would be passed on from one gold standard country to another via changes in their internal price levels.[38]

It is quite apparent that if a nation wishes to protect itself from foreign price and cyclical disturbances, it must isolate its price level from those of other countries, for this is the channel through which these disturbances are transmitted.[39] To accomplish this, a nation should subscribe to a monetary system with variable exchange rates. In this way, if significant price changes occur abroad, the incidence of the correction will fall on the exchange rate rather than on the internal price level.

The fact that Keynes was willing to sacrifice the advantages of a fixed exchange rate to foreign trade attests to the priority he assigned to the retention of monetary autonomy and the stability of internal prices. The stability of prices, he said, is so vital to the functioning of free economic systems that they cannot survive without it. He noted that,

> modern individualistic society, organized on lines of capitalistic industry, cannot support a violently fluctuating standard of value, whether the movement is upwards or downwards. The arrangements presume and absolutely require a reasonable stable standard. Unless we can give it such a standard, this society will be stricken with a mortal disease and will not survive. [40]

A stable price level is especially significant for capital formation. A high level of national income cannot be achieved unless there exists a substantial and ever-expanding volume of investment. However, investment must be financed out of savings and savings depend on the confidence that people have in the value of the monetary unit. Thus, by encouraging investment, which in turn stimulates a higher level of national income, a stable price level helps to promote national prosperity. A stable price level also has a positive effect on the all-important expectations and anticipations of the business community. [41] On the other hand, price instability, especially deflation, worsens business expectations and leads to cutbacks in productive activity. Consequently, to the extent that falling prices or the prospect of declining prices can be replaced by stable price expectations, this will have a beneficial effect on economic activity in general. [42]

Keynes believed that unemployment, industrial disputes, and business bankruptcy owed their occurrence in large measure to the instability of prices. Therefore, if prices could be stabilized, these evils, especially unemployment, could largely be eliminated. So convinced was he of the need for stable domestic prices and of the effectiveness of a fluctuating exchange rate in achieving that end that in later years he came to defend "exchange instability and disparity in national price levels in the name of Full Employment dogma." [43]

A final argument cited by Keynes for favoring a fluctuating exchange rate and a stable internal price level over a fixed exchange rate and an attending fluctuating domestic price level was that whereas the whole national output is affected by the internal value of money, only a portion of national production is affected by the value of the exchange rate. Because of the preponderance of domestic transactions, most nations stand to gain a much greater advantage from a stable price level than from a fixed rate of exchange. [44] In fact, Keynes questioned whether it might not also be more advantageous for countries doing a large volume of foreign trade to stabilize the internal rather than the external value of their currencies. Although Keynes, during the early 1920s, had recognized the advantages of a fixed rate of exchange, toward the end of the decade he questioned whether it was, indeed, quite as important as he had thought. Writing in the *Treatise on Money*, he observed,

So far as foreign trade is concerned, I think that the advantage of fixing the maximum fluctuations of the foreign exchanges within quite narrow limits is usually much overstated. It is, indeed, little more than a convenience. It is important for anyone engaged in foreign trade that he should know for certain, at the time that he enters into a transaction, the rate of forward exchange at which he can cover himself. . . . It is not important that the rate of exchange at which he covers himself this year should be exactly the same as the rate at which he covered himself for a similar transaction last year. [45]

SUMMARY

In summary, Keynes was further opposed to the traditional gold standard system because fixed exchange rates are disruptive of domestic stability, especially at a time when wide disparities characterize the price levels of its member countries. In the economic setting of the post–World War I period, fixed exchange rates could be maintained only by sacrificing domestic price stability. As the price levels prevailing abroad varied, a given member country had to adjust its own internal price level to them, if it was to keep intact the external value of its currency. But such variations in a nation's domestic prices had dire consequences for national prosperity, especially when these adjustments were of a deflationary character. In such circumstances, the fixed value of the exchange could be maintained only by fostering general contraction with its attending unemployment and other economic disruptions.

To remove these destabilizing influences, Keynes recommended that the fixed exchange rates of the gold standard be replaced with a system of flexible exchange rates. In this way, adjustments between internal and external price levels could be achieved through an alteration of the exchange rate, thereby minimizing the effects on the domestic sector of the economy.

Keynes's opposition to a fixed exchange mechanism and his preference, instead, for a standard that would provide a more flexible system of exchange rates evidences his concern for keeping external considerations from impinging on the national prosperity. Whether Keynes was diagnosing the pre-war economic problems of India or those of the war weary nations of Europe, characteristically, his prescription emphasized monetary management and national self- determination. Although he was cognizant of the advantages associated with an international monetary system like that of the pre-1914 era, he was even more aware of the havoc and disorder visited by such a standard on the internal sector of the economy. Basically, it was his desire to shield the home economy from these disturbances that caused Keynes to reject the gold coin standard and to urge in its place a modified version that would permit each nation greater latitude over its own monetary affairs. In time, this same preoccupation with the promotion of domestic economic objectives and insistence on national self-determination would lead Keynes to an open break with the free trade dogma.

In the next chapter, added evidence will be presented to illustrate the high priority Keynes assigned to the attainment of domestic well-being and to national self-determination in economic matters by reviewing briefly his opposition to the restoration of the British pound to its pre-war parity of exchange in the spring of 1925.

NOTES

1. It is interesting to note that in this work Keynes not only sets forth his opposition to the gold standard, but also gives a very lucid insight into the nature of his later monetary thinking. Schumpeter, for one, pointed out that there are certain elements in this work that permeate much of Keynes's later writings. In his view, much of Keynes's general outlook on monetary phenomena and monetary policy as expressed in this work foreshadowed many of the ideas he expressed in his *Treatise on Money*, which appeared in 1930. Schumpeter suggested that if one were to add the theoretical implications of the English experience of the 1920s to the theory of *Indian Currency and Finance*, one would get the substance of the Keynesian ideas of 1930. See J. A. Schumpeter, *Ten Great Economists from Marx to Keynes* (New York: Oxford University Press, 1951), 264–65.

2. See chapter 2 of *Indian Currency and Finance* for a complete treatment of the gold exchange standard. Schumpeter believes that this is the foremost work in the field. He says, "I think it fair to call this book the best English work on the gold exchange standard." See Schumpeter, *Ten Great Economists from Marx to Keynes*, 265; also, see the article by J. S. Nicholson dealing with gold exchange standard, "The Report on Indian Finance and Currency in Relation to the Gold Exchange Standard," *Economic Journal* 24, no. 94 (June 1914): 236–47.

3. Indian currency had been a perplexing question ever since 1873, the date marking the abandonment by the world of the bimetallic standard. India went off the silver standard in 1893 and in 1899 the Fowler Commission, the second of its kind within a ten-year period, recommended that India adopt a gold coin standard of the British type. The recommendation was never carried out, and, instead, the monetary system that was ultimately established was one fashioned out of ad hoc administrative measures adapted to meet particular exigencies as they occurred. The net resultant of these actions was a gold exchange system. See R. F. Harrod, *The Life of John Maynard Keynes* (New York: Harcourt, Brace, 1951), 165.

4. J. M. Keynes, *Indian Currency and Finance* (London: Macmillan, 1913), 30.

5. Keynes, *Indian Currency and Finance*, 20.

6. L. R. Klein, *The Keynesian Revolution* (New York: Macmillan, 1947), 2.

7. India did not have a central bank at this time. Keynes strongly recommended the establishment of such an institution, but without success. See Keynes, *Indian Currency and Finance*, 232–39.

8. Keynes, *Indian Currency and Finance*, 71.

9. In the period from April 1922 to January 1923, the *Manchester Guardian Commercial* sponsored a series of twelve supplements on the problem of European reconstruction. These installments contained articles by leading authorities on such topics as finance, industry, trade, labor, and similar subjects bearing on the rehabilitation of Europe. In addition to being the editor of these works, Keynes was himself an active contributor.

10. J. M. Keynes, "The Stabilization of the European Exchanges, a Plan for Genoa," *Manchester Guardian Reconstruction Supplement*, 3.

11. J. M. Keynes, "The Stabilization of the European Exchanges, a Plan for Genoa," p. 4.

12. J. M. Keynes, "The Amalgamation of the British Note Issues," *Economic Journal* 36, no. 150 (June 1928): 322.

13. Keynes, "The Amalgamation of the British Note Issues," 325.

14. J. M. Keynes, "The Problem of the Gold Standard," *The Nation and Athenaeum* 36, no. 25 (March 21, 1925): 866.

15. J. M. Keynes, *A Treatise on Money*, vol. 2 (New York: Harcourt, Brace, 1930), 309.

16. Keynes, *A Treatise on Money*, 285.

17. J. M. Keynes, "The Return towards Gold," *The Nation and Athenaeum* 36, no. 21 (February 21, 1925): 708.

18. J. M. Keynes, *A Tract on Monetary Reform* (New York: Harcourt, Brace, 1924), 174.

19. Keynes, "The Problem of the Gold Standard," 866.

20. Keynes, "The Problem of the Gold Standard," 866.

21. Keynes, *A Treatise on Money*, vol. I, 164.

22. J. M. Keynes, "The Committee on the Currency," *Economic Journal* 35, no. 138 (June 1925), 302–3.

23. Keynes, *A Treatise on Money*, vol. I, 214–15.

24. J. M. Keynes, "The Future of the Foreign Exchanges," *Lloyds Bank Limited Monthly Review* 6, no. 68 (October 1935): 533.

25. Keynes, *A Treatise on Money*, vol. II, 304.

26. Keynes, *A Treatise on Money*, vol. II, 306–7.

27. For a consideration of the evils associated with monetary instability, see Keynes, *A Tract on Monetary Reform*, chapter 1.

28. Keynes, *A Tract on Monetary Reform*, 155.

29. Keynes, *A Tract on Monetary Reform*, 159–60.

30. Keynes, *A Tract on Monetary Reform*, 159.

31. Keynes, *A Treatise on Money*, vol. I, 166.

32. Keynes, *A Tract on Monetary Reform*, 160–62.

33. Keynes, *A Tract on Monetary Reform*, 163–64.

34. Keynes, *A Tract on Monetary Reform*, 161.

35. Keynes, *A Treatise on Money*, vol. I, 357–63.

36. F. C. James, "Some Practical Effects of the Doctrines Suggested by Mr. John M. Keynes Prior to 1930," in *The Economic Doctrines of John M. Keynes* (New York: National Industrial Conference Board, 1933), 3.

37. G. Haberler, *The Theory of International Trade* (London: William Hodge, 1936), 46.

38. See L. Fisher, "Are Booms and Depressions Transmitted Internationally through Monetary Standards?," *Bulletin de L'institut International de Statistique* (The Hague) (1935): 1–32.

39. It should be understood that a system of fluctuating exchange rates does not preclude all changes in the internal price level arising out of foreign trade activity. A flexible exchange rate mechanism can eliminate only the general shifts in income and domestic prices such as those occurring under the gold standard; however, relative price changes are another matter. Under any monetary system, relative changes are also required in the domestic price structure. These are made necessary by the redistribution of demands in the process of international adjustment and by factors not directly related to the balance of payments. Therefore, to affect these changes in relative price relationships, absolute changes in prices, defined in terms of the national currency, will be required. Thus, some price adjustment is required even in this type of monetary arrangement; however, the amplitude of the total price fluctuation required therein is much less than that necessitated by a system of rigid exchange rates. See P. B. Whale, *International Trade* (London: Thornton Butterworth, 1952), 24–25.

40. J. M. Keynes, "The Objective of International Price Stability," *The Economic Journal* 103, nos. 210–11 (June–September 1943): 185–87.

41. Schumpeter, *Ten Great Economists from Marx to Keynes*, 273.

42. Keynes, "Currency Policy and Unemployment," 611.

43. P. Cortney, *The Economic Munich* (New York: Philosophical Library, 1949), 205.

44. J. M. Keynes, "The Bank Rate," *The Nation and the Athenaeum* 36, no. 23 (March 7, 1925): 790 and 792.

45. Keynes, *A Treatise on Money*, vol. II, 333.

Chapter Two

Keynes's Opposition to the Restoration of the British Pound to the Pre–World War I Parity of Exchange

Keynes was a bitter foe of Great Britain's return to the gold standard at the pre-war parity of exchange. He was unalterably opposed to this policy from the time the British government first hinted its intention to restore the pound to its former value, which it did in the spring of 1925 to the fall of 1931 when it was finally forced to abandon the gold standard.

Keynes was against Great Britain's return to the gold standard at the pre-war parity of exchange, because British costs and prices at the time exceeded those prevailing in other countries. To justify the higher rate of exchange, British internal prices would have to be brought into line with those of other countries. This adjustment could be effected either through a deflation of prices at home or through an inflation of prices abroad. But the latter was not too likely, because the United States was the dominant monetary power in the world at that time and it was reluctant to initiate expansionary credit policies of the magnitude required to insure such an adjustment. Thus, Great Britain was left with the alternative of internal deflation. But such a policy of forced deflation ran counter to Keynes's economic philosophy and so, under the circumstances, he was forced to reject restoration of the pound to its pre-war value.

Since Keynes's opposition to Great Britain's return to the gold standard was inextricably connected to his aversion to deflation, no meaningful explanation of his stand on this question can be had without some reference to his attitude toward deflation. As a matter of fact, Keynes's attitude toward deflation went far beyond his position on the gold question. Professor Harrod felt that Keynes's views on deflation had a critical bearing on the reformulation of his entire economic thought. Keynes's warning in the early 1920s against the evils of deflation, he says, may be considered as heralding the work that was to absorb his interests for the next fifteen years and lead him far from his original starting point.[1]

Keynes first expressed his views on deflation in an article he prepared late in 1922 titled "The Stabilization of the European Exchanges II." This work appeared in the eleventh installment of the *Manchester Guardian Commercial Supplements on European Reconstruction* and was reproduced the following year in the *Tract on Monetary Reform*. In that work, he noted that, whereas rising prices constitute an injustice to rentiers and discourage savings, falling prices inhibit production and lead to unemployment. Although both types of instability have their characteristic disadvantages, Keynes regarded deflation as having the more serious consequences for the home economy.[2] "Inflation is unjust and deflation is inexpedient," he said.[3] But of the two, he added, perhaps deflation is the worse, since in an impoverished world it is a more serious matter to provoke unemployment than to disappoint the rentier.

Deflation fosters unemployment largely by discouraging business investment. Modern business is conducted in large measure with borrowed capital, but if entrepreneurs are faced with the prospect that their investments will in time be worth only a fraction of their original value, lengthy productive processes involving large money outlays are discouraged, thereby reducing output and employment.[4] Paradoxically, in a period of deflation there exists a greater possibility of reward in not producing and undertaking risk than in producing and incurring all kinds of uncertainty. Under circumstances such as these it is clearly more profitable for the entrepreneur to withdraw from "the risks and exertions of activity," as Keynes put it, by converting his assets into cash and to await "in country retirement the steady appreciation promised him in the value of his cash."[5] Therefore, concluded Keynes, downward price adjustments are bad enough, but a deliberate policy of deflation is even worse. For insofar as the business community believes that the monetary authority really intends to carry out a declared deflationary policy, they are more likely to lose confidence in the existing level of prices and are therefore more certain to restrict output and employment.

Keynes was further opposed to a policy of deliberate deflation because of the existence at that time of large internal debt in most European capitals.[6] Should deflation occur under such circumstances, he noted, money incomes would be appreciably reduced. But owing to the fixed nature of the service charges on the public debts, taxes could not be correspondingly reduced; hence, such a deflationary policy would place an intolerable strain on the productive classes of society.[7] In effect, the fixed income groups, for example, rentiers and government bond holders, would profit at the expense of the working classes, since they would now receive a larger share of the real national income.[8]

By so changing the real value of the existing monetary standard, Keynes felt that the process of deflation redistributes wealth in a manner detrimental both to business and social stability.[9] Deflation involves a transfer of wealth from the borrowing to the lending classes. This is particularly lamentable, in Keynes's estimate, because the transfer is affected from the active to the inactive classes of society. But such a situation is not likely to exist for any extended period, he warned, because "the active and working elements in no community, ancient or modern, will consent to hand over to the rentier or bond holding class more than a certain proportion of the fruits of their work."[10]

Thus, the restoration of the British pound to its pre-war parity was fundamentally an aspect of the broader question of inflation versus deflation. The issue at hand was whether Great Britain should leave the value of sterling at its then prevailing level or restore it to its pre-war parity. The former alternative would leave the internal purchasing power of the currency intact, whereas the latter would seek to augment it through a process of deliberate deflation.[11]

With the issue more clearly defined, we now turn to a survey of the events leading to the restoration of the gold standard in Great Britain in the spring of 1925.

The first real clash between Keynes and those who advocated the restoration of the gold standard in Great Britain at its pre-war value occurred in the summer of 1923 when the Bank of England raised the bank rate from 3 to 4 percent. This action did not appear to be at all consistent with the prevailing economic situation, since Great Britain was in the throes of a severe depression at that time. When unemployment is increasing, enterprise is disheartened and prices are declining, that is hardly the time to tighten credit.[12] And so, Keynes took the bank authorities to task, charging that "the raising of the Bank Rate to 4 percent is one of the most misguided movements of that indicator which have ever occurred."[13]

But if raising the interest rate was not a move calculated to encourage business recovery, what was the bank's justification for taking this action? The authorities offered no explanation, but Keynes contended that it was to be found in the decline of the dollar exchange by about 2 percent. This action, he charged, was just another phase of the deflationary policy that the Bank of England had initiated some eighteen months earlier[14] for the purpose of restoring sterling to its pre-war dollar value.[15]

Although the Bank of England's attempt to raise the general level of British interest rates would, in time, enhance the exchange value of sterling, this improvement would be made at the expense of the home economy. Any improvement in the British exchange rate could be accomplished only through deflation and its attending business depression and unemployment. In fact, Keynes charged that this deliberate deflationary policy was directly to blame for Great Britain's failure to keep pace with the economic revival in the United States during the first half of 1923. [16] Unfortunately, however, the Bank authorities deemed it "more important to raise the dollar exchange a few point than to encourage flagging trade." [17] In espousing this policy, lamented Keynes, "the Bank of England, acting under the influence of a narrow and obsolete doctrine, has made a grave mistake." [18] The "narrow and obsolete doctrine" to which Keynes was referring was the manipulation of the interest rate for the purpose of effecting adjustments in a country's external affairs rather than for the promotion of stable internal prices and high levels of output and employment.

As Great Britain continued to move irresistibly toward the restoration of the gold standard at the pre-1914 parity, Keynes became more vehement in his protests. The reason for his antagonism was the same now as it had been earlier. The then current level of British domestic prices relative to those prevailing in other countries was inordinately high, and to return to the gold standard at the pre-war parity would necessitate a deflation of wide proportions. Writing in the *New Republic* in the spring of 1925, he observed,

> I believe that our price level is too high, if it is converted to gold at the par of exchange, in relation to gold prices elsewhere, and if we consider the prices of those articles only that are not the subject of international trade and of services, that is, wages, we shall find these are materially too high—not less than 5 percent and probably 10 percent. Thus, unless the situation is saved by a rise of prices elsewhere, the Chancellor is committing us to a policy of forcing down money wages by perhaps two shillings to the pound. [19]

To indicate the magnitude of the disparity between British wages and those prevailing elsewhere, Keynes contrasted the wages received by steel workers in Great Britain with those of countries on the continent. In early 1925, skilled iron and steel workers were receiving the equivalent of 1£ 18s per week in Belgium, 1£ 13 s in France, and 2£ 2s 6d in Germany; in Great Britain the weekly pay for shorter hours and for the average of both skilled and nonskilled workers amounted to 3£ 3s. To illustrate further the extent of the difference between British and other European wage rates, Keynes cited the rates paid by an American overseas firm to factory workers on its payroll in several European countries during the latter part of 1924. The relationship between these rates that were converted into gold at the then prevailing rates compares favorably with the one noted above. Whereas in Great Britain the daily wage rate amounted to $2.28, in Germany it was $1.55, in France $1.24, in Belgium $1.14, and in Italy $0.96.

Although gold wages in Great Britain were considerably higher than those prevailing in other countries, the level of real wages there was not commensurately higher. The reason for this is that the prevailing British rate of exchange overstated the internal purchasing power of sterling. In effect, gold bought much less in Great Britain than elsewhere. The British price level in 1925, as measured by the gold cost of living index, showed a far greater increase over the pre-war period than did the price levels of other European countries. For example, whereas the gold cost of living in Germany in 1925 was 25 percent higher than it was in 1913 and 21 percent higher in Italy, it was 79 percent higher in Great Britain. Thus, the basic problem for the British rested not in relatively higher real wages, as was popularly thought at the time, but to the fact that the gold cost of living had risen much higher in Great Britain than it had in other countries.

Thus, if Great Britain was to raise the value of its exchange, the purchasing power of the pound would clearly have to be enhanced. But this could be accomplished only through a lowering of the domestic price level. However, as was noted earlier, this would impose serious burdens upon the economy. First of all, the real burden of the debt would, in Keynes's estimate, be increased by 10 percent. Second, money wages would have to be reduced by about 10 percent. This in itself would be of no real consequence provided the reduction of other costs and prices would be similarly carried out across the board. This, though, was not likely, owing to the many rigidities built into the internal cost and price structure. Consequently, any attempt to reduce the level of money wages would, Keynes thought, lead to industrial strife. [20] Interestingly, Keynes warned in this regard the following prophecy that did, in fact, come to pass in the General Strike of 1927.

> The working classes attacked first are faced with a depression of their standard of life, because the cost of living will not fall until all the others have been successfully attacked too, and therefore, they are justified in defending themselves. . . . Therefore, they are bound to resist as long as they can; and it must be war, until those who are economically weakest are beaten to the ground. [21]

Furthermore, Keynes argued that unless the adjustment of internal prices and costs kept pace with the improvement in the exchange rate, the cost price relationship of British exports, for example, coal and textiles, would be distorted. Given a higher exchange value for sterling, British export prices would have to be lowered. But unless the internal costs associated with the production of these goods were correspondingly reduced, the British export industries would be unable to compete in foreign markets. Only when sufficient depression and unemployment had been realized in the export industries to bring internal costs, particularly wages, into line with prices could the competitive status of the British export industries be restored. [22]

Lastly, Keynes pointed out, as he had done earlier in the *Tract on Monetary Reform*, that the mere declaration of a deflationary policy would be sufficient to inhibit home industry and commerce. Given the certainty that prices will fall, producers will curtail their operations and postpone any capital improvements they may have contemplated. On the demand side, prospective buyers would postpone the acquisition of goods and services in anticipation of still-lower prices. Therefore, concluded Keynes, the threat of falling prices is bad enough, but the certainty of such deflation must surely aggravate unemployment and retard productive activity. In contemplating the depressing effect that restoration of the gold standard would have on output and employment, Keynes quipped, "a cheerful programme! Would the public fall down and worship the gold standard with gratitude and awe."[23]

Instead of forcing the internal price level to conform to the higher exchange rate, Keynes preferred that the adjustment be effected the other way around. He recommended that the British forego restoration of the gold standard at the old par of exchange and permit, instead, the external value of the currency to seek its own level. In this way, disruptions of the home economy would be kept to a minimum. In articles he prepared for the *Nation and Athenaeum* and for the *New Republic* in the spring of 1925, Keynes observed,

> I believe that it would be much better for us, as well as much easier, to let our exchange adjust itself to the present level of our prices and wages, which have now been fairly steady for some time.[24] It seems to me wiser and simpler and saner to leave the currency to find its own level for some time longer than to force a situation where employers are faced with the alternative of closing down or of lowering wages, cost what the struggle may.[25]

Despite Keynes's admonition that the time was not propitious for Britain's resumption of the gold standard at the pre-war parity, the financial community (the City) and the British public remained steadfast in their conviction that this was the proper course for the nation to follow. In a way, this attitude was difficult to comprehend because most Britons were not unmindful of the dangers associated with a restoration of the gold standard. According to Keynes, most people appreciated the dangers and the complexities of the case and sincerely wished that they had not talked so much about the blessings of hurrying back to par. "It is in this chastened mood," he added, "that the British public will submit their necks to the golden yoke,—as a prelude, perhaps, to throwing it off forever at not a distant date."[26]

Turning again to a review of some of the more important developments that preceded Great Britain's return to the gold standard, it is significant to note that throughout most of 1924 the Federal Reserve Banks pursued a cheap money policy. The Federal Reserve Bank of New York reduced its rediscount rate from 4.5 percent in May, 1924 to 3 percent in August of that same year. The rediscount rate remained at that level until February 1925, at which time it was raised to 3.5 percent. During this period, the Bank of

England had the alternative of either easing credit to bolster home employment or keeping credit restricted to enhance the value of the sterling exchange. Unfortunately, in Keynes's estimate, the authorities decided on the second course of action.

As a result of the easy money policy being pursued by the Federal Reserve Banks between May 1924 and February 1925, dollar prices during this period rose by about 10 percent. In that interval the Bank of England's bank rate remained at 4 percent, with the result that there occurred little change in the volume of credit. Although British prices rose somewhat in sympathy with the American advance, the increase during this period amounted to only 4 percent.[27] This difference between the movement of the American and British price levels together with the exchange dealings of speculators who were anticipating Great Britain's return to the gold standard at the pre-war parity caused the sterling exchange rate to appreciate by about 8 percent by the closing months of 1924.

In January 1925, the exchange touched 1 = \$4.78; however, subsequent action by the Federal Reserve Banks made further appreciation difficult. As noted earlier, the Federal Reserve Bank of New York in February 1925 raised its discount rate from 3 to 3.5 percent. Meanwhile, the Bank of England, intent on completing the task it had set for itself, raised its bank rate to 5 percent. Although this was not a popular consequence of the bank's policy to return to the gold standard, public clamor for the resumption of the gold standard at the pre-war parity continued unabated. In the early months of 1925, there occurred mounting pressure from both the financial community and the general public to implement the recommendations of the Cunliffe Committee of 1918 and of the Currency Committee of 1924 that Great Britain return to the gold standard at the pre-war parity.

Notwithstanding the inability of sterling to register further gains against the dollar, Great Britain in the spring of 1925 reinstituted the gold standard. Winston Churchill, who was Chancellor of the Exchequer at that time, announced in his budget speech on April 27, 1925, that the Bank of England would resume the free sale of gold at the old parity price of £3:17 : 10½ per standard ounce. Churchill's announcement that Great Britain would return to the gold standard at the pre-war parity meant, in effect, that the official value of the pound would be raised from the then prevailing rate of prevailing rate of 1£ = \$4.40 to 1£ = \$4.86, an increase of about 10 percent.

Although restoration of the pound to its pre-war parity was thus officially realized, a very serious obstacle had to be overcome before it could be made truly effective. To justify the pound's higher external value, internal prices and costs would have to be reduced by at least 10 percent. But if this was so, why did the British authorities take such precipitate action in raising the external value of the pound?

Keynes assigned much of the blame for this untimely action on the failure of the Committee on the Currency to distinguish between the significance of the index of wholesale prices and that of the index of internal purchasing power. In urging the restoration of the gold standard at the pre-war parity of exchange, the Committee based its recommendation on the fact that the wholesale price index was adjusting itself to the improvement that had been taking place in the exchange value of sterling. It reasoned that since the prices of commodities entering into wholesale trade were adapting themselves to an improvement in the exchange, all other prices would similarly adjust themselves to this appreciation in the external value of sterling. [28] For this reason it was thought that an immediate return to the gold standard at the pre-war parity could be accomplished without difficulty.

But the fact that the British wholesale price index compared favorably with the behavior of the wholesale price index of the United States and other countries did not warrant, in Keynes's estimate, the conclusion that the internal purchasing power of their respective currencies bore the same relationship to one another as in the pre-war period and that therefore a return to the pre-1914 rate of exchange between the dollar and the pound was justified. Keynes argued that a comparison of wholesale price indices does not provide a true indication of the relative purchasing power of different currencies.

Actually, there cannot be too much variation between the wholesale price levels of different countries. Keynes noted that nearly two-thirds of all the commodities entering into the calculation of wholesale price indices are traded in highly organized international markets; [29] hence, after allowing for tariffs and transportation costs, the prices of those goods must be the same for all countries when defined in terms of a common currency. [30] In effect, the prices of all internationally traded commodities cannot differ materially from one center to another. [31] And because wholesale indices are largely comprised of these same commodities moving in international trade, it follows that they, too, must be approximately equal.

If there do occur fluctuations in the ratio of one country's wholesale price index to that of another, these changes must correspond closely to the fluctuations in the exchange rates between their currencies; conversely, if there occur changes in the rate of exchange between two currencies, their wholesale price indices must accordingly adjust. For example, if the external value of sterling is increased, British wholesale prices would have to be reduced. If prices of British goods moving in wholesale trade were, under these circumstances, to remain the same, the real sterling prices of these goods would exceed world prices because of the higher cost of sterling exchange. Consequently, if a given nation's currency costs more, then the prices at which its merchants sell their wares in international markets will have to be correspondingly reduced, assuming, of course, that no price increases occur in other countries. In short, if a nation's exchange value is altered, its wholesale price level will have to be correspondingly adjusted.

All of the above adjustments take place in accordance with the Purchasing Power Parity Theory of the Foreign Exchanges, which, simply stated, holds that the rates of foreign exchange between two currencies move in the same way as the ratio of their respective international or wholesale index numbers. The theory is really a truism and cannot be seriously questioned. Unfortunately, however, some economists, notably Gustav Cassel, tried to extend the theory to the internal purchasing power of money as well. Under this variation it is held that the rate of exchange between two currencies moves in the same fashion as the ratio of their respective purchasing power indices. Keynes, as will be noted below, considered this to be an illicit extension of the Purchasing Power Parity Theory and placed much of the blame for Britain's restoration of the gold standard on this interpretation.

In returning to the gold standard at an overvalued exchange rate, the British authorities felt that the adjustment of British wholesale prices to world prices, in accordance with the Purchasing Power Theory of the Foreign Exchanges, would compensate for this overvaluation. Keynes, though, was little impressed by this line of reasoning, because it failed to consider adequately the adjustments that would have to be made in purely internal prices.

If the prices of all goods—those that enter into domestic as well as into foreign trade—were to adjust to a new rate of exchange, including those commodities that enter into wholesale trade, for example, cotton, copper, and other raw materials, there would be little difficulty in moving to a new level of exchange. However, not all commodity prices are quite so sensitive to such exchange variations. For example, there are certain costs (e.g., housing, taxes, interest, railway charges, and wages) that respond slowly, if at all, to an improvement or deterioration of the exchange rate. These costs do not enter directly into international trade and for this reason, according to Keynes, may differ from their counterparts in other countries.[32]

But though these services are mostly exchanged within the economy and are largely insulated from foreign competition, they can have an important impact on international trade. For example, if there occurs an increase in the exchange value of a given currency, the costs of these services per unit of output must be reduced; otherwise, they will place that nation's exports at a competitive disadvantage. The export industries will find themselves in a situation where their production costs will continue to be high and the prices they receive for their goods will decline because of the appreciated value of their exchange. Keynes describes this squeeze in the following terms.

> An improvement in the sterling exchange necessarily lowers all the 'unsheltered' prices, and if this is unaccompanied by forces tending to depress the "sheltered" prices to an equal extent, those who produce in the 'unsheltered'

industries are in obvious difficulties, because they are selling at the 'unsheltered' price level and, in part at least, buying and consuming at the 'sheltered' price level.[33]

This is the kind of difficulty Keynes foresaw for Great Britain's export industries when the Treasury decided to return to the gold standard at the pre-war parity. Keynes felt that the sheltered and other internal prices were not sufficiently low to warrant the higher value for sterling exchange. Keynes maintained that only when domestic costs could be sufficiently reduced to enable exporters to sell at a lower price level would such a return to parity be justified. The question of parity, observed Keynes, involves a consideration of the prices of not only commodities entering into foreign trade, but also those that do not or only do so indirectly. In his judgment, it would have been far more realistic to consult the cost of living index, in which sheltered prices play a more dominant role, than the wholesale price index for determining whether the time was propitious for a return to the gold standard at the pre-war parity.[34]

Had the Committee on the Currency recognized this distinction between the behavior of goods that enter directly into international trade, for example, raw materials, and those that do not or do so only indirectly, for example, railway costs, wages, and construction costs, Keynes believed it unlikely that the Committee would have made the mistake it did. Unfortunately, the Committee reasoned that all prices behaved in the same fashion as those on the wholesale level; hence, if these prices were adjusting themselves to the higher exchange value, so, too, would all other prices. Fundamentally, the committee's error was rooted in its illicit extension of the Purchasing Power Parity Theory of the Foreign Exchanges to the purchasing power of money itself, as Keynes indicates in the following observation made in his *Treatise on Money.*

> At the time of Great Britain's return to the gold standard the Treasury and the Bank of England were led to the false conclusion that, because of the Wholesale Index, which was almost the same thing as the British International Index, was moving rapidly into adjustment—as an International Index necessarily must—with the movement of the gold exchanges, therefore, the same thing was true of prices generally.[35]

In a subsequent passage in the same volume Keynes noted,

> I do not believe that Great Britain would have returned in 1925 to the Gold Standard at the pre-war parity if it had not been for the habit of regarding the Wholesale Standard as a satisfactory indicator of general purchasing power.[36]

Keynes took farther exception with the Currency Committee on grounds that although it fully recognized that the pound was overvalued and that a further downward adjustment of prices was necessary, it failed to disclose how much deflation was required and how the British price and cost structure was to be reduced in order to make the internal value of the currency conform to its enhanced external value.

Keynes suspected that the Committee hoped to reduce internal prices and costs through the instrumentality of a higher bank rate. The process of adjustment would work out in the following manner. An increase in the bank rate would immediately lead to a contraction of credit, which, if sufficiently widespread, would lead to a reduction of employment. If sufficient unemployment could be generated, wages could be forced downward under the pressure of hard economic facts even in the sheltered industries.[37] Given such lower wage costs, British exporters would again be in a position to sell their wares at the lower prices prevailing in the international market. At this point, the British internal price and cost structure would be brought into balance with that prevailing abroad and the higher exchange value could now be sustained.

This process of adjustment sounds entirely plausible, if one is willing to disregard the toll it exacts from the labor force. But apart from its heavy social costs, this process of adjustment is of dubious value, for it fails to take cognizance of the highly inelastic character of the British industrial system. The mobility of labor and the flexibility of wage rates assumed by this adjustment mechanism were simply non-existent in post-war Great Britain. On this point Keynes says,

> I suspect that their conclusions (those of the Committee on Currency) may be based on theories, developed fifty years ago, which assumed a mobility of labour and a competitive wage level which no longer exist; and that they have not thought the problem through over again in the light of the deplorably inelastic conditions of our industrial organism today.[38]

In earlier periods, asserted Keynes, the pressure exerted by the loss of profits and the unemployment of the productive factors operated more quickly and effectively than they did in the 1920s to bring about a desired income deflation. Even in that environment the resistance to a downward revision of wage rates was considerable, but in the altered economic environment of the post-war world, wherein trade unions and a proletarian electorate were extremely strong and articulate, this resistance was even stronger.[39]

If the value of all transactions expressed in monetary terms could be lowered simultaneously to correspond with the appreciation of the exchange, there would have been no problem. But such was not the case, for not all prices could adjust themselves in the same way to changes in the external

value of the currency.[40] Prices and costs would adjust to the new exchange
rate at varying rates and in different degrees.[41] This essentially was the crux
of the problem. Because of this lack of flexibility in the internal cost and
price structure, the deflation required for the restoration of the pound to its
pre-war value would create many frictions that would, in turn, lead to a
discouragement of production and employment. This, then, would be the
consequence, observed Keynes, of "the so called sound policy, which is
demanded as a result of the rash act of pegging sterling at a gold value, which
it did not—measured in its purchasing power over British labour—possess as
yet."[42] It is a policy, he said, "from which any humane or judicious person
must shrink."[43]

SUMMARY

In summary, the above account of Keynes's opposition to the restoration of
the gold standard by the British Treasury at the pre-war parity of exchange
gives further credence to the contention that he was primarily concerned with
the promotion of high levels of economic activity at home and was opposed
to pursuing policies in the external sector that would jeopardize the realization of those objectives. Although Great Britain's return to the gold standard
at the pre-war value of sterling would be a great boon to an international
financial center such as London, Keynes felt that the price the domestic
economy would have to pay in terms of deflation and unemployment would
more than offset that external advantage. Therefore, to minimize internal
disruptions, he urged that the external value of sterling be made to conform
to its internal value and not the other way around. By having the incidence of
the adjustment between the internal and external sectors of the economy fall
on the latter, the government could then be largely free to pursue policies
best designed to promote the domestic welfare.

NOTES

1. R. F. Harrod, *The Trade Cycle* (Oxford, Oxford University Press, 1936), 314.
    2. This view is somewhat surprising, if one considers that only three years prior to this time
inflation gave Keynes greater cause for concern. In his *Economic Consequences of the Peace*,
published in 1919, Keynes had argued that the great injustice of inflation is that it confiscates
arbitrarily and, in the process of redistributing the wealth of the community, impoverishes some
and enriches others.
    3. J. M. Keynes, *A Tract on Monetary Reform* (New York: Harcourt, Brace, 1924), 40
    4. J. M. Keynes, "Currency Policy and Unemployment, "*The Nation and the Athenaeum*
33, no. 19 (August 11, 1923): 611.
    5. Keynes, "*A Tract on Monetary Reform*," 156–57.
    6. Keynes, "Currency Policy and Unemployment," 611.
    7. D. Dillard, *The Economics of John Maynard Keynes* (New York: Prentice-Hall, 1948),
304.

8. J. M. Keynes, "The Stabilization of the European Exchanges—II," *Manchester Guardian Reconstruction Supplement* 11 (December 7, 1922): 658.

9. Keynes, *A Tract on Monetary Reform*, 155

10. Keynes, "The Stabilization of the European Exchanges—II," 658.

11. On the question of immediate currency stabilization versus currency appreciation for the European exchanges in the early post-war period, Keynes had earlier noted: "It would be better to return to more modest values in order that the risk of a fiasco and a breakdown may be as little as possible. Furthermore, an appreciating currency by lowering home prices, may have a depressing effect on trade, and by constantly increasing the real burden of the National Debt will aggravate the already nearly insoluble problem of the National Budget." See J. M. Keynes, "The Stabilization of the European Exchanges, a Plan for Genoa," *Manchester Guardian Reconstruction Supplement*, 4–5.

12. J. M. Keynes, "Bank Rate and Stability of Prices," *The Nation and Athenaeum* 23, no. 16 (July 21, 1923): 530.

13. J. M. Keynes, "Bank Rate at 4 Per Cent," *The Nation and Athenaeum* 33, no. 15 (July 14, 1923): 502.

14. Keynes estimated that the actual deflation during this period amounted to 10 percent.

15. J. M. Keynes, "Is Credit Abundant?," *The Nation and Athenaeum* 33, no. 14 (July 17, 1923): 470.

16. J. M. Keynes, "The Measure of Deflation," *The Nation and Athenaeum* 33, no. 17 (July 28, 1923): 558.

17. Keynes, "Bank Rate at 4 Per Cent," 502.

18. Keynes, "Bank Rate at 4 Per Cent," 502.

19. J. M. Keynes, "England's Gold Standard," *The New Republic* 42, no. 546 (May 20, 1925): 339.

20. J. M. Keynes, "The Gold Standard," *The Nation and Athenaeum* 37, no. 5 (May 2, 1925): 129.

21. J. M. Keynes, *The Economic Consequences of Mr. Churchill* (London: The Hogarth Press, 1925), 9.

22. J. M. Keynes, "Great Britain's Cross of Gold," *The New Republic* 44, no. 563 (September 16, 1925): 88.

23. J. M. Keynes, "The Policy of the Bank of England," *The Nation and the Athenaeum* 35, no. 16 (July 19, 1924): 501.

24. J. M. Keynes, "Is Sterling Overvalued," *Nation and Athenaeum* 37, no. 1 (April 4, 1925): 28.

25. Keynes, "England's Gold Standard," 339.

26. J. M. Keynes, "Is Sterling Overvalued—II," *The Nation and the Athenaeum* 37, no. 3 (April 18, 1925): 86.

27. J. M. Keynes, "The Bank Rate," *The Nation and Athenaeum* 36, no. 23 (March 7, 1925): 790.

28. Keynes, *The Economic Consequences of Mr. Churchill*, 11.

29. Keynes, *The Economic Consequences of Mr. Churchill*, 11.

30. J. M. Keynes, *A Treatise on Money*, vol. I (London: Macmillan, 1930), 69–70.

31. J. M. Keynes, "The Gold Standard—A Correction," *The Nation and Athenaeum* 37, no. 6 (May 9, 1925), 170.

32. J. M. Keynes, "Monetary Policy—Relation of Price Levels," *The Times of London*, September 4, 1925, p. 20. Also see J. M. Keynes, "The First Fruits of the British Gold Standard," *The New Republic* 47, no. 600 (June 2, 1926): 54.

33. J. M. Keynes, "The Committee on the Currency," *Economic Journal* 35, no. 138 (June 1925): 301.

34. Keynes, "The Gold Standard—A Correction," 170.

35. Keynes, *A Treatise on Money*, vol. I, 74–75.

36. Keynes, *A Treatise on Money*, vol. 1, 74–75.

37. Keynes, *The Economic Consequences of Mr. Churchill*, 17.

38. Keynes, "The Committee on the Currency," 302.

39. Keynes, *A Tract on Monetary Reform*, 1831.

40. Keynes, *The Economic Consequences of Mr. Churchill*, 11.
41. Keynes, "The First Fruits of the Gold Standard," 345.
42. Keynes, *The Economic Consequences of Mr. Churchill*, 17.
43. Keynes, *The Economic Consequences of Mr. Churchill*, 17.

Chapter Three

Keynes's Search for a Managed Monetary Standard

In view of his dissatisfaction with the ability of the traditional gold standard to promote the well-being of the domestic economy, Keynes, during the 1920s, recommended in its place a type standard that would make possible the realization of many of the objectives cited in the earlier chapters of this section. He thought that these could be best achieved through the instrumentality of a consciously managed currency. It should be noted, however, that although Keynes's managed currency proposals were opposed to the so called automatic gold standard of the pre-war period, they did not completely exclude gold. Keynes did, in fact, retain an important reserve function for gold in his monetary arrangements. In this connection he said,

> I retain for gold an important role in our system. As an ultimate safeguard and as a reserve for sudden requirements, no superior medium is yet available. But I urge that it is possible to get the benefit of the advantages of gold, without irrevocably binding our legal tender money to follow blindly all the vagaries of gold and future unforeseeable fluctuations in its real purchasing power. [1]

Conscious control of the monetary standard is imperative, Keynes contended. In one of his more colorful passages of the *Tract on Monetary Reform* he observed,

> We can no longer afford to leave it in the category of which the disturbing characteristics are possessed in different degrees by the weather, the birth rate, and the Constitution,—matters which are settled by natural causes or are the resultant of separate action of many individuals acting independently, or require a Revolution to change them. [2]

Keynes's interest in a managed monetary standard did not have its origin in the post–World War I era. In fact, this was one of his prime preoccupations even during the earliest phase of his career. This is evidenced by his very first work, which he prepared while a young instructor at Cambridge. This effort, titled "Recent Economic Events in India," dealt with the monetary disturbances that took place in that country in 1907 and 1908 and their relation to the management of the rupee.[3]

During 1908, India experienced an unfavorable balance of trade. This imbalance was caused principally by a harvest failure in that year and a large increase in the coinage that had taken place in the previous year as a result of a prosperous export trade and an influx of foreign capital. These developments had stimulated the sale of Council Bills in London, which, when encashed in India, swelled the volume of currency in circulation. The harvest failure served to increase the volume of imports while the increased money supply led to an inflation of prices that, by discouraging exports, added further to India's balance of payments problems. Unfortunately, India had no sizable gold reserve with which to meet this external imbalance, and as a result, the exchange value of the rupee headed toward a serious depreciation. This prospect, however, was averted by the unprecedented intervention of the Indian secretary of state in the exchange market when he made available sufficient resources for the support of the rupee.[4]

Keynes commended the secretary's action in not permitting free market forces to run their natural course, which in this instance would have led to a severe depreciation of the external value of the rupee. Thus, even at this early date Keynes's attitude toward monetary management was clear. He regarded the currency system not as a mechanism that should be automatic and free from tampering, but as a device that should admit of management for the purpose of obtaining a desired end.[5]

Keynes's early preference for a managed currency is further exhibited in an article he prepared for the *Economic Journal* in late 1914 on monetary problems of the early war period. In it he argued that it was needless for civilized countries to expose themselves "to sudden and arbitrary disturbances of their social and economic systems by leaving fluctuations of the monetary standard outside their control, when they might be within it."[6] Such control is entirely possible for "it is easy to invent modes of regulating the value of the standard which, however far from perfection, are at least better than what we have at present."[7] Only the public will to accept this conscious direction remains to be attained and this, he asserted, is not in the too distant future.

> It is . . . a possible consequence of the present war . . . that some international
> standard will be forced on the principal countries of the world. If it prove one
> of the after-effects of the present struggle, that gold is at last deposed from its

despotic control over us and reduced to the position of a constitutional monarch, a new chapter of history will be opened. Man will have made another step forward in the attainment of self-government in the power to control his fortunes according to his own wishes. . . . A new dragon will have been set up at a new Colchis to guard the Golden Fleece from adventures. [8]

Keynes had earlier made a similar prophecy concerning the inevitable acceptance by society of a managed monetary system in his *Indian Currency and Finance*, wherein he stated,

The time may not be far distant when Europe, having perfected her mechanism of exchange on the basis of a gold standard, will find it possible to regulate her standard of value on a more rational and stable basis. It is not likely that we shall leave permanently the most intimate adjustments of our economic organism at the mercy of a lucky prospector a new chemical process, or a change of ideas in Asia. [9]

Despite Keynes's earlier anticipation of a struggle in the post–World War I period between a managed and a so called automatic gold standard, none came to pass. Like it or not, managed money was a *fait accompli*. There was no issue at stake, for the monetary and banking systems that emerged during the post-war era dealt largely in paper money and credit, the volume of which was, in fact, consciously controlled. As Keynes pointed out, "In the modern world of paper currency and credit there is no escape from a 'managed' currency, whether we wish it or not." [10]

The so called automatic gold standard could not exist in this period, because the value of gold was no longer determined by a variety of independent forces, as had been the case prior to the war. During the pre-war period, the intrinsic value of gold was largely determined by the demand of the arts and the hoards of Asia. The value of gold during that time did not depend on the policy decisions of any single institution. But all this was changed in the post-war world with the rise of the United States as the dominant gold holding power. With most nations off the gold standard, the supply of gold would have been redundant, if the United States had chosen to restrict the gold holdings to her real needs. This, of course, the United States did not do, for if she were to limit her demand for the yellow metal, and thereby permit its value to fall to its natural value, her own standard would be seriously depreciated. Therefore, to maintain the value of gold at an artificial level, the Federal Reserve Banks were obliged to bottle up a sizable portion of the world's supply. But in so doing, they destroyed the automatic character of the standard. Thus, concluded Keynes, since the value of gold depends on the policy of the Federal Reserve Board, or at most, the policies of the three or four most powerful central banks, gold has become de facto a managed standard. [11]

Another reason cited by Keynes for the passing of the automatic nature of the gold standard during the post-war period was the impounding of gold by the Federal Reserve Banks. This resulted from their practice of sterilizing the inflow of gold to the United States. Instead of regulating their discount rates according to the inflow and outflow of gold and varying the proportion of their gold reserves to their liabilities, the Banks chose to disregard these measures and accepted gold without permitting it to cause an inflation of credit and prices. In so preventing gold movements from exercising their full impact on credit and prices, the Federal Reserve Board destroyed the automatism of the gold standard.

U.S. monetary and credit policy at that time was not determined by reference to the above criteria, as would be expected under the "automatic" gold standard, but by the requirements of stable prices, trade, and employment, as Keynes pointed out in his *Tract on Monetary Reform*:

> In practice the Federal Reserve Board often ignores the proportion of its gold
> reserve to its liabilities and is influenced, in determining its discount policy, by
> the object of maintaining stability in prices, trade, and employment. Out of
> convention and conservatism it accepts gold. Out of prudence and understand-
> ing it buries it. [12]

This policy was not peculiar to the United States alone. In Great Britain, too, strides were being made at that time toward the ideal of regulating the bank rate and credit policy by reference to the internal price level rather than by reference to the pre-war criteria of the amount of money in circulation, the status of the gold reserves, or the value of the dollar exchange.

In the light of conditions obtaining in the post-war world, particularly in the United States, Keynes concluded that there could be no issue between a managed and an automatic standard, since the former had already supplanted the latter, as he notes in the following observation in the *Tract on Monetary Reform*:

> In truth, the gold standard is already a barbarous relic. All of us, from the
> Governor of the Bank of England downwards, are now primarily interested in
> preserving the stability of business, prices and employment, and are not likely,
> when the choice is forced on us, deliberately to sacrifice these to the outworn
> dogma, which had its value once, of £3:17 : 10½ per ounce. Advocates of the
> ancient standard do not observe how remote it now is from the spirit and the
> requirements of the age. A regulated non-metallic standard has slipped in
> unnoticed. It exists. [13]

The real issue in Keynes's mind was not whether the monetary standard should be managed, but for what purpose it should be managed. Should it be managed for the objective of securing a stable internal price level or a stable exchange rate? Actually, Keynes's concept of a managed standard took into account both objectives. It was to provide "a method for regulating the supply of currency and credit with a view to maintaining so far as possible, the stability of the internal price level."[14] It also made provision for a system "for regulating the supply of foreign exchange so as to avoid purely temporary fluctuations, caused by seasonal or other influences and not due to a lasting disturbance in the relation between the internal and external price level."[15]

Although Keynes included the stabilization of the exchange rate as one of the objectives to be achieved by a managed currency, this in no way contradicts his earlier position on the primacy of a stable internal price level,[16] as noted the following statement:

> At any rate, my scheme would require that they [the Treasury and the Bank of England] should adopt the stability of sterling prices as their 'primary' objective—though this would not prevent their aiming at exchange stability also as a secondary objective by cooperating with the Federal Reserve Board in a common policy.[17]

Keynes emphasized that his advocacy of exchange stability as a secondary objective would in no way impair the realization of his first objective. Rather, it would simply be a concomitant of stable prices in both Great Britain and in the United States. His contention was that "so long as the Federal Reserve Board was successful in keeping dollar prices steady, the objective of keeping sterling prices steady would be identical with the objective of keeping the dollar exchange steady."[18] However, Keynes warned that should the Federal Reserve Board fail to keep dollar prices stable, sterling prices should not be made to follow them simply for the sake of maintaining a fixed parity of exchange.

Additional proof that Keynes was entirely consistent in advocating both a stable internal price level and a stable exchange rate may be had by considering the type of exchange stability he sought. The exchange stability favored by Keynes was unlike the long period stability associated with the international gold standard. His objective was to eliminate seasonal and other passing variations not caused by lasting disturbances between internal and external price levels. In short, Keynes favored a stabilization of the exchange rate only for short periods of time. In the long run, however, the exchange should be left free to adjust to the relation existing between the internal and external price levels.[19]

Having set forth the objectives of his monetary system, Keynes then outlined the criteria to be employed by the Treasury and the Bank of England for determining whether fiscal and monetary policies were being properly directed toward the realization of those ends.

The first norm suggested by Keynes was an index number of prices compiled in a way to indicate the behavior of a standard composite commodity. The authorities would then seek to contain variations in this index within certain prescribed limits just as they tried before the war to keep the price of gold from varying by more than a certain amount. However, Keynes did not rely exclusively on this price index, since the action resulting from this indicator might be unduly delayed. It is not the past but the future rise or decline in prices that has to be counteracted.

Therefore, in addition to actual price movements, Keynes suggested that the authorities utilize the following barometers in determining appropriate fiscal and monetary policies: the state of employment, the volume of production, the effective demand for credit, the structure of interest rates, the volume of new security issues, the amount of cash in circulation, the flow of foreign trade, and the level of the exchange. All these statistics, said Keynes, should be analyzed for the purpose of achieving stable domestic prices. [20]

A more critical task commanding Keynes's attention was the development of a modus operandi that would help to achieve simultaneously a stable domestic price level and a stable exchange rate. The crux of the problem here was to promote long term price stability and short-run exchange stability. In other words, the objective was to dampen the excessive sensitivity of the exchanges to temporary influences, as was possible under the gold standard, but without at the same time leaving the internal economy open to all the vagaries attending fluctuations in the value of gold.

Keynes believed that it was possible to stabilize the exchange rate without at the same time having to subject the internal economy to the disequilibrating effects of gold and capital movements, if a number of modifications were made to the monetary and banking system that emerged after the war. These innovations included manipulation of gold buying and selling prices, regulation of forward exchange dealings, spreading the gold points, control of the rate of long term foreign lending, separation of gold reserves from bank note circulation, and augmenting the size of central bank reserves. These monetary control devices were largely developed by Keynes in the period from 1920 to 1930 and are treated principally in his *Tract on Monetary Reform* (1923) and his *Treatise on Money* (1930).

Concerning the regulation of the buying and selling prices of gold, Keynes suggested that the Bank of England quote such prices weekly just as it stipulated the rate of discount every Thursday morning. These quotations might remain unchanged for a considerable period of time; however, unlike the practice of the pre-war era, they would not be pegged for all time. In determining these gold prices, Keynes at first recommended that a spread of 0.5 percent be established between the buying and selling prices. Later he suggested a range of at least 2 percent. The significance of having the Bank of England stand ready to exchange gold for sterling at stipulated prices is that this guarantee would minimize fluctuations in the rate of exchange over the short run. For example, if the exchange rate of sterling for dollars had a tendency to soften, this depreciation of sterling could not go beyond a certain point, namely, the gold export point for sterling. For once the exchange rate reached this level, it would be cheaper to convert sterling notes for gold at the Bank of England and remit the metal to the United States. By so having the Bank of England place a flooring below and a ceiling on the gold value of the pound over short intervals, the exchange rate would be largely insulated from the pressures of every minor movement. However, it should be cautioned that while the exchange rate would be stabilized over the short run, it would not be so stabilized over the long run, for this would be tantamount to surrendering the stability of the internal price level.

In order to keep the domestic price level steady, the Central Bank would have to determine whether it should adjust the value of the exchange rate by altering its gold buying and selling prices or whether it should adjust its discount rate. For example, if at the prevailing bank rate and level of gold prices there occurs an influx or efflux of gold that is disruptive of domestic prices, the monetary authority will have to determine whether this gold movement is due to the operation of internal or external forces. Assuming that there occurs an outflow of gold from the country, how is this outflow to be stopped and prices stabilized? If this loss of gold appears to be caused by a tendency of sterling to depreciate in terms of commodities, that is, by internal inflationary pressures, the proper remedy is to raise the bank rate. If, on the other hand, this gold outflow can be explained by a tendency of gold to appreciate abroad in terms of goods and services, that is, by lower foreign prices, the correct prescription is to raise the gold buying price.

By raising the value of gold in terms of sterling, more pounds would be surrendered to the foreign customer for the same amount of gold as heretofore. This action would have the effect of bringing the higher British prices into balance with those prevailing in other countries without any need for internal adjustment. In short, a devalued pound would enable the British to compete in foreign markets without having to subject their economy to serious deflation. Once this balance between local and world prices is achieved, the gold outflow will be stemmed and may, in fact, be reversed.

Under the orthodox gold standard, when gold appreciated in terms of foreign commodities and, as a result, started to flow abroad, this outflow was usually checked by a decline in the domestic price level. In the monetary system proposed by Keynes, however, such a disruption of the domestic price level was unnecessary, for the Central Bank would effectively bring it into balance with the price levels prevailing abroad by simply surrendering more of its cheapened currency for the same quantity of gold.

The second recommendation made by Keynes for managing the currency dealt with forward exchange operations. In addition to its quotations for the purchase and sale of gold, Keynes urged that the Bank of England quote rates at which it would be prepared to sell three months forward exchange on one or two selected financial centers. [21] These prices would be established at a reasonable discount or premium on the spot quotation, depending on the relative standing of the interest rates in the two centers. Other factors affecting the spread between spot and forward quotations would include financial uncertainty, political risk, the demand and supply of forward exchange, and the size and extent of competition in the various foreign money markets.

Apart from these latter considerations and assuming only that the interest rate in New York is 3 percent higher than in London, the price of dollars purchased forward should be 3 percent per annum cheaper than spot dollars in terms of sterling. This means that an individual who is desirous of converting sterling into forward dollars under these conditions should be able to obtain them at a discount on the spot price, whereas a person wishing to exchange dollars for forward sterling would have to pay a premium on the spot price in order to make up for the lower-interest return obtainable in London. In the absence of any disturbing influences, Keynes noted that given two money markets in which unlike rates of interest prevail, "forward quotations for the purchase of the currency of the dearer money market tend to be cheaper than spot quotations by a percentage per month equal to the excess of the interest which can be earned in a month in the dearer market over what can be earned in the cheaper (market)"[22] and the forward quotations for the purchase of the currency of the cheaper money market will tend to be higher by this amount.

To eliminate as much risk as possible from the Central Bank's forward exchange operations, Keynes suggested that it deal in both the spot and forward markets. Every sale of forward exchange should be accompanied by a corresponding spot purchase of the currency being traded. In this way, the bank can escape the risk of loss. Similarly, every purchase of forward exchange should be matched by a corresponding spot sale of the currency being exchanged. However, not every forward transaction need be covered by a corresponding spot purchase or sale, provided that a forward sale of exchange on a particular center may be matched with a forward purchase on that same center. By so offsetting these forward contracts one against the other, it will not be necessary for the bank to assume an open or speculative position.[23] Moreover, such a matching of contracts will obviate the need to transfer funds in either direction, which is, of course, one of the important objectives of such forward dealings.

To handle such forward exchange operations, the Central Bank would have to maintain a certain amount of cash resources or borrowing facilities in the financial centers on which it buys and sells exchange. This fund should be large enough to sustain any loss that might be incurred by the Bank in its operations. In fact, losses are to be contemplated, because at times the Central Bank may arbitrarily have to set rates that are moving counter to market forces. But even allowing for these losses, the fund would not have to be quite so large as one set up for the purpose of maintaining the exchange value of a currency. It would be a revolving fund in that it would be automatically replenished at the maturity of the forward contracts.

The establishment of a well-developed forward exchange market, Keynes thought, would help to facilitate the flow of commerce between nations. By enabling traders to determine in advance the value of their transactions in terms of their own currency, a forward exchange market would help to eliminate much of the uncertainty that usually attends a fluctuating exchange rate. Dealings in forward exchange would permit traders to enjoy the certainty provided by a system of fixed exchange rates, despite fluctuations that might subsequently occur in the exchange rate. Thus relieved of the need to provide a fixed exchange rate for the advantage of the foreign trade community, the authorities could more freely devote themselves to promoting monetary and fiscal policies attuned to their domestic needs.

A third proposal made by Keynes for managing a nation's currency system centered on the control of short term capital movements. Under the prewar gold standard system, domestic equilibrium was often disrupted from the outside by the existence of different interest rate structures in the various international financial centers. Because of these variations, short term balances would move from those centers offering a relatively low rate of interest to those financial capitals offering a higher rate of return. To control these inward and outward capital flows, the level of bank rate, though corresponding to domestic needs, would have to be altered. The Central Bank would have to set aside its own domestic monetary objectives and adjust its interest rate to the world level. Thus a nation's monetary policy was often determined by reference to external considerations—a prospect very much opposed by Keynes. For if a nation's interest rate is to be determined by outside forces, it may be impossible for it to achieve domestic investment equilibrium. According to Keynes, "This will happen if its foreign balance is inelastic, and if, at the same time, it is unable to absorb the whole of its savings in new investment at the world rate of interest."[24]

It is quite clear, therefore, that if a nation was to achieve some degree of autonomy in the determination of its interest rate policy, it would have to exercise control over short term capital movements. This Keynes hoped to accomplish in part via the forward exchange mechanism. The plan envisaged by him would have the Central Bank regulate within limits the movement of capital funds by entering into forward exchange operations. Through its buy and sell quotations for forward exchange, the Central Bank would influence the gain or loss resulting from the exchange of one currency for another and in this way could control the movement of funds between different financial centers. Thus freed from the necessity of employing its bank rate to satisfy external requirements, the Central Bank could then utilize this device for the promotion of stable prices, full employment, and other purely domestic objectives.

To illustrate the manner in which Keynes's plan would help curb capital flows, let us assume that the Central Bank lowers its bank rate to a level below that prevailing in foreign financial centers. To take advantage of the higher interest rate that would be obtainable in foreign financial centers, bankers and other holders of balances that are available for short term investment will be inclined to place them in foreign bills or to deposit them abroad. However, this type of investment involves considerable risk in a system of fluctuating exchange rates because of the unfavorable movements in the exchange. Therefore, to protect himself from such a possibility, the holder of these foreign investments may enter into a contract to sell foreign exchange thirty or ninety days forward, depending on the maturity of his investments. In this way, the owner of such balances could move his funds from one financial center to another in the knowledge that his earnings from the higher interest rate would be completely safeguarded.

It was Keynes's thought that if this element of safety provided by forward exchange dealings could in some way be reduced or eliminated, this might inhibit some balances from moving from country to country in quest of higher interest earnings. The way to do this, he observed, would be to have the Central Bank set the price of forward exchange at a level that would offset any gain in interest realized from the foreign investment of funds. In effect, should the discount on the forward exchange be sufficiently large to eliminate the gain in interest, no one could gain from the higher interest rates prevailing abroad, except by taking an open position and assuming an exchange risk. Since few investors would be likely to remit funds temporarily from one money market to another on any large scale simply to take advantage of a 0.5 or 1 percent per annum differential in the interest rate, while exposing himself to a possible exchange loss, this alteration of forward exchange prices would serve to restrict the migration of short term balances.

By adjusting the buying or selling rate on forward exchange, the Central Bank could make short term interest rates at home stand temporarily in such relation (within limits) to similar rates abroad as it might deem advisable. By neutralizing the differential between its own interest rate and those rates prevailing abroad, the Central Bank would tend to inhibit the movement of funds between international financial centers. Thus relieved of the need to employ the bank rate as a means of preserving equilibrium in its balance of payments and stability of its exchange, the monetary authority could then utilize this mechanism exclusively for satisfying internal economic requirements, especially the maintenance of high levels of employment. That the main function of bank rate should be the promotion of purely domestic objectives, and not the regulation of the exchange rate, was clearly indicated by Keynes, as noted in the following observation:

> I have expressly excluded from my devices changes in bank rate and in the volume of domestic credit, which were the main instruments of pre-war policy. It is the outstanding lesson of our post-war experience that these methods must be entirely discarded as a means of regulating the exchanges. They required for their success certain special conditions which, no longer obtain, and may have been responsible even in pre-war days for much damage. It is essential that they should be employed in future with exclusive regard to internal conditions and, in particular, the state of employment.[25]

Although variations in the price of forward exchange could be effective in discouraging the movement of funds when the exchange rate was at a level somewhere between the gold points, Keynes recognized that it was not equally effective when the value of the exchange rested at one of these extremes. So long as the exchange was at some intermediate point, there was a likelihood that it might move up or down. If the owner of international balances transferred his funds abroad at such a level of, them exchange, he would run the risk of not being able to repatriate them at the same rate of exchange. Thus, in determining whether or not he should avail himself of the higher rate of return obtainable abroad, the holder of these balances would have to offset this advantage by the possibility of an exchange loss. Often, this risk was enough to inhibit a substantial outward flow of short term capital.

However, the situation was altogether different when the exchange rate reached either the gold expert or import point. For example, if the dollar-sterling exchange rate were anchored at the gold export point for sterling, an interest rate in London higher than the one prevailing in New York would induce a flow of funds from New York to London. For as the exchange touches this point, there is no threat, barring a devaluation of the pound, that the value of sterling will drop below this level. At this level, the owners of sterling balances are fairly confident that they will be able to return home their capital without incurring any exchange loss.[26] In fact, there may even be some likelihood that during the period of the loan sterling will appreciate in terms of dollars; hence, the owners of these funds stand to realize an exchange profit in addition to the higher-interest return. The same situation, of course, would hold in the opposite direction.

Keynes noted that when the exchange rate is fixed within very narrow limits, as is usually the case in the international gold standard, loans in different national currencies are virtually identical, because the two currencies are interchangeable without cost at a rate of exchange known in advance. Since there is very little risk involved in making such loans, bank balances migrate freely in response to differences in interest rates.[27]

Clearly, if the movement of short term balances between foreign financial markets was to be discouraged, the element of certainty attending these transactions would have to be eliminated or at least reduced. An element of doubt or expense would have to be injected into these transactions. One way of accomplishing this, said Keynes, was to widen the margin between the gold points. This notion of spreading the gold points was not novel to Keynes's thinking of the 1920s. Actually, he had made this recommendation in his *Indian Currency and Finance* in 1913 as a means of coping with floating international balances. In that work, he indicated that differences in interest rates between financial centers will not lead to short term capital movements when their costs of remittance are high. Specifically, he pointed out that although the interest rate might go as high as 7 or 8 percent on excellent security, fully 5 percent more than could be obtained in London, the cost of transferring funds between India and London would largely wipe out that advantage. Keynes estimated that the cost of remittance per rupee amounted to 3/32 d or .6 percent. But to recoup this amount on a three-month loan, say, the rate of interest in India would have to be about 2.5 percent higher than in London. Therefore, notwithstanding the substantially higher interest rate obtainable in India, there was little incentive to transfer British funds to that country under these circumstances. Funds might be further inhibited from moving between the two countries, he observed, if there existed any danger of an exchange fluctuation or if gold were not freely obtainable.

These cost and risk factors are extremely significant, for they determine the real gold point spread. This spread Keynes defined as the maximum spread between the best and worst terms on which two currencies may be exchanged. It is the existence of this difference between the terms on which one currency is exchanged for another and the terms on which this transaction may be later reversed that serves to dampen the sensitivity of capital flows to interest rate differentials under the gold standard and thereby permits unlike interest rate structures to obtain at least to some degree in different money markets.[28]

The margin between the gold points is a function of two factors—doubt and cost. The first element consists of the uncertainty attending the future terms of exchange between two currencies. Such uncertainty may exist, for example, when the Central Bank fails to guarantee the parity value of its currency. The cost factor is made up of two components. The first is the difference between the Central Bank's buying and selling prices for gold. The second cost element consists of those expenses associated with transferring gold from one locale to another, for example, freight charges, insurance, and loss of interest while in transit. In general, the maximum cost range for different pairs of countries during the late 1920s varied from one-half to one and one-half percent. This margin between the gold points, that is, the maximum spread between the best and worst terms on which two currencies could be exchanged, was extremely significant, for it helped to protect a nation's money market from being upset "by every puff of wind which blows in the money markets of other countries."[29]

To widen further the spread between the gold points, and thus further insulate each nation's money market from monetary developments abroad, Keynes suggested that "the difference between a Central Bank's obligatory buying and selling prices of gold should be made somewhat greater than hitherto, say 2 percent, so that there would be at least this difference between the gold points irrespective of the actual cost of transporting gold."[30] Such a widening of the spread between the gold points would increase the range within which the exchange rate could fluctuate. The wider the range over which the exchange may vary, the greater the possibility that the holder of foreign balances may incur an exchange loss in transferring his funds from one financial center to another. Faced with this possibility of a greater exchange loss, the more reluctant owners of such balances will be to send them abroad in quest of a higher interest return. Moreover, a widening of the gold points will further lessen the possibility of widespread capital movements, because the farther apart they are set, the fewer will be the occasions on which the exchange will reach either of these limits. The less frequently this occurs, the less often can a prospective lender of international funds be able to make a loan with the certainty that he will be able subsequently to reverse this transaction without danger of incurring an exchange loss.[31]

To the extent that a widening of the gold points increases the possible amplitude of exchange fluctuations and reduces the frequency with which the exchange rate moves to the gold points, bank balances are likely to be less sensitive to variations in interest rates abroad. Thus relieved of the need to deal with the disequilibrating effects of floating balances, the Central Bank is in a better position to pursue an autonomous monetary policy aimed at the attainment of domestic stability, which was, of course, the primary objective of Keynes's managed currency proposal.

To protect further the home economy from the disequilibrating movement of international funds, Keynes suggested that the monetary authority control the rate of long term lending, that is, the rate at which purchases of foreign securities are made. To accomplish this, he recommended that the Bank of England place an embargo on new issues floated in London whenever the situation so dictated. He also suggested that the Treasury impose a punitive tax on the income derived from securities purchased on foreign exchanges.[32]

The last feature of Keynes's managed currency scheme dealt with the size of Central Bank reserves and measures for augmenting them. Keynes was opposed to setting aside a minimum reserve of gold against the note issue,[33] since such a requirement sterilizes a like amount of the precious metal which the monetary authority might otherwise use to meet temporary or sudden deficits in its balance of payments.[34] Keynes further disagreed with the theory of tying up the gold reserve with the note issue on grounds that such a practice did not promote national economic objectives. The real purpose of stipulating the amount of gold to be held against the volume of notes was to indicate to the Central Bank that when the minimum reserve of gold to notes was reached, a curtailment of credit was in order, if it was to maintain the value of its legal tender money at lawful parity. Although adherence to this ratio preserved convertibility, it did not equally guarantee the stability of prices. As Keynes points out, "This method belongs indeed to a period when the preservation of convertibility was all that one thought about, and before the idea of utilizing bank rate as a means of keeping prices and employment steady had become practical politics."[35]

The effect of relating the gold reserve to the note issue is to make the amount of gold available to meet international emergencies and indebtedness dependent on the amount of paper in circulation despite the fact that there is no direct nexus between the two. (Neither did Keynes discern any nexus between the amount of paper money in circulation and the gold reserve. The amount of money in circulation, he thought, should be determined by the state of trade, prices, and employment.) Keynes believed that gold should be used exclusively as a reserve for correcting the influences of a temporarily adverse balance of payments and in this way insure the day to day stability of the exchange.[36] Given more substantial gold reserves, Keynes believed that the Central Bank could more effectively offset unfavorable developments in the balance of payments and thus be in a position to pursue more autonomous monetary policies.

In addition to increasing the Central Bank's free or excess reserves, Keynes urged that large liquid balances be held in foreign centers and that these balances be permitted to experience wide fluctuations. He also suggested that overdraft facilities be arranged among central banks and that borrowing and lending arrangements be established between them and a Supernational Bank, for which he provided the blueprint.[37]

SUMMARY

In summary, it may be noted that the principal feature of the managed currency scheme developed by Keynes during the 1920s was that it sought to achieve external equilibrium in a way that would not interfere with the promotion of full employment and stable prices in the internal sector of the economy. By contrast, external balance under the gold standard could be realized only by forcing the domestic economy into line with the external sectors. Often a nation was obliged to sacrifice its domestic objectives for the sake of maintaining the value of its exchange at parity or to preserve balance in its foreign accounts.

Being primarily concerned with the attainment of full employment and stable internal prices, Keynes was opposed to the implementation of a monetary policy that would sacrifice these objectives simply to insure the maintenance of external equilibrium. In his estimate, the bank rate should be employed for the satisfaction of domestic and not international requirements.

Certainly, Keynes recognized that external equilibrium could not be disregarded; however, he felt that it should not be accomplished at the expense of domestic well-being. If adjustments between a nation's internal and external sectors had to be made, these, he insisted, should be effected in the latter, as witness his suggestions that the Central Bank should alter its gold buying and selling prices; quote buying and selling prices for forward exchange; and widen the spread between the gold points in order to cope more effectively with capital flows; and increase the amount of gold reserves at its disposal for combating temporary exchange rate fluctuations and balance of payments disturbances. By bringing the external sector into balance with the home economy, instead of the other way around, the Central Bank would then be free to pursue its monetary policies independently and free of interference and pressure from without. Not only would the monetary authority be relieved of any anxieties respecting the transmission of external disturbances into the internal sector, but the monetary authority would also be in a position to utilize the bank rate exclusively for the advancement of purely domestic policies.

Keynes's quest for national monetary independence and insulation of the domestic economy from disruptive external forces through a managed monetary standard illustrates his abiding desire to promote first and foremost the well-being of the domestic economy. Ultimately, it was this prior concern with the problems of the domestic sector, particularly in terms of employment, that caused him to part company with the classicists on the issue of free trade—a proposition to be established in the subsequent chapters of this book.

NOTES

1. J. M. Keynes, *A Tract on Monetary Reform* (New York: Harcourt, Brace, 1924), 173.
2. Keynes, *A Tract on Monetary Reform*, 40.
3. J. M. Keynes, "Recent Economic Events in India," *Economic Journal* 19, no. 73 (March 1909): 51–67.
4. J. M. Keynes, "Recent Economic Events in India," 66–67.
5. R. F. Harrod, *The Life of John Maynard Keynes* (London: Macmillan, 1951), 146.
6. J. M. Keynes, "The Prospects of Money, November, 1914," *Economic Journal* 24, no. 96 (December 1914): 626–27.
7. Keynes, "The Prospects of Money, November, 1914," 626–27.
8. J. M. Keynes, "The Prospects of Money, November, 1914," 620–27.
9. Keynes, *Indian Currency and Finance* (London: Macmillan, 1913), 100–101.
10. Keynes, *A Tract on Monetary Reform*, 170.

11. Keynes, *A Tract on Monetary Reform*, 166–68.

12. Keynes, *A Tract on Monetary Reform*, 197.

13. Keynes, *A Tract on Monetary Reform*, 172–73.

14. Keynes, *A Tract on Monetary Reform*, 177.

15. A. F. Smithies, "Reflections on the Work and Influence of John M. Keynes," *The Quarterly Journal of Economics* 115 (1951): 588.

16. Keynes, *A Tract on Monetary Reform*, 186.

17. Keynes, *A Tract on Monetary Reform*, 186.

18. Austin Robinson, "John M. Keynes," *The Economic Journal* 107 (1947): 63.

19. Keynes, *A Tract on Monetary Reform*, 188–89.

20. Keynes dealt extensively with the question of the forward exchange in his article "The Forward Market in the Foreign Exchanges," which appeared in the *Manchester Guardian Commercial Supplements on Reconstruction* in Europe on April 20, 1923. Keynes also treated this question in his *Tract on Monetary Reform*, chapter 3; in the *Treatise on Money*, 323–27; and in his article "The Future of the Foreign Exchanges," in *Lloyd's Bank Monthly Review*, on October 1935 (VI, N.S. 68): 527-535.

21. Keynes, *A Tract on Monetary Reform*, 124.

22. R. F. Mikesell, *Foreign Exchange in the Postwar World* (New York: The Twentieth Century Fund, 1954), 163.

23. J. M. Keynes, *A Treatise on Money*, vol. II (London: Macmillan, 1930), 304.

24. R. G. Hawtrey, *The Art of Central Banking* (London: Longmans, Green, 1932), 414.

25. Keynes, "The Future of the Foreign Exchanges," 531.

26. Keynes, *A Treatise on Money*, vol. I, 324.

27. Keynes, *A Treatise on Money*, vol. II, 319.

28. See Keynes, *Indian Currency and Finance*, 243–51; also, "Stabilization of the European Exchanges—A Plan for Genoa," 4.

29. Keynes, *A Treatise on Money*, vol. II, 325.

30. Keynes, *A Treatise on Money*, vol. II, 325.

31. It should be noted that a widening of the gold points, as suggested by Keynes, would not have resolved completely the problem of disequilibrating short term capital movements. A wider spread between the gold points would provide an even greater inducement to convert funds into the weaker currency whenever the exchange approached one of the gold points, since it would offer a greater possibility for exchange appreciation than would a more narrow spread of the gold points. Although a wider spread of the gold points would reduce the frequency with which balances are transferred, the amount of money involved in these transfers when the exchange touches one of these points would be increased, because of the possibility of a greater exchange profit. For a fuller discussion of this matter see C. R. Whittlesey, *International Monetary Issues: The Art of Central Banking* (New York: McGraw-Hill, 1937), 419.

32. Note the similarity between Keynes's suggestions of the 1920s with attempts by the U.S. government in the summer of 1963 to stem the outflow of capital.

33. J. M. Keynes, "The Amalgamation of the British Note Issue," *Economic Journal* 38, no. 150 (June 1928): 321–28.

34. Again note the similarity between Keynes's proposal made in the 1920s with the suggestion of the Council of Economic Advisers in 1961 that the United States divorce its gold reserve from its currency and bank deposits and use them instead for dealing with balance of payments problems.

35. Keynes, *A Treatise on Money*, vol. II, 210.

36. Keynes, *A Treatise on Money*, vol. II, 209–13.

37. These notions were later incorporated by Keynes's Clearing Union proposals of the 1940s.

The Evolution of Keynes's Thinking on Foreign Trade from World War I to World War II

The purpose of this section will be to track the development of Keynes's foreign trade views from the early phase of his career from around World War I to his disenchantment with free trade in the years just prior to the outbreak of World War II.

Trained at Cambridge in the classical tradition by the renowned Alfred Marshall, Keynes, not surprisingly, subscribed to the tenets of free trade. His allegiance to the doctrine during the early phase of his career was grounded in the Law of Comparative Advantage and the efficiency that results from the international division of labor.

His support for free trade was clearly evident in his *Economic Consequences of the Peace*, in which he criticized the terms of the treaty for allowing the French to develop their own steel making facilities to process the iron ore from Alsace-Lorraine, a region that had been ceded to them, when those facilities were already available in eastern Germany. In his view, the ore should have been exported to Germany, processed there, and the finished product made available to the French and all of the other needy countries of Europe.

Keynes's writings in the *Manchester Guardian Commercial Supplements* and the *Tract on Monetary Reform* clearly show that free trade was essential for Europe's post-war recovery. What made trade for Europe so compelling was the fact that much of its territory had been partitioned into smaller states, none of which were self-sustaining and would have to trade with each other if they were to survive under the new political arrangement.

However, with Britain's home economy in difficult straits and her balance of payments stubbornly refusing correction through orthodox measures, Keynes, in the late 1920s, started to question the ability of free trade to resolve the country's external difficulties. And so, in his *Treatise on Money*, which was published in 1930, he suggested that Britain pursue a more restrictive trade policy by altering the relative prices of her imports and exports.

Whereas Keynes's endorsement of a more restrictive trade policy was "enshrouded in elaborate theoretical language" in the *Treatise on Money*, his support for restricted trade, as expressed in the Macmillan Report of 1930, was much less cryptic. Later, with Britain's balance of payments rapidly deteriorating and practically extinct by early 1931, Keynes came out in favor of a revenue tariff in March of that year, one that he hoped would ameliorate the foreign balance and provide funds for the Treasury for the expansion of public works projects.

Keynes's support for a revenue tariff was short lived, because of Britain's abandonment of the gold standard in September of that same year. The subsequent devaluation of the sterling exchange provided the British the same advantage, if not more, than would have the introduction of a revenue tariff and so he asked that consideration of his proposal be deferred. But did the fact that he abandoned the tariff mean that he was any less committed to protecting Britain's external interests? It's not at all likely.

Nevertheless, with the gradual improvement in Britain's trade balance, Keynes became somewhat more receptive to free trade. But when the World Economic Conference in London in June 1933 failed to act favorably on his proposal for a worldwide expansion program, he receded once again from free trade and urged Britain to forsake any effort to resolve her financial and economic problems through international cooperation and try, instead, to resolve them independently.

The conditions of the twentieth century, he argued, were different from those of the past. Many of the arguments in support of free trade, albeit valid at an earlier time, were no longer applicable to Great Britain. Accordingly, he urged her to minimize her trade and financial contacts and resolve her problems autonomously.

Chapter Four

Keynes's Early Free-Trade Views

Keynes's early thinking on the question of free versus restricted foreign trade was entirely orthodox. Although Keynes did not in any of his early writings specifically consider the comparative merits of free and restricted foreign trade, his sentiments were decidedly partial to a liberal trade policy. This may be confirmed by a review of his early post–World War I contribution, *The Economic Consequences of the Peace*,[1] wherein he dealt with the Versailles Conference and the Peace Treaty fashioned there.

According to the terms of the Peace Treaty, Germany was required to cede to France the region of Alsace-Lorraine, an area that accounted for about 75 percent of her pre-war iron ore output. Although Keynes conceded that the Germans should surrender this rich territory, he felt that a large amount of the ore mined there should be freely exported to Germany for processing, since she already had a substantial steel making capacity. Most of Germany's blast furnaces and steel foundries were located in the interior of the country and so were not relinquished with the iron ore fields in the Alsace-Lorraine region. Since France did not possess adequate steel making facilities, Keynes's proposal certainly had economic merit. But owing to political considerations, it was extremely doubtful that France would agree to such a proposition. Having recovered the ore deposits of Lorraine, she would now surely attempt to develop steel making facilities within her own borders.

The contemplated French action was in direct contradiction to the principles of free trade, notably the Law of Comparative Advantage, and was roundly condemned by Keynes. Such a policy, he asserted, would reduce the amount of steel to be produced and thereby retard the European reconstruction. If only political considerations could remain subservient to economics, lamented Keynes, the principles of free trade could be made to operate and thus achieve the greatest advantage for all nations concerned.[2] This senti-

ment, so eloquently expressed in the following argument, provides one of the
first written indications of Keynes's early free trade philosophy.

> In fact, here, as elsewhere, political considerations cut disastrously across
> economics. In a regime of Free Trade and free economic intercourse it would
> be of little consequence that iron lay on one side of a political frontier, and
> labor, coal and blast furnaces on the other. But, as it is, men have devised ways
> to impoverish themselves and one another, and prefer collective animosities to
> individual happiness. It seems certain, calculating on the present passions and
> impulses of European capitalistic society, that the effective iron output of
> Europe will be diminished by a new political frontier (which sentiment and
> historic justice require), because nationalism and private interest are allowed
> to impose a new economic frontier along the same lines. These latter consider-
> ations are allowed, in the present governance of Europe, to prevail over the
> intense need of the Continent for the most sustained and efficient production to
> repair the destructions of war, and to satisfy the insistence of labor for a larger
> reward.[3]

The strongest expression of Keynes's free trade convictions in *The Economic Consequences of the Peace* is to be found in its closing pages, where
he recommends the formation of a Free Trade Union under the auspices of
the League of Nations. All participating nations would permit the free importation of goods produced by other members of the association. The nucleus
of this alliance, he suggested, should be made up of Germany, Poland, the
new states formerly contained in the Austro-Hungarian and Turkish Empires,
and the mandated states. He urged that membership in the union by these
states be made compulsory for a period of ten years, and that participation by
other nations be left voluntary. Although Keynes expected some of these
other nations to oppose membership in the organization, he hoped "that the
United Kingdom, at any rate, would become an original member."[4]

The reason for Keynes's proposing such a free trade union is that it would
compensate at least in part for the organization and efficiency lost by the
creation of new but economically incomplete national states. In keeping with
the orthodox view that self-sufficiency is practical only for countries with
vast diversified areas, Keynes agreed that the partition of the empires of
Germany, Austria-Hungary, Russia, and Turkey into some twenty sovereign
powers no longer made possible such national autonomy. If these newly
formed states were to survive, economic cooperation was essential. Moreover, Keynes thought that a free trade union comprising the whole of central,
eastern, and southeastern Europe, Siberia, Turkey, and the United Kingdom
might do as much for the peace and prosperity of the world as the newly
formed League of Nations.[5]

Keynes's advocacy of a multilateral free trade system for Europe established unequivocally his early belief in the efficacy of the classical free trade

argument. In fact, so convinced was he of the benefits to be derived from the free international flow of goods that he urged his own nation to join the free trade union proposed by him.

It is significant to note that Keynes did not at this time foresee any conflict between the promotion of Great Britain's internal economic welfare and its participation in an open free trade system. Britain had prospered in the past as a free trader and it was not yet apparent why she might find a free trade system less advantageous in her post-war economic setting.

Keynes remained steadfast in his free trade convictions throughout the early 1920s. As in his *Economic Consequences of the Peace*, he adhered to the view that free trade was essential for European economic recovery. In commenting on the relevance of free trade for the reconstruction of Europe, Keynes showed himself to be a staunch supporter of the classical doctrine, as the following passage will attest.

> We must hold to Free Trade, in its widest interpretations as inflexible dogma, to which no exception is admitted, wherever the decision rests with us. We must hold to this even where we receive no reciprocity of treatment and even in those rare cases where by infringing it we could in fact obtain a direct economic advantage. We should hold to Free Trade as a principle of international morals and not merely as a doctrine of economic advantage.[6]

These sentiments calling for nations to be selfless and magnanimous in the implementation of free trade principles are unmistakably those of a free trader in the classical tradition.

Further evidence of Keynes's preference for free trade at this time may be gleaned from two pronouncements he made on behalf of the Liberal Party's campaign during the general election of November 1923. During the campaign, Mr. Stanley Baldwin, the Conservative Party candidate, came out in favor of protection as a means of combating the existing unemployment in Great Britain. Keynes took exception with Mr. Baldwin and in doing so presented an eloquent defense on behalf of free trade. In fact, it has been said that nowhere in his writings is the classical influence better illustrated than in those arguments he presented on behalf of free trade.[7] In answering the Conservatives, Keynes cited two fundamental truths on which the validity of a free trade policy is based.

The first is the familiar Law of Comparative Advantage, which he describes in the following terms:

> It is better to employ our capital and our labour in trade where we are relatively more efficient than other people are, and to exchange the products of these trades for goods in the production of which we are relatively less efficient.[8]

Keynes contended that this principle is readily understandable, because every sane person abides by it. In his economic life, each person performs those functions for which he is best qualified and leaves to others those operations that they are capable of doing better than he can. Admittedly, there are certain exceptions to this principle, which Keynes clearly recognized. Like most free traders, he agreed that protection might be justified on certain non-economic grounds such as national defense. He also concurred with the view that such a policy might be warranted for supporting vital industries and for dealing with the dumping of goods from abroad. Perhaps the greatest concession he made to protectionism was his admission that such a policy might also be justifiable in meeting "the competition from imports from countries with depreciating currency."[9] By and large, though, Keynes's defense of the Law of Comparative Advantage was much like that of any student nurtured on the principles of classical economics.

The other important truth advanced by Keynes on behalf of free trade is that imports are beneficial to a country's economy. In this regard, he says,

> The second great principle is that there can be no disadvantage in receiving useful objects from abroad. If we have to pay at once, we can only pay with the export of goods and services, and the exchange would not take place unless there was an advantage in it. Every export, which is not paid for by an import, represents a decrease in capital available within the country.[10]

Clearly, Keynes's views at this time were contrary to those of the Mercantilists, for unlike them he did not attach much significance to a favorable balance of trade. Keynes was opposed to imposing any restrictions on the flow of imports for the purpose of obtaining a favorable balance of trade, since this was tantamount to sending goods to the rest of the world without receiving payment for them. Imports, he said, are a payment for exports and to put obstacles in their way is to be as crazy as a businessman who tried to prevent his customers and his debtors from paying their bills.[11]

The difference between a nation's exports and imports represents foreign investment. But, argued Keynes, such a diversion of capital abroad at a time when Great Britain was herself in critical need of resources was not in the national interest, as noted in his following contention:

> With our shortage of housing and the need of factories and equipment to render efficient our growing supply of labour, we need to keep more capital at home, and so arrange matters that our surplus resources are occupied in increasing our own equipment for future production and for the shelter of our population. There is already, in my opinion, too much encouragement to the export of our capital. With our diminished savings and our increasing needs we are not in the position in which we used to be for sending out goods to the rest of the world and getting back, for the time being, nothing whatever in return.[12]

Although Keynes is avowedly developing still another argument for free trade, there is a discernible new undercurrent of thought in this passage. Unlike his earlier pronouncements on behalf of free trade, Keynes now seems to be more disposed to gearing foreign trade activity to domestic needs. He appears to be somewhat less insistent than he was in the *Economic Consequences of the Peace* that nations, particularly his own, be selfless in pursuing liberal trade policies. Implicitly, he seems to be saying that Great Britain's altered post-war economic status no longer permits her to continue in her pre-war role of international financier and that she must now conserve capital for home needs. Very significantly, the statement also confirms his long held conviction, as noted in his arguments against the traditional gold standard, that domestic needs supersede those of an external character; in this instance, foreign investment should be diverted to domestic investment.

In returning to Mr. Baldwin's argument during the campaign of 1923 that a protectionist trade policy will augment employment at home, Keynes points out that if tariff barriers are raised, as urged by Mr. Baldwin and the Conservatives, this will contract the volume of trade. [13] Protection simply constitutes an effort to extract from foreign customers a money price in excess of the competitive price, and such an attempt to charge a higher price, argues Keynes, can only serve to reduce the volume of imports. But if imports are reduced, he continues, exports must similarly be cut back, because the two are necessarily equal unless, of course, they are to be given gratuitously to foreigners. To summarize the argument in Keynes's own words,

> Protection must mean—to this there is no exception—an attempt to limit the volume of trade; it must mean charging the foreigner more at the expense of doing less trader with him. And insofar as the keeping out of an import does not involve a corresponding restriction of exports, it must drive some capital out of the country. [14]

Therefore, Keynes concludes that instead of expanding the volume of activity, a protectionist policy contracts it and thereby further aggravates the problem of unemployment.

Parenthetically it should be noted that Keynes did at this time admit the possibility that a protectionist trade policy could increase the amount of work to be performed. [15] By rendering the Law of Comparative Advantage inoperative, a protectionist policy reduces the level of productivity and so requires the employment of additional labor to produce the same volume of goods that would be realized under a free trade policy. However, while a reduction in the volume of imports will increase the amount of work to be performed, it will not augment the level of national income. [16] In this regard, Keynes noted,

> If Protectionists merely mean that under their system men will have to sweat and labour more, I grant their case. By cutting off imports we might increase

the aggregate of work; but we should be diminishing the aggregate of wages. The protectionist has to prove, not merely that he has made work, but that he has increased the national income. [17]

Thus, Keynes concluded that "if there is one thing that Protection cannot do, it is to cure Unemployment." [18] There are some arguments for protection, he said, to which there are no simple refutations, but the claim that it can cure unemployment involves the protectionist fallacy in its grossest and crudest form. If imports are receipts and exports are payments, how can we expect to better ourselves, he asked, by diminishing our receipts? In his inimitably dramatic style he pondered, "Is there anything that a tariff could do, which an earthquake could not do better?" [19]

Keynes remained a staunch supporter of free trade during the mid-1920s not because of any allegiance to the laissez-faire philosophy, but because a nation enjoys a maximum advantage only when it employs its resources in those areas where it has a comparative advantage. This, he felt, was the only course a nation could legitimately take.

Although Keynes remained an advocate of free trade, it appears that he started to entertain some misgivings about it in the latter part of the decade. In an address entitled "Am I a Liberal?," which he delivered at the Liberal Party Summer School at Cambridge, he voiced his reservations in the following terms:

> In my opinion there is now no place except in the left wing of the Conservative Party, for those whose hearts are set on old-fashioned individualism and laissez-faire in all their rigour—greatly though these contributed to the success of the 19th century. I say this not because I think that these doctrines were wrong in the conditions which gave birth to them, but because they have ceased to be applicable to modern conditions. [20]

In spite of his misgivings about the applicability of the laissez-faire doctrine for the altered economic setting of the 1920s, Keynes during this period remained a staunch advocate of a free trade policy. He continued to espouse this point of view not because of any allegiance to the laissez-faire philosophy, but because of his conviction that a nation enjoys a maximum advantage when it employs its resources in those areas where it has a comparative advantage. In effect, he favored free trade, because he felt that this was the only course a nation could legitimately take, as noted in the following assertion:

> I no longer believe in the political philosophy which the Doctrine of Free Trade adorned. I believe in Free Trade because, in the long run and in general, it is the only policy which is technically sound and intellectually tight. [21]

These, though, are among Keynes's last published words in support of free trade. From this point onward he became increasingly skeptical about the appropriateness of this policy, especially for Great Britain whose economic fortunes continued to deteriorate .

SUMMARY

Inasmuch as Keynes had been trained at Cambridge by Alfred Marshall, one of the leading economists of his time, in the classical tradition, it is not surprising that he should be in favor of free trade during the early part of his career. In addition, economic conditions in Europe in the immediate post-war years were such as to add practical support to his position.

From a theoretical standpoint, Keynes favored free trade for all of the usual reasons, most notably the Law of Comparative Advantage, and the greater efficiency that results from the specialization and division of labor.

In *The Economic Consequences of the Peace*, Keynes faulted the Peace Treaty for having Germany cede Alsace Lorraine, a region rich in iron ore deposits, to the French while permitting her to retain her blast furnaces and steel making facilities, which were located further to the east. Instead of exporting ore to Germany for processing, the French were intent on developing their own steel making capacity at a time when Europe was in immediate need of all the output that could be produced. In terms of the Law of Comparative Advantage, this strategy made no sense. If the ceding of Alsace-Lorraine was a political expedient, Keynes argued, then provision should have been made for the free flow of iron ore to Germany and finished steel to France and the rest of Europe

The partition of Germany, the Austro-Hungarian Empire, Russia, and Turkey into some twenty sovereign powers similarly called for the expansion of free trade. Given their small sizes, these nations, unlike a well-diversified country, could not survive on their own. They would have to specialize in those areas where they enjoyed a comparative advantage and then trade their goods with each other. Accordingly, Keynes, again in *The Economic Consequences of the Peace*, urged the formation of a free trade union under the auspices of the League of Nations. For only by being able to exchange each other's goods freely would it be possible to regain the efficiency lost by the break-up of the larger nations.

In advancing further his argument for free trade during this period, Keynes argued that countries should not put up barriers against imported goods. For it made no sense to send goods to the rest of the world and ask for nothing in return for the time being. At the same time though he warned Britain not to run up too large a trade surplus, because a part of the resulting foreign investment should be used, instead, for satisfying domestic needs. On the surface, this advice seems to be incongruous with the tenets of free trade, but is entirely consistent with Keynes's long held view that domestic considerations should supersede those of an external character.

Ironically, he took exception with Stanley Baldwin's contention that protectionism could help to resolve Great Britain's unemployment—an argument he himself would later support. Nevertheless, at the time Keynes, relying on the Law of Comparative Advantage, argued that protection was not a cure for unemployment. He did admit that protectionism might create more work because of the loss of efficiency; however, in the end it would also lead to a lower national income and that, in turn, would lead to lower spending and more unemployment.

As of the mid-1920s, Keynes was still among the ranks of the free traders, even though he was becoming an increasingly outspoken critic of laissez-faire economics. Although "old fashioned individualism and laissez faire" contributed to the success of the nineteenth century, those doctrines, he argued, were no longer applicable to modern times.[22] But despite his misgivings with laissez-faire, he continued to adhere to the doctrine of free trade, as noted the following assurance he gave to the Liberal Summer School at Cambridge in August 1925:

> I no longer believe in the political philosophy which the Doctrine of Free Trade (laissez faire) adorned. I believe in Free Trade because, in the long run and in general, it is the only policy which is technically sound and intellectually tight.[23]

These, though, are among Keynes's last published words in support of free trade. From this point onward he became increasingly skeptical of this policy, especially for Great Britain, whose economic fortunes continued to deteriorate.

NOTES

1. This work, published in 1920, was widely acclaimed by the public because it disclosed to a far greater extent than anything up to that time the proceedings at the Versailles Conference, where the treaty with Germany was being drafted. Keynes, who attended these meetings as a member of the British Treasury delegation, showed himself to be no meek author, but a brilliant writer who was determined to deliver his message to the world and be heard. The gospel he sought to preach, according to Professor Harrod, was that the treaty was "an act of wickedness and folly." It was hypocritical and against the principles enunciated in the *Armistice*. See R. F. Harrod, *The Life of John M. Keynes* (London: Macmillan, 1951), 255; and H. C. O'Neil, "Men on Today," *Today and Tomorrow* 1 (1931): 130–35.

2. J. M. Keynes, *The Economic Consequences of the Peace* (New York: Harcourt, Brace and Howe, 1920), 99–100.

3. Keynes, *The Economic Consequences of the Peace*, 99.

4. Keynes, *The Economic Consequences of the Peace*, 265.

5. Keynes, *The Economic Consequences of the Peace*, 268.

6. J. M. Keynes, "The Underlying Principles," *Reconstruction in Europe*, January 4, 1923, 717.

7. L. R. Klein, *The Keynesian Revolution* (New York: Macmillan, 1947), 10.

8. J. M. Keynes, "Free Trade," *The Nation and Athenaeum* 34, no. 8 November 24, 1923): 302.

9. Keynes, "Free Trade," 302.

10. Keynes, "Free Trade," 302.

11. Keynes, "Free Trade," 302.

12. J. M. Keynes, "Free Trade for England," *The New Republic* 37, no. 472 (December 19, 1923): 86.

13. Keynes, "Free Trade," 302.

14. Keynes, "Free Trade for England," 87.

15. See J. M. Keynes, "Free Trade and Unemployment," *The Nation and Athenaeum* 35, no. 9 (December 1, 1923): 335–36; and J. B. Condliffe, "The Value of International Trade," *Economics* 5 , no. 18 (May 1938): 130.

16. Although Keynes in the early 1920s agreed that a protectionist policy would not increase a nation's real income, it is questionable whether he would have held to this view after he had written his *General Theory of Employment, Interest and Money*, in an economy with wide-spread capital and labor displacement the employment of these resources would, other things being equal, raise the level of its income, because it would lead to a net gain in domestic output. The situation might be otherwise, of course, if these resources were simply being transferred from other pursuits, as in a condition of full employment.

17. Keynes, "Free Trade and Unemployment," 335.

18. Keynes, "Free Trade for England," 87.

19. Keynes, "Free Trade and Unemployment," 336.

20. The address, titled "Am I a Liberal?," was reproduced in *The Nation and Athenaeum* 37, no. 19 (August 8, 1925), especially 564.

21. Keynes, "Am I a Liberal?," 564.

22. John M. Keynes, "The End of Laissez-Faire I," *The New Republic* 48, no. 612 (August 25, 1926): 13–15. Also see "The End of Laissez-Faire II," *The New Republic* 48, no. 613 (September 1, 1926); and "Laissez-Faire Versus Nation Building," *The New Republic* 37, no. 472 (December 19, 1923): editorial page.

23. Keynes, "Am I a Liberal?," 564.

Chapter Five

Keynes's Views on Commercial Policy in his Treatise on Money

During the next few years, Keynes lost faith in the free trade philosophy that he had so ably articulated in the past and found that protectionism had much more to commend it than he had formerly thought.[1]

Keynes's shift of allegiance was motivated by the economic conditions prevailing in Great Britain in the late 1920s. During that time, Great Britain was being plagued by chronic unemployment and a depressed state of activity at home, while externally she was finding it increasingly difficult to balance her accounts.[2] The latter problem was of special concern to Keynes. In fact, a number of prominent British economists, among whom numbered W. H. Beveridge, J. R. Hicks, L. C. Robbins, and F. C. Benham, alleged at the time that Keynes was first attracted to protection as a means of solving Britain's external imbalance—a condition he largely attributed to the restoration of the pound to its pre-war parity.[3] In time, Keynes was to favor a restrictionist trade policy for other considerations as well. He subsequently looked on tariffs as an alternative to devaluation,[4] as a stimulant to domestic employment, and as a means of augmenting the national revenue.[5]

The first hint of Keynes's new attitude toward protectionism is to be found in his *Treatise on Money* where in he makes "a rather hesitant case for the tariff."[6] To establish this fact is by no means easy, for as Sir William Beveridge pointed out, it is entirely possible for a protectionist to read the *Treatise* without finding in it any support for protection. According to Sir William, "To anyone, indeed, who believed almost any of the common arguments for Protection, the whole of Mr. Keynes's *Treatise* with its subtle analysis of economic reactions, would be incomprehensible."[7] Nevertheless, if one can get close enough to peer through the finely spun veil of Keynesian subtlety, one may readily discern a. preference on his part for such a commercial policy.

In view of the relevance that external equilibrium had for Keynes's change of attitude toward protectionism, an understanding of what that concept involves is essential for an explanation of his new position.

Keynes's notion of external equilibrium, as set forth in the *Treatise on Money*, contains two important elements—the volume of foreign lending and the size of the foreign balance. *Foreign lending* Keynes defines as the excess of the amount of money put at the disposal of foreigners by the nationals of a particular country through the net purchase of investments abroad over the corresponding amount expended by foreigners for investments situated in the home country.[8] It may, perhaps, be best described as a nation's balance of transactions on capital account, exclusive of gold. The foreign balance, according to Keynes, is equal to the difference between the value of home-owned output of goods and services placed at the disposal of foreigners and the value of the corresponding foreign owned output placed at the disposal of the home country. It actually amounts to the balance of trade on income account.[9] This balance is positive when a part of one nation's current output is transferred to other countries, instead of being utilized at home, and negative when the flow of goods is in the opposite direction.

Since the international balance sheet must always balance, gold is required to offset any difference between the amount of foreign lending and the value of the foreign balance. Thus, when the volume of foreign lending exceeds the value of the foreign balance, equilibrium is achieved through the exportation of gold equal to this difference, that is, foreign lending equals the foreign balance plus the gold export. On the other hand, when the foreign balance exceeds the amount of foreign lending, equilibrium is attained by the importation of gold equal to this difference; that is, the foreign balance equals foreign lending plus the gold import.

Although both of the above cases illustrate how equilibrium may be achieved in the international accounts, they do not demonstrate a true condition of external balance. Equilibrium cannot exist so long as there occurs any gold movement either into or out of a country.[10] It obtains only when the foreign balance is exactly equal to the volume of foreign lending. When this happens, foreign investment, which Keynes defines as that part of a nation's savings made available to other countries, is equal to foreign borrowing.

Given this condition of external equilibrium, Keynes in the *Treatise* maintains that internal equilibrium is achieved when home savings are equal to home investment. Internal and external equilibrium are simultaneously realized, he says, when home investment equals home savings and foreign investment (which is equal to the foreign balance) is equal to the excess of total savings over home savings (which is equal to the amount of foreign lending).[11] Thus, Keynes's concepts of internal and external equilibrium, as expressed in the *Treatise*, are both intimately related to the behavior of savings and investment.

The equality of savings and investment had different implications in the *Treatise on Money* and in the *General Theory*. In the former, this equality was achieved through a variation of the interest rate and assumed only one level of output. In the latter, this equality was achieved through a variation in spending; determined the level of employment; and applied to any level of output.

Despite the significance of their equality, Keynes observed that there is no direct or automatic relationship between the foreign balance and foreign lending. Although there are certain interrelations between them, basically they respond to independent sets of forces. Contrary to the then popular British view, Keynes held that the size of the foreign balance is not a function of the amount of foreign lending, but is determined by the relative prices of internationally traded goods at home and abroad. The fact that the volume of foreign lending varies, argued Keynes, does not mean that the foreign balance will automatically adjust itself to it immediately and without any appreciable disturbance of internal prices and income. Equilibrium between these values, he contended, depends on gold movements and the consequent alteration of interest rates.[12] As to the volume of lending, Keynes held that it is determined by relative rates of interest at home and abroad and the prevailing state of confidence.[13] Thus, if there occurs a discrepancy between the foreign balance and the volume of foreign lending, this condition of external disequilibrium will be due either to a disturbance of relative price levels or to a falling out of line of relative interest rates.[14]

A nation's ability to cope with a condition of external disequilibrium, whether it is caused by a falling out of line of relative interest rates or a disturbance of relative price levels, was, according to Keynes, largely limited to its power to alter interest rates and the terms of lending.[15]

For example, if there occurs a decline in the price level abroad, not accompanied by a similar alteration of the domestic price level, the demand for that nation's exports will decline and the demand for its imports will increase. This will lead to a deterioration of that country's foreign balance and, assuming further that there occurs no corresponding change in the volume of foreign lending, will bring about a condition of external disequilibrium. To correct this imbalance and to stem the attending gold outflow, the monetary authority will raise interest rates. The higher interest rate structure should serve to reduce the nation's volume of foreign lending and at the same time indirectly cause the general price level, the volume of home savings, and the foreign balance to fall to levels below what they were in money terms before prices fell abroad. When these adjustments have been completed a new level of equilibrium will be realized. Apart from the new money values that now prevail, Keynes maintained that nothing will be changed in real terms and that the new equilibrium would not differ significantly from the old.[16]

Should the external imbalance be caused by a downward movement of interest rates at home and abroad, the monetary authority will again have to resort to the bank rate to effect the necessary correction. However, the adjustment will not be restricted to the interest rate structure. Variations in the interest rate will have a significant bearing on price and income levels because of the effect they will have on investment activity. An increase in the bank rate at home will tend to diminish the amount of lending abroad. At the same time, though, it will also discourage borrowers from making investments at home, with the result that current savings now exceed total investment. But according to Keynes's formulation in the *Treatise*, an excess of savings over investment will have a deflationary effect on the economy, with the result that prices, profits and ultimately earnings of the productive factors must fall. The reduced money costs of production are now more competitive in relation to those abroad (assuming, of course, no offsetting adjustments take place) and will, therefore, help to increase the foreign balance.[17]

Thus, the instrument of bank rate provides a two pronged attack against external disequilibrium. On one front it discourages foreign lending and eases the gold outflow; on the other, it helps to increase the foreign balance by reducing domestic money costs of production relative to those prevailing abroad. On both counts; therefore, the higher bank rate drives the volume of foreign lending to equality with the foreign balance.[18] As in the earlier case, external equilibrium will be restored by the monetary authority by finding that interest rate that equates the foreign balance with the volume of foreign lending and additionally the level of savings with the level of investment.

Although the above abbreviated account of the process whereby balance is restored to a nation's external accounts does not consider the many transitional difficulties involved, Keynes was very much aware of them. He was quick to point out, for example, that the restoration of equilibrium in the external sector may have an adverse effect on internal equilibrium. Thus, if home investment and home saving were equal under the old interest rate, [19] they would be made unequal at the new level of interest; hence, the first effect of the monetary authority's effort to restore external equilibrium would be to disrupt the internal balance.[20] Although Keynes did not rule out the possibility that the monetary authority could succeed in achieving simultaneously internal and external equilibrium through a rate of interest that[21] would, in the long run, equate the foreign balance with foreign lending and home savings with home investment,[22] he stressed that there would still exist considerable friction and disharmony between the two conditions of equilibrium. He also noted that in an international currency system such as gold considerations of internal equilibrium are subordinated to those of external equilibrium. The primary duty of the central bank is to preserve the parity of the national currency with the international standard. The maintenance of this parity is incompatible with any long continuance of external disequilibrium. However, the central bank is under no similar compunction to maintain internal equilibrium, and so, Keynes says, "internal equilibrium must take its chances, or rather, the internal situation must be forced sooner or later into equilibrium with the external situation."[23]

According to Keynes, the degree of disharmony between internal and external equilibrium is largely dependent on the size of foreign lending relative to the amount of total saving together with its sensitivity to small changes in relative interest rates at home and abroad, and the susceptibility of the foreign balance to small changes in relative prices. The duration of the disharmony between the two depends on the facility with which changes can be effected in the internal money costs of production. If the volume of foreign lending, the foreign balance and the internal money costs of production are sensitive to small variations in the interest rate, prices and the level of employment, respectively, then the task of maintaining simultaneously both internal and external balance will not be a difficult one.[24]

However, contrary to the then prevailing theory, Keynes doubted that such sensitivity did, in fact, exist. Although he acknowledged that the volume of lending could be influenced in some countries, he maintained that the money costs of production were not flexible, especially when downward adjustment was required. Thus the foreign balance in many countries did not readily adjust to the requirements of the external situation.[25] As a result, it was not an easy matter for most nations to achieve internal and external equilibrium simultaneously in the post-war world.

Ideally, Keynes thought that a nation should be able "to bend the position of external equilibrium to suit the conditions of its own internal equilibrium."[26]

In the pre–World War I period, Keynes observed, the antagonism between internal and external equilibrium was not quite as acute as it was in the 1920s. In fact, in the pre-war period, he said, "no one troubled much about anything but the condition of external equilibrium." But since the war, he added "the progress of ideas about monetary management and the importance of stabilizing the Purchasing Power money have led to a more general concern about the preservation of internal equilibrium, without its being realized how far the one is compatible with the other."[27] The degree to which a single country can dominate the international situation and the period for which it can afford to disregard external disequilibrium, for example, by allowing gold to flow freely into or out of the economy, Keynes said, depends on its financial strength. Prior to the first World War, Great Britain enjoyed such power to influence the international situation to accord with its own domestic needs. In the post-war period, Keynes thought, the United States and to a lesser degree France were in a similar position to disregard the needs of external equilibrium (at least for a time) in the interests of their own internal equilibrium. By contrast, and contrary to Keynes's own convictions, Great Britain of the post-war period was forced "to disregard internal equilibrium in the effort to sustain a self-imposed external equilibrium which was not in harmony with the existing internal situation."[28]

Although Keynes's views concerning commercial policy were undergoing change at this time, his basic economic philosophy remained intact. Keynes had been a champion of monetary management before World War I and he continued to adhere to this view during the late 1920s. But whereas he had not in the pre-war period given too much consideration to the possibility of a conflict between the pursuit of an autonomous monetary policy and the attainment of external equilibrium, in the altered post-war economic setting he recognized that such a problem could easily develop. Yet he did not waver from his original position. He continued to accord top priority to national, monetary management even if it meant forcing the position of external equilibrium to suit internal needs. Thus, Keynes's rejection of free trade and his subsequent embrace of protectionism were entirely consistent with the implementation of his economic philosophy.

With the theoretical structure of the *Treatise on Money* thus established, it is now possible to consider Great Britain's external difficulties of 1929–1930 within that frame work and to review the means suggested by Keynes for their solution.

In diagnosing Britain's external problems, Keynes found two factors at work: the existence of higher gold costs of production in Great Britain relative to those in other countries and the prevalence of higher interest rates abroad compared to those at home. Whereas the former condition led to a reduction in Britain's foreign balance, the latter encouraged a volume of foreign lending in excess of the amount warranted by her balance of payments requirements. Thus, the net result was a condition of external disequilibrium in which the volume of foreign lending exceeded the amount of the foreign balance.

To cope with this condition of external disequilibrium, Britain was constrained to raise the level of interest rates in the hope of reducing the volume of foreign lending to bring it into balance with her foreign balance. But this could not be accomplished without at the same time creating other difficulties. In raising the interest rate to the international level, the Bank of England might force it above its natural rate with the result that this would destroy the equality between savings and investment. Thus, although a higher interest rate would be effective in restoring external balance, it might do so only by engendering internal disequilibrium with its attending profit deflation[29] and unemployment.

In the pre–World War I period, Britain would not have experienced such disharmony between internal and external equilibrium for too long a period.

But in the post-war era, Britain had lost her position of financial preeminence. She was now a mature country in which population had ceased rapidly to expand. In that type of setting, Keynes felt, investment could profitably absorb home savings only at declining rates of interest. By contrast, younger nations could, because of their more vigorous growth patterns, absorb savings at higher rates of interest. As a result, an ever increasing proportion of Britain's savings was being attracted abroad. But such a siphoning of savings from Britain could be continued only if she could raise her foreign balance. Unfortunately, though, Britain was finding it difficult to do so at this time because of her high domestic costs of production. Another obstacle that served to make the demand for her exports inelastic was the growing tendency on the part of foreign countries to raise their tariff walls in an effort to solve their own external problems.[30]

In this regard, Keynes noted,

> I leave it to the reader to work out in detail what a pickle a country might get into if a higher rate of interest abroad than can be earned at home leads to most of its savings being lent abroad, whilst at the same time there are tariffs abroad against most of its exports and a tendency to raise these tariffs from time to time to balance the gradually rising level of costs in the protected countries due to the inflow of gold from the lending country.[31]

In effect, Keynes's position was that countries that enjoy a favorable balance of trade on income account, but an unfavorable balance of transactions on capital account, should permit a lending country (such as Great Britain was during the late 1920s) to increase its level of exports and not impede it by placing tariff obstacles in its way. Unless a lending country is thus given an opportunity to expand its exports, it will suffer a condition of external disequilibrium. Under these circumstances, a lending country may have no alternative but to augment its foreign balance forcibly by reducing its imports through the expediency of tariffs.[32]

On the assumption that British wages and other internal production, costs could not be reduced to increase the foreign balance and that the attractiveness of foreign over domestic investment continued unabated, Keynes pointed out that this would lead to an outflow of gold and an increase in the bank rate that, in turn, would lead to chronic depression and unemployment. From this eventuality, he said, there are but four ways to escape:

1. to increase the value of the foreign balance by reducing money costs of production through increased efficiency;[33]
2. to increase the value of the foreign balance by diminishing the volume of imports through tariffs or similar measures;

3. to increase home investment by establishing through means of a subsidy, or other similar arrangement, a differential rate of interest for home investment as compared with foreign investment; and
4. to stimulate investment throughout the world, both home and abroad, by an international cheap money policy.[34]

Although a good case could be made on behalf of each of these methods for achieving external balance, Keynes was more favorably disposed toward the second and third alternatives. He felt that the imposition of a tariff, as provided in the second alternative, would reduce imports without commensurately reducing exports and home investment, thus leading to an increase in the favorable balance of trade. This increase in foreign investment, Keynes maintained, would largely represent "a net gain to the wealth of the community."[35] This view contrasted sharply to Keynes's pronouncement of the early 1920s when, in defense of free trade, he argued that exports not paid for by imports took away from a nation's capital.

Although Keynes did not in the *Treatise* explain why he now thought that an increase in exports and a decline in imports would be beneficial to the home economy, we may speculate that it may have been caused by the different character of aggregate demand in the two periods. During the early 1920s, there was no shortage of aggregate demand in Great Britain, because of the need to rebuild the economy after four years of war. In those circumstances it did not make sense, at least from a national economic standpoint, to divert much needed resources abroad. In the latter part of the decade, however, the supply situation had improved and the nation could more readily afford to export a part of its production. But the high domestic costs of production and overvaluation of the sterling exchange made it difficult for British industry to market its wares abroad.

With the possibility of raising the level of demand through an increase in exports thus precluded, Keynes may have sought to accomplish this objective through a diversion of demand from foreign to import competing goods. The resulting amelioration of the balance of trade, like an increase in investment, would lead to an increase in the demand for current domestic output while at the same time would add nothing—at least immediately—to the supply of goods. Hopefully, then, the expansion of activity in the import-competing industries would generate an increase in employment and income and in this sense make possible a net gain for the domestic economy.

In the third alternative, Keynes recommended the granting of a subsidy to prospective home investors to make up for the difference between the market rate of interest and the natural rate of interest.[36] Under the then prevailing conditions, the market rate of interest would have to be maintained at a higher level in order to discourage foreign lending and thereby help insure external equilibrium. However, a higher market rate of interest would discourage home investment. To increase home investment and bring it into balance with savings, a lower rate of interest would be clearly required, and to this end Keynes recommended a subsidy or some equivalent form of assistance for home investors. The alternative to a differential rate of interest for home as compared with foreign investment, according to the theoretical framework of the *Treatise,* was deflation, unemployment, and business losses. For the community as a whole, Keynes said, the real choice was between an increment of wealth that would yield a lower effective rate of return or no increment at all.[37]

By selecting the second and third alternatives over the first and fourth alternatives as solutions for Britain's external problem, Keynes appears to favor an expansion of home activity to an increase of foreign trade, although the two are not, of course, mutually exclusive. His reason for favoring a solution to Great Britain's problems through restrictions rather than through an expansionist trade program was significantly influenced by his thinking on the mature economy.

Keynes pointed out that Great Britain was an old country and no longer enjoyed the vibrant economic growth of the pre-war period. Despite this maturity, her people continued to save at a rate far in excess of their internal investment requirements. Keynes estimated that the British continued to save about 10 percent of national income—a rate more attuned to the capital needs of an expanding economy. Although British savings were in excess of domestic investment requirements, this was not completely reflected in the level of interest. If Great Britain were a closed system, the natural rate of interest, that is, the rate that equates total savings and investment, would have been at a level substantially lower than the one then prevailing. In an open system, however, the level of the British interest rate was under no such compulsion to decline, since a substantial part of home savings could be channeled to countries enjoying more vigorous economic growth.

Given the existence of higher interest rates abroad, Keynes noted that equilibrium under laissez-faire conditions would require that a large and ever increasing proportion of British savings find their way abroad. Theoretically, this increase in foreign lending could, in time, be offset by enlarged interest receipts from earlier investments; hence, there would be no need to strive for greater exports. The foreign balance, through the medium of these expanded investment earnings, could, after a time, keep pace with the increased volume of foreign lending. Keynes cautioned, however, that there is an interim period during which the increased foreign lending cannot be readily matched by higher earnings on external investments.[38] In these circumstances, there is no alternative but to increase exports relative to imports.

Unfortunately, it was not easy for Britain at this time to augment its exports in accordance with its balance of payment requirements. Apart from the economic collapse of 1929, which was rapidly enveloping the major industrial nations of the world, Keynes felt that Britain was not likely to realize this objective because of the tariff walls in foreign markets, the disappearance, in a more competitive industrialized world of the special advantages once peculiar to British manufacture, and the existence of higher real wages in Britain as compared to those of her European competitors. These factors, particularly the latter two, were symptomatic of Britain's mature status. In this setting, Keynes concluded, "one cannot but feel a doubt whether the attainment of equilibrium on the lines of an expanding trade surplus will in fact be practicable."[39]

Keynes agreed that the attainment of equilibrium through the traditional principles would be the ideal solution, but, he was quick to add, "if we could get it." If social and political forces precluded such a possibility, he would not be averse to achieving equilibrium through the unorthodox media of offering differential terms of interest for home as opposed to foreign investment and the imposition of tariffs. With no other alternatives in sight, Keynes was more disposed to embracing protection, as the following important passage strongly suggests.

> It may be that the attainment of equilibrium in accordance with our traditional principles would be the best solution,—if we could get it. But if social and political forces stand in the way of our getting it, then, it will be better to reach equilibrium by such a device as differential terms for home investment relatively to foreign investment, and even, perhaps, such a falling from grace as differential terms for home produced goods relatively to foreign-produced goods, than to suffer indefinitely the business losses and unemployment that disequilibrium means. Of the two types of devices indicated above, I much prefer that of differential rates for home and foreign lending to that of differential prices for home and foreign goods, for I believe that there is a much greater scope for this device without risking injurious reactions in other directions, and, in some cases indeed, with positive social advantage. But I am coming round to the view that there is also room for applying usefully some method of establishing differential prices for home and foreign goods. [40]

Although Keynes did not explicitly state that he favored the imposition of protective tariffs on imports or subsidies on exports, this inference is clear, for how else could differential prices for home and foreign goods be established? To the extent that tariffs would lead to a reduction of imports without an adverse effect on exports, and insofar as subsidies would expand exports without similarly effecting imports, they would both serve to increase the foreign balance and thus help the economy to attain external equilibrium, that is, an equality between its foreign balance and the volume of its foreign lending.[41]

SUMMARY

In summary, it may be concluded that with the British home economy in difficult straits and with the balance of payments stubbornly refusing correction through orthodox means, Keynes, during the late 1920s, was driven to a serious consideration of a restrictive foreign trade policy. Faced with a loss of markets abroad and a mature economy at home, Britain was finding it increasingly difficult to live under the rules of a multilateral free trade system. However efficacious free trade may have been in the past, this policy no longer served Britain's present economic interests.

In Britain's altered economic circumstances of the late 1920s, Keynes for the first time expressed a willingness to modify and, perhaps, even supplant the open free trade system under which Britain had waxed so prosperously in earlier times, with a more consciously guided trading system. Admittedly, Keynes's position in the *Treatise* left him somewhat short of an open break with free trade, but then neither did he favor its continuation with his earlier conviction and fervor. Keynes was obviously experiencing a change of heart and despite his guarded endorsement of a restricted trade policy, he continued to move inexorably in that direction in the months ahead.

NOTES

1. R. Hinshaw, "Keynesian Commercial Policy," in *The New Economics*, edited by S. Harris (New York: A. A. Knopf, 1947), 316.
2. J. M. Keynes and H. D. Henderson, *Can Lloyd George Do It?* (London: Nation and Athenaeum, 1929), passim.
3. W. H. Beveridge et al., *Tariffs: The Case Examined* (London: Longmans, Green, 1932), 76–77.
4. Beveridge et al., *Tariffs*, 77.
5. J. M. Keynes, "Proposals for a Revenue Tarrif," *New Statesman and Nation* 1, no. 2 (March 7, 1933): 53–54.
6. Hinshaw, "Keynesian Commercial Policy," 316.
7. Beveridge et al., *Tariffs*, 81.
8. J. M. Keynes, *A Treatise on Money*, vol. I (London: Macmillan, 1930), 131–32.
9. Keynes, *A Treatise on Money*, vol. I, 132.
10. Keynes, *A Treatise on Money*, vol. I, 163.
11. Keynes, *A Treatise on Money*, vol. I, 151–63.
12. According to certain neoclassicists, for example, Ohlin and Beveridge, Keynes underestimated the degree to which it was possible for the foreign balance of a country to adapt itself to foreign transfers without any special devices such as gold flows. In their view, variations in the volume of foreign lending stimulate corresponding changes in the size of the foreign balance directly, automatically, and with minor assistance from gold movements. See Beveridge et al., *Tariffs*.

To put the question to the inductive test, Professor Taussig made a number of studies of nineteenth- and early twentieth-century examples of countries that experienced wide variations in their volume of foreign lending. As expected, he found that foreign lending and the foreign balance almost inevitably moved together; however, in examining the question of how far monetary adjustments had to be pushed to effect this equality, no conclusive answer was forthcoming. At times the evidence seemed to support Professor Ohlin's thesis and at times that subscribed to by Keynes. See F. Taussig, *International Trade* (New York: Macmillan, 1927), passim, and Keynes, *A Treatise on Money*, vol. I, 329–30.

It was only after the appearance of *The General Theory of Employment, Interest and Money* that economists, particularly Mrs. Joan Robinson and Professor R. F. Harrod, began to realize more fully that the rapid adjustment of a country's balance of payments, which Professor Taussig had observed to take place independently of price and monetary changes, was the result of induced movements of income and employment. The Keynesian income and expenditure analysis was found to provide a far more realistic account of the adjustment mechanism of the balance of payments than did the traditional price-specie flow doctrine. For an extensive treatment of the income approach to the restoration of equilibrium in the balance of payments, consult the following sources: L. A. Metzler, "The Theory of International Trade," in *A Survey of Contemporary Economics*, ed. H. S. Ellis (Philadelphia: Blakiston, 1948), 211–22; J. Robinson, *Essays in the Theory of Employment* (London: Macmillan, 1937), chapter 1; R. F. Harrod, *International Economics*, 2nd ed. (London: Cambridge University Press, 1939), chapter 5; F. Machlup, *International Trade and the Foreign Trade Multiplier* (Philadelphia: Blakiston, 1943), passim; J. Viner, *Studies in the Theory of International Trade* (New York: Harper & Bros., 1937), chapter 6; R. Nurkse, "Domestic and International Equilibrium," in *The New Economics*, ed. S. Harris (New York: Alfred A. Knopf, 1947), 264–92.

13. See J. Robinson, *Essays in the Theory of Employment*, 187.

14. Keynes, *A Treatise on Money*, vol. I, 326.

15. Keynes, *A Treatise on Money*, vol. I, 163.

16. Keynes, *A Treatise on Money*, vol. I, 326.

17. Keynes, *A Treatise on Money*, vol. I, 214–15.

18. Keynes, *A Treatise on Money*, vol. I, 215.

19. J. M. Keynes in the *Treatise* believed that the equality of savings and investment depended on the interest rate mechanism.

20. Keynes, *A Treatise on Money*, vol. I, 164.

21. According to Keynes's construction in the *Treatise*, the market rate of interest is synonymous with the international and natural rates of interest at the point where both internal and external equilibrium obtain. The international rate he defines as that rate which obviates gold movements and the latter he defines as that rate which insures an equality between total savings and total investment (see Keynes, *A Treatise on Money*, vol. I, 331–32).

22. Keynes, *A Treatise on Money*, vol. I, 214.

23. Keynes, *A Treatise on Money*, vol. I, 164.

24. Keynes, *A Treatise on Money*, vol. I, 165.

25. Keynes, *A Treatise on Money*, vol. I, 165.

26. Keynes, *A Treatise on Money*, vol. I, 164.

27. Keynes, *A Treatise on Money*, vol. I, 166.

28. Keynes, *A Treatise on Money*, vol. I, 165.

29. Keynes, *A Treatise on Money*, vol. I, 185.

30. Keynes, *A Treatise on Money*, vol. I, 347–48.

31. Keynes, *A Treatise on Money*, vol. I, 348.

32. Beveridge et al., *Tariffs*, 81.

33. This was referred to as "Rationalization" in Great Britain during the decade of the 1920s.

34. J. M. Keynes, *A Treatise on Money*, vol. II (London: Macmillan, 1930), 186–87.

35. Keynes, *A Treatise on Money*, vol. II, 186.

36. Keynes, *A Treatise on Money*, vol. II, 186–87.

37. Note in this connection attempts on the part of the Kennedy Administration in 1961 to set the short term interest rate at higher levels to forestall the outflow of short term capital abroad and to set the long term interest rate at a lower level in order to encourage home investment.

38. Keynes, *A Treatise on Money*, vol. II, 188–89.

39. Keynes, *A Treatise on Money*, vol. II, 189.

40. Keynes, *A Treatise on Money*, vol. II, 189.

41. Beveridge et al., *Tariffs*, 81–82.

Chapter Six

Keynes's Endorsement of Protectionism as a Solution to Britain's Economic Problems

Whereas Keynes's endorsement of a restrictive trade policy in the *Treatise on Money* was "enshrouded in elaborate theoretical language,"[1] his support of this measure was much less disguised in his subsequent pronouncements, especially in the *Report of the Committee on Finance and Industry*.

In the fall of 1929, Mr. Snowden, the Labour Chancellor of the Exchequer, formed the Committee on Finance and Industry to inquire into the abnormal industrial depression that had been rampant in Britain for some time. Appointed to this Committee were such prominent persons as Lord H. P. Macmillan, who served as its chairman, Ernest Bevin, Reginald McKenna, and J. M. Keynes. Before the group could begin its deliberations, however, the British economy was further jolted by the convulsions in the American stock market. As a result of these developments on Wall Street, the scope of the Committee's study was broadened to include international economic considerations as well. Accordingly, the British Treasury announced in its minute of November 5, 1929, that the Committee on Finance and Industry was established "to inquire into banking, finance and credit, paying regard to the factors both internal and international that govern their operation, and to make recommendations calculated to enable these agencies to promote the development of trade and commerce and the employment of labour."[2]

In taking part in this study during late 1929 and 1930, Keynes had an opportunity to expound many of the ideas and theories he had developed in his completed but yet unpublished *Treatise on Money*. Keynes had just finished four years of intensive research and study on the central problems of money and finance and this experience served him well in his deliberations

with the Committee. In fact, the theoretical framework supporting his thinking in the Committee's report, especially in "Addendum I," was taken directly from the *Treatise*.

Keynes played an extremely important role in questioning witnesses appearing before the Committee, in offering his own personal testimony to the
group and in drafting the final report. The final *Macmillan Report*, though
bearing some marks of compromise, was largely structured along Keynesian
lines and incorporated a majority of the proposals suggested by Keynes in his
numerous publications of the 1920s and in the *Treatise on Money*. Among
Keynes's recommendations accepted by the Committee were a managed currency system that would seek to stabilize output and employment at a high
level by influencing the flow of savings into home and foreign investments;[3]
control over the long term investment market;[4] rejection of the gold coin
standard;[5] the divorce of gold reserves from the note issue;[6] the utilization of
gold reserves solely for meeting deficits in the international balance of payments;[7] the permitting of wider swings in the size of the Central Bank's gold
reserves as a means of reconciling foreign exchange stability[8] with domestic
credit stability; and, in general, the pursuit of an autonomous monetary policy.[9]

Keynes was not equally successful, though, in convincing the Committee
of the need for a larger spread, between the gold points and for fixing the
forward exchange rates on selected financial centers as means for controlling
international capital movements. Neither was he able to win the full Committee's endorsement of his public works plan nor his suggestion of a tariff and
export bounty scheme of the type he had previously considered in the *Treatise on Money*. Strange as it may seem, Keynes, who had long been one of
Britain's most outspoken critics of the gold standard, did not press for its
abandonment. But this was only because he and other members of the Committee, notably Ernest Bevin, were convinced that there was not even a
remote chance that the public would accede to such a move. It is ironic to
note, however, that Britain did abandon the gold standard scarcely three
months after the appearance of the Committee's report.

Despite the fact that the main body of the *Macmillan Report* reflected
much of his own thinking, Keynes felt that its recommendations did not go
far enough. And so, in concert with a number of other dissident Committee
members, including Reginald McKenna and Ernest Bevin, he prepared an
appendix to the report titled "Addendum I," in which he gave fuller expression to his views. As intimated earlier, Keynes's concern in this minority
report was with such matters as the control of capital flows, the undertaking
of massive public works, and the adoption by Great Britain of a restricted
trade policy. Since our concern is principally with the latter, our review of
"Addendum I" will largely focus on it.

According to the conclusions of the full committee, the best hope for a solution to the economic problems of the world at large was an expansive monetary policy that would increase purchasing power and encourage the spirit of enterprise and the undertaking of new investment. Although Keynes and his dissenting colleagues did not dispute the validity of this recommendation for a closed system, they questioned whether it was good advice for Britain. Because Britain's economic affairs were very much interrelated with those of other countries, they felt that the Central Bank's power to pursue an independent policy, unfettered by foreign considerations, was extremely limited.[10] In effect, policies that might be advantageous for Britain might not be equally acceptable to other nations and because of this conflict her monetary authority might be compelled to abandon them.

Keynes and his group reasoned that if the monetary authority should reduce the interest rate on long term obligations or if the government should attempt to stimulate the economy directly, for example, through a public works program, either of these actions would place a strain on the Bank of England, unless, of course, similar policies were pursued by other nations.[11] A cheap money policy in Britain would make investments abroad more attractive and thus encourage a volume of foreign lending in excess of the foreign balance. A public works program would, by stimulating the level of national income, expand imports and thereby reduce the foreign balance.[12] The pursuit unilaterally of either or both of these policies could set in motion an outward gold flow and consequently lead to a condition of external disequilibrium, as outlined earlier by Keynes in his *Treatise*. Faced with a condition of external imbalance, the Bank of England could not pursue for too long a period an easy money policy. But if the bank were thus forced to abrogate its expansive money policy, the domestic recovery would be aborted.

The implications of the relationship between a nation's efforts to stimulate economic recovery at home and its external balance are quite clear. A nation can implement an expansive monetary policy or undertake large public expenditures only so long as they do not induce large gold outflows and thereby upset its external equilibrium. To guarantee the success of an internal expansion program, a nation must either strengthen its balance of trade surplus or take measures to reduce its volume of lending abroad. However, Keynes and his associates doubted that a nation could, with the available monetary instruments, simultaneously promote an expansion of activity at home and maintain balance in its external accounts. They pointed out that if the Central Bank and the state were to implement programs to abate the depression and restore employment to a more satisfactory level, additional measures would have to be devised to augment the foreign balance or reduce the volume of foreign lending in order to safeguard external equilibrium.

Turning to a consideration of these measures, Keynes and his colleagues concluded that there were really three alternatives available for raising home employment and insuring external equilibrium. Two of them were designed to increase the foreign balance and one to increase the volume of home investment. Specifically, these measures called for a reduction of domestic wages; the restriction of imports; the granting of assistance to the export industries; and the encouragement of domestic enterprise through the extension of subsidies to private investment or through some other form of state action.[13]

As noted earlier, the reduction of wages would be largely accomplished through the instrumentality of the bank rate. An increase in the interest rate would contract credit and this would have an adverse effect on current business activity and investment. The curtailment of economic activity would, in turn, lead to a loss of employment and a decline in the wage level.

As might be expected, Keynes and his supporters were not too well disposed to this course of action. It will be recalled that Keynes's earlier opposition to the restoration of the gold standard in Britain was due in large measure to his abhorrence of deflation.

In keeping with his pronouncements made during the early and middle 1920s, Keynes argued against a reduction of labor's income because it would create a serious social injustice.[14] There was little to commend a solution that would have reduced wages while leaving unaffected other classes of income. In fact, rentiers, bond-holders, and others whose money incomes were fixed by contract would stand to realize an increase in their level of real income as a result of the deflation. Moreover, if all nations were to initiate wage cuts for achieving external equilibrium, this policy would benefit no one. Such universal wage-cutting, he reasoned, would merely reduce prices further and "rivet on the shoulders of the debtors a heavier burden of monetary obligation."[15] Even more significant, perhaps, in explaining Keynes's rejection of this approach was his preference of inflation over deflation, if such a choice had to be made, in dealing with economic problems.

This point of view was clearly reflected in the observation made by Keynes and his dissenting colleagues that there was a better chance of solving Britain's external difficulties through a recovery of world prices than through a further reduction of home costs. They did not feel that lower export costs could sufficiently stimulate Britain's foreign trade to be of much value to her. A policy designed to direct increased purchasing power into the proper channels, both home and abroad, with a view to restoring equilibrium at the prevailing level of costs would, they maintained be a saner approach than trying to cut internal costs at a faster rate than the rest of the world. Significantly, Keynes's emphasis here, as later in the *General Theory*, was on the demand rather than on the supply side of the market.

Lastly, Keynes and his associates ruled out a reduction of wages on grounds that such a policy would not add to the level of employment.[16] Although Keynes had not yet fully developed the argument contained in the *General Theory* that a general wage reduction cannot increase employment because of its adverse effect, on demand, he surely intimated that line of reasoning in the Addendum, as the following passage clearly shows:

> It is impossible to calculate in advance what increase of employment could be expected from a given average reduction of wages. But the relation of the one to the other might disappoint the expectations of many people, inasmuch as a false analogy is often drawn from the obvious great advantages to an individual employer of a reduction of the wages which he has to pay. For each employer perceives quite clearly the advantages he would gain if the wages which he himself pays were to be reduced, but not so clearly the disadvantages he will suffer if the money incomes of the customers are reduced. Just as it is to the advantage of each producer that every product should be cheap except his own, similarly it is to his advantage that all costs and wages should be high except those which he himself incurs since the demand for his product comes from the incomes which are paid out as costs by other producers.[17]

Although Keynes and his fellow dissidents opposed a reduction of money wages, they recognized that if Britain was to achieve external equilibrium, some adjustment of money incomes was unavoidable. They pointed out that it would be foolhardy to think that the nation could continue to adhere to the existing level of money incomes irrespective of the value of money.[18] But if wage reductions were to be shunned, what other alternatives could the authorities fall back on to contract the gold value of money incomes? The signatories to the Addendum suggested two practical courses of action: devaluation and a scheme of tariffs plus export bounties.[19] Through these means it was hoped that incomes and costs in gold terms might be sufficiently reduced to stimulate the size of the foreign balance and thereby enable the Bank of England to pursue without encumbrance a program of monetary expansion.[20]

The first of these alternatives was considered to be the most advantageous method because it would reduce the gold parity of sterling while leaving money incomes at their current levels. Devaluation would reduce the real value of all classes of income uniformly without recourse to any other measures. Also, it would have the advantage of providing an immediate and direct benefit to the export and import competing industries that were in dire need of assistance at the time. But despite these advantages, a devaluation of the currency was not a completely satisfactory solution for an international banking country such as Great Britain. Being a creditor nation, she was owed large sums from abroad fixed in terms of sterling; hence to effect such a devaluation would mean that external debts would be written down by an amount equal to the devaluation of the pound.[21] Moreover, it was reasoned that such action would further impair international confidence and so was rejected.

The second alternative, calling for a scheme of import tariffs and export bounties, was more favorably received. Keynes and his confreres felt that this approach could secure for Britain the same advantages as a devaluation of sterling. The imposition of tariffs, by making foreign goods more expensive, would reduce the value of a given level of money income as effectively as could a devaluation of the currency. Keynes and his friends cited two advantages for this approach; first, it would be fair, since every type of money income would be equally affected; and second, it would involve no disturbance to confidence and no loss of understanding with Britain's foreign creditors.[22] Like devaluation, the introduction of a tariff would, by discouraging imports, help bring about an improvement in the foreign balance, assuming, of course, no offsetting decline in British exports. Actually, an increase in exports was anticipated. For under the proposed plan, it was hoped that the competitive position of British goods in world markets could be enhanced through the granting of subsidies or other forms of indirect aid to the export industries. This assistance would be made available by the government and would be financed by the revenue derived from the tariff on imports. Thus, a system of import tariffs plus export bounties would, by discouraging imports and stimulating exports, augment the foreign balance.

The higher trade balance would then stand in better relation to the volume of foreign lending and would, therefore, facilitate the attainment of external equilibrium. Protected in this way from a loss of the precious metal, Keynes and his colleagues noted that the Bank of England could then promote a cheap money policy designed to secure the full employment of manpower and resources. In addition to safeguarding external equilibrium and insuring the continuance of a condition of monetary ease, a protectionist trade policy would, by causing home produced goods to be substituted for foreign commodities, help to bring about an increase in the level of home employment and income.

Plagued with a surplus of labor and a plant capacity she could not fully utilize, owing to the relative standing of production coats and interest rates at home and abroad, Great Britain, in the signatories' judgment, could not subscribe unconditionally to a policy of free trade. They felt that in the prevailing economic circumstances the arguments in favor of free trade simply did not apply. To be effective, a free trade policy must operate in a climate of full employment. Given a condition of widespread unemployment and economic slack, Keynes and his associates maintained that production, employment, and even productivity could be more readily increased through protectionism than through a free trade policy. They affirmed this view in the following unequivocal terms:

The fundamental argument for unrestricted free trade does not apply without qualification to an economic system that is neither in equilibrium nor in sight of equilibrium. For if a country's productive resources are normally fully employed, a tariff cannot increase output, but can only divert production from one direction to another. Whilst there is a general presumption that the natural direction for the employment of resources, which they can reach on their merits and without being given special advantages at the expense of others will yield a superior national dividend. But if this condition of full employment is neither fulfilled nor likely to be fulfilled for some time, then the position is totally different, since a tariff may bring about a net increase of production and not merely a diversion.

It appears to us, therefore, that, if imports were to be controlled, whether by a tariff with compensation for exports or by Import Boards, or in some other way and home produced goods substituted for them, there is a presumption, so long as present circumstances last, that this would mean a net increase of employment and of national productivity.[23]

Thus, for the second time in the short span of a year or so, Keynes controverted his contention of 1923 that protection cannot increase the level of home employment. Keynes's change of view was caused in large measure by Great Britain's economic plight of the late 1920s and by his belief that the conditions necessary for the free flow of goods between nations no longer obtained at this time. Keynes pointed out that the free trade argument, like the Bank Rate doctrine, implied a flexibility of wages and costs. However, this fluidity no longer existed and so in the altered economic circumstances of the late 1920s Keynes no longer believed it was impossible to raise the level of employment through a protectionist policy.

Another factor responsible for Keynes's change of heart, according to Professor R. F. Harrod, was his saving and investment analysis of unemployment, which he had recently formulated in the *Treatise on Money*.

Briefly, this explanation maintained that an excess of savings over investment[24] was deflationary and because of its adverse effect on prices led to business losses and a resulting cut back in output and employment.[25] Clearly, to correct this imbalance between savings and investment, either savings would have to be reduced and consumption increased, or investment would have to be raised to a higher level. In the *Treatise*, Keynes defined the foreign trade balance as a. part of investment;[26] hence, any increase in the excess of exports over imports would exert the same beneficial effect on domestic output and employment as would an improvement in the level of home investment.

Therefore, to the extent that restrictive trade measures add to the balance of trade, and thereby increase investment, they lead to an improvement in home output and employment. Moreover, a protectionist policy helps to revive business confidence, especially in the import competing industries, and so further stimulates domestic investment activity. If one adds to this the fact that a restrictive trade policy helps bring about an expansion of domestic activity without need for a reduction of money wages and without turning the terms of trade against the home country, it becomes even more apparent why Keynes should, at this time, turn away from free trade and embrace protection.

Keynes and his associates were not unmindful of the adverse effects that a restrictive trade policy might have on the demand for British exports. They readily conceded that if Great Britain were to use her improved balance of trade to exact gold from other nations, this would force a contraction of credit abroad and an attending reduction in the demand for her wares. If, on the other hand, Britain were to utilize her favorable balance of trade to increase home investment (an expansion she could not have undertaken in the absence of a simultaneous restriction of imports), her demand for imports of raw materials and foodstuff would increase, and in this way would help to provide foreigners the necessary income to purchase her output. Similarly, if Britain were to increase her volume of foreign lending commensurately with the improvement in her foreign balance, the need for a contraction of credit abroad would be lessened and the demand for British exports could thereby be sustained.

In addition to the direct benefits a program of import tariffs and export bounties would exert on home employment and the foreign trade balance, Keynes and his fellow dissidents thought that such a scheme "would run well in double harness" with the third class of remedy proposed by them, namely, an expansion of home investment. As a matter of fact, they felt that the undertaking of an expansive domestic investment program without a concurrent restrictive trade policy might very well be self-defeating.

Although an increase in investment would initially have a beneficial impact on employment, it could also place a heavy burden on the balance of trade. An increase in investment could, by diverting resources and causing prices to rise, hamper the export industries. A large capital development program might further impair the balance of trade by encouraging an increase in imports of raw materials and consumer goods, especially foodstuffs, to satisfy the demands of the newly employed.

Although Keynes and his associates recognized these dangers, they were not unduly concerned. They discounted the first possibility on grounds that Britain still had considerable unutilized industrial plant and so there was no immediate danger of a push-up in prices. [27] In answer to the second difficulty, they noted that an increase in imports could accompany any attempt to increase home employment.

Any increase in employment is likely to induce an increase in the imports of raw materials for the home industries and an increase in the demand for consumer goods. These increases are to be expected and should not deter the undertaking of an expansive program to increase the level of employment.

Nonetheless, Keynes and his colleagues saw in these potential dangers sufficient reason for not embarking too rashly on large-scale investment programs without providing at the same time for the payment of the concomitant and necessary increment of imports.[28] Accordingly, they recommended that if the recovery of domestic output should proceed to a point where the external equilibrium was threatened, the Bank of England should then take appropriate steps to insure that the rate of foreign lending not exceed the available trade balance. Thus, if Britain could expand investment at home, while simultaneously controlling her trade balance through a scheme of import tariffs and export subsidies and her volume of foreign lending through Central Bank control, she could enjoy the double advantage of an increase in home and foreign investment, while avoiding the disturbing effects of both on her international balance.[29]

SUMMARY

In sum, with Britain's home economy continuing to suffer widespread unemployment of manpower and resources and her external sector showing further signs of deterioration, Keynes abandoned his cautious tariff position of the *Treatise on Money* and openly came out in favor of a restrictive trade policy following the worldwide financial crisis of 1929. Although the upheaval of late 1929 did, no doubt, help galvanize Keynes's thinking on this issue, the fact of the matter is that he had already taken a long step in the direction of protection. Unlike most industrial nations, Britain, during the 1920s, had been plagued with a lingering economic malaise and because all other measures had failed, Keynes was prepared to recommend a stronger prescription in the form of protection.

Keynes favored a restrictive trade policy as an alternative to money wage and salary reductions, the standard classical recommendation for an economy suffering disequilibrium, on grounds that such an approach would stimulate home employment through an improvement in the balance of trade and make possible the undertaking of a domestic capital expansion program, while at the same time safeguarding Great Britain's external equilibrium.

He rejected a downward revision of money incomes and other costs of production because deflation would be too disruptive of internal economic relations. Moreover, he was more disposed to seeking a solution to economic problems through an expansion, of aggregate demand than through adjustments on the supply side of the market—a preference that later was to come into full focus in the *General Theory*. To minimize the impact on the internal sector of the economy, Keynes sought to have the brunt of the correction take effect in the external sector through a decrease in imports and an increase in exports. The resulting improvement in the foreign trade balance would stimulate home employment and insure external equilibrium without recourse to changes in money incomes and disruptions in existing economic relations.

Keynes's preference for a restricted trade policy marks unmistakably the high priority he had assigned to the promotion of domestic well-being earlier in his career. Just as he had rejected the gold standard because of the frequent disruptions it visited on the home economy in terms of fluctuations in interest rates, prices and employment, Keynes was now opposed to measures for safeguarding the foreign balance that would have an adverse effect on the home economy. As in his earlier monetary thinking, he preferred that the necessary corrections be made in the external sector. In short, domestic economic objectives should not be sacrificed for external considerations, be it the safeguarding of the gold standard or the maintenance of external equilibrium.

Significantly, too, Keynes's recommendation that the Bank of England exercise control over the volume of foreign lending—a proposal he had made earlier in his *Treatise on Money*[30] — points out once again his conviction that a nation's monetary arrangements should not be left to the operation of blind market forces, but should admit of some form of conscious control. In large measure, it was his desire to chart the national economic course instead of leaving it to be buffeted about by free, insensitive market forces that led him ultimately to espouse protection. In effect, Keynes's support of a restricted trade policy was entirely consistent with his economic philosophy at the time. The fact that he was disposed to subordinate international to domestic needs—a recurrent theme in this work—was also an important factor in explaining his disenchantment with free trade and his movement toward protectionism.

NOTES

1. R. Hinshaw, "Keynesian Commercial Policy," in *The New Economics*, ed. S. Harris (New York: A. A. Knopf, 1947), 316.

2. Committee on Finance and Industry (Macmillan), *Report of the Committee on Finance and Industry*, Cmd. 3897 (London: H.M. Stationery Office June, 1931), 1.

3. Committee on Finance and Industry (Macmillan), *Report of the Committee on Finance and Industry*, 118–19.

4. Committee on Finance and Industry (Macmillan), *Report of the Committee on Finance and Industry*, 119–20.

5. Committee on Finance and Industry (Macmillan), *Report of the Committee on Finance and Industry*, 121–22.

6. Committee on Finance and Industry (Macmillan), *Report of the Committee on Finance and Industry*, 137–43.

7. Committee on Finance and Industry (Macmillan), *Report of the Committee on Finance and Industry*, 122.

8. Committee on Finance and Industry (Macmillan), *Report of the Committee on Finance and Industry*, 141.

9. Committee on Finance and Industry (Macmillan), *Report of the Committee on Finance and Industry*, 132.

10. J. M. Keynes et al., "Addendum I to the Report of the Committee on Finance and Industry," in *Report of the Committee on Finance and Industry*, Cmd. 3897 (London: H. M. Stationery Office, 1931), 190.

11. Keynes et al., "Addendum I," 191.

12. Cognizance should be taken, of course, of the feedback effect on the expanding nation's balance of trade. The increased demand for imports would raise foreign incomes and, depending on income and price elasticity of demand considerations, the higher incomes abroad could lead to larger purchases of the expanding country's goods.

13. Keynes et al., "Addendum I," 192.

14. Keynes et al., "Addendum I," 193–94, 208.

15. Keynes et al., "Addendum I," 196.

16. As previously noted, Keynes had expressed the conviction that wage reductions should not be used as a means of achieving equilibrium throughout the 1920s. He reaffirmed this view in two articles that appeared early in 1930. See J. M. Keynes, "The Question of High Wages," *Political Quarterly* 1, no. 1 (January 1930): 118–19, and "British Industry, Unemployment and High Wages," *Barron's—The Financial Weekly* 10, no. 12 (March 24, 1930): 22.

17. Keynes et al., "Addendum I," 194.

18. Keynes et al., "Addendum I," 198.

19. Keynes et al., "Addendum I," 199–200.

20. Keynes et al., "Addendum I," 193.

21. Keynes et al., "Addendum I," 199.

22. Keynes et al., "Addendum I," 200.

23. Keynes et al., "Addendum I," 201.

24. Unlike the treatment of savings and investment in the *General Theory* wherein the two are always equal, Keynes in the *Treatise* defined these concepts in such a way that they could at times be unequal to one another.

25. For a consideration of the effects exerted by a disparity between savings and investment on business activity and employment see J. M. Keynes, *A Treatise on Money*, vol. 1 (London: Macmillan, 1930), 171–84, 279–92; *A Treatise on Money*, vol. II (London: Macmillan, 1930), 206–8; and "An Economic Analysis of Unemployment," in *Unemployment as a World Problem*, ed. Q. Wright (Chicago: University of Chicago Press, 1931), 20–29.

26. Keynes, *A Treatise on Money*, vol. II, 132.

27. Of course, it might be asked, if there was indeed unutilized industrial capacity in Britain at the time, what incentive would there be for an increase in investment? Although they did not so indicate, perhaps Keynes and his friends were relying on a capital improvement program to provide the major impetus.

28. Keynes et al., "Addendum I," 205.

29. Keynes et al., "Addendum I," 203.

30. Keynes, *A Treatise on Money*, vol. II, 313.

Chapter Seven

Keynes's Proposal for a Revenue Tariff

During the early months of 1931, the economic situation in Great Britain was becoming progressively worse. One-fourth of the nation's industrial plant was idle and a similar proportion of her industrial labor force was unemployed. The government's budget was in precarious balance, so much so, in fact, that serious consideration was being given to a cutback in public expenditures. Although not fully understood at the time, such a perverse policy would have further aggravated the general economic situation.

In the international sector, Britain's export industries were finding it increasingly difficult to compete in foreign markets because of their higher wage and other production costs. Her balance of payments position was being further impaired by the continued outflow of funds abroad where investment prospects were brighter. Britain's external position was further aggravated by the unwillingness of creditor nations such as France and the United States to lend abroad in the same way that Britain had in the period prior to the war. As a result of all these difficulties, Britain was rapidly being forced into the position of a debtor nation. By 1930 her surplus balance on international account had fallen to £39,000,000 and by early 1931 had become virtually extinct.

To deal with these internal and external problems, two approaches were possible: a decrease in the cost of output or an increase in the demand for output. Either of these approaches would help restore a proper margin of profit and thereby stimulate output and employment, which, it was agreed, was the key to the solution of all Britain's problems.

Keynes was opposed to the first course of action for the same reasons he had advanced in the *Macmillan Report.* He argued that although a reduction in wages and other production costs may appear to be advantageous to a single entrepreneur, it overlooks both the consequences of the reduction of his customer's income and of the lower production costs, which his competitors will similarly enjoy. Moreover, a general decrease in wages would lead to social injustice and violent resistance, since it would serve to benefit one class at the expense of another. True to his earlier convictions, Keynes believed that the solution to Britain's difficulties was to be found in an expansionist policy. Nonetheless, in the prevailing circumstances, Keynes recognized that such a policy might not be practicable because of the additional burdens it would impose on the trade balance, the exchange value of sterling, the budget, and the state of confidence. Although expansionary monetary and fiscal policies would, by increasing the level of profits and the volume of employment, ultimately exert a favorable effect on these factors, he acknowledged that in the beginning the results might be different.

Keynes conceded that the undertaking of expansive policies in the existing economic climate would cause a further deterioration of Great Britain's trade balance. Such a program would, by inflating domestic prices, further hamper the export industries in their efforts to compete in foreign markets. At the same time, the expanded domestic activity together with the higher level of internal prices would serve to increase the level of imports and thereby aggravate the trade balance. The promotion of an easy money policy would have a further adverse effect on Britain's external position, since, by lowering the level of interest, it would encourage more capital to seek foreign outlets.

The resulting deterioration of the trade balance and the increase in the volume of foreign lending would cause the exchange value of sterling to depreciate and might so aggravate the situation as to force Great Britain off the gold standard. Such an eventuality, Keynes thought, would be unfortunate for both Great Britain and the rest of the world, since he counted heavily on her to lead the world back to recovery.

In his judgment, the exiting economic slump was worldwide in character and had been largely caused by the failure of the United States and France to provide the kind of financial leadership Great Britain had made available to the world in the pre–World War I era. Keynes placed much of the blame for the prevailing international depression on the reluctance of the American and French authorities to lend their surplus on international account to other nations.

Because of their refusal to lend abroad, the United States was able to amass about one-half and France about one-fourth of the world's gold supply. This concentration of gold in the hands of the United States and France, Keynes argued, was primarily responsible for the disastrous decline in the level of international prices and the attending economic collapse. [1]

If the world was to back off from the brink of disaster, the leadership vacuum would first have to be filled. Only Britain, Keynes felt, was qualified to fill this void. But to resume her position of financial leadership, she would herself have to be strong. If full confidence was to be restored in London, it was imperative, Keynes insisted, that the value of sterling remain intact and that Great Britain continue on the gold standard. Although Keynes had long been on opponent of the gold standard and fixed exchange rates, he favored their retention now in order to alleviate international anxieties. In this connection he noted,

> No domestic cure today can be adequate by itself. An international cure is essential; and I see the best hope of remedying the international slump in the leadership of Great Britain. But if Great Britain is to resume leadership, she must be strong and believed to be strong. It is of paramount importance, therefore, to restore full confidence in London. . . . For these reasons I . . . believe that our exchange position should be relentlessly defended today, in order, above all, that we may resume the vacant financial leadership of the world which no one else has the experience or the public spirit to occupy, speaking out of acknowledged strength and not out of weakness.[2]

In addition to its harmful effects on the trade balance, an expansionary policy, Keynes agreed, would have adverse repercussions on the budget and the state of confidence. By increasing the amount of borrowing for financing public works and other employment creating schemes, an expansive fiscal policy would further unbalance the budget. The ensuing deficit would have an unsettling effect on investors, because it would raise the prospect of higher taxes and thus engender a further loss of business confidence. Although of a temporary duration, the budget imbalance and the resulting loss of business confidence were not matters to be taken lightly. Even though he was convinced that expansive monetary and fiscal policies were absolutely essential to recovery, Keynes acknowledged that they could not be undertaken unless accompanied by other measures that would neutralize their adverse side effects.

If Great Britain could find some way of increasing her volume of exports, this would help to alleviate the pressure on the trade balance and accord her greater latitude in initiating an expansionary monetary policy, though admittedly it would still leave the budget problem unresolved. However, in the prevailing circumstances, Keynes thought that it was too much to hope for any increase in British export sales because of the deflation that such an attempt would entail. Moreover, even if domestic wages and other costs could be adjusted downward, there was no guarantee that Britain's action would not be duplicated by other nations and thus offset any advantage she might otherwise enjoy.[3] With the possibility of strengthening the British foreign trade balance through a revitalization of the export industries largely precluded,[4] Keynes turned to the other alternative—a restriction of imports.[5] "If I knew of a concrete, practicable proposal for stimulating our export industries, I should welcome it," he said, "(but) knowing none, I fall back on a restriction of imports to support our balance of trade and to provide employment."[6]

In his estimate, the only measure that could possibly assist the balance of trade and at the same time neutralize all the dangers inherent in an expansionary policy was the introduction of a revenue tariff.[7] Such a measure, Keynes argued, would add to the balance of trade surplus, safeguard the exchange value of the pound, and thereby help to restore confidence in the financial leadership of London. In addition, it would add to the level of employment, help ease the strain on the budget and thereby bolster confidence in the business community.

Keynes reasoned that a revenue tariff would ease the pressure on the budget by providing a large portion of the funds for financing the increased public expenditures needed for coping with the unemployment situation.[8] He proposed that two flat rates of duty be imposed on the whole range of imports of food, raw materials, and manufactures. Foodstuffs and raw materials would be taxed at 5 percent and semi-finished and manufactured goods would be subject to an ad valorem levy of 15 percent. These imports, according to Keynes's calculations, should net the Exchequer between 50 and 75 million pounds. In addition to providing the government much needed revenue, Keynes's tariff proposal would have a beneficial impact on public confidence. For it could obviate the need for deficit financing and the prospect for higher personal and business income taxes. It would further engender confidence in the business sector, especially in the import competing industries, by lessening the amount of foreign competition.

By reducing the inflow of foreign goods, the tariff would clearly provide a much needed fillip to the trade balance and thereby enable the authorities to pursue expansionary programs with equanimity.[9] As indicated earlier, an expansionary monetary policy could not be undertaken without a concurrent improvement in the trade surplus. An easy money policy would be likely to set off an outflow of capital to foreign money markets because of the higher interest rates obtainable there. But unless this increased foreign lending were offset by a comparable increase in the foreign trade surplus, the external balance would be upset. The resulting gold outflow and depreciation of the sterling exchange would weaken confidence in the financial position of London and conceivably lead to the abandonment of the gold standard—the very things to be avoided if Great Britain was to lead the world back to recovery.

Keynes felt that the tariff, by relieving the pressure on the balance of trade, would permit Britain a much needed margin to pay for the more essential imports that a domestic expansion program would entail. The increased trade surplus would, by permitting some increase in foreign lending, permit London to finance loans to debtor countries. Keynes readily acknowledged that Britain would, by restricting her imports, take purchasing power away from the rest of the world; however, he felt that she would at the same time restore it to them through the medium of increased loans. Keynes summed up his arguments in these terms,

> By relieving the pressure on the balance of payments it (the revenue tariff) will provide a much needed margin to pay for the additional imports that a policy of expansion will require and to finance loans by London to necessitous debtor countries. In these ways, the buying power that we take away from the rest of the world by restricting certain imports we shall restore it with the other hand. Some fanatical Free Traders might allege that the adverse effect of import duties on our exports would neutralize all this; but it would not be true. [10]

Through the advantages thus accorded by the tariff to the budget, the state of public confidence and the trade balance, Keynes hoped to bolster the British economy and make London financially strong. Keynes did not believe that the tariff could, of itself, solve all of Britain's difficulties; however, he supported it because he believed that it would accord her a margin of strength and a breathing space in which to formulate a program to combat both domestic and international problems. Accordingly, he noted,

> I have reached my own conclusion as a result of continuous reflection over many months, without enthusiasm, as the result of the gradual elimination of the practicable alternatives as being more undesirable. Nor do I suppose for one moment that a revenue tariff by itself will see us out of our troubles. Indeed, I mainly support it because it will give us a margin of resources and a breathing space, under cover of which we can do other things. [11]

Although Keynes advanced his tariff proposal principally as a means for making possible the expansion of activity at home without fear of unsettling disturbances in the external sector, he noted that one of the happy concomitants of this measure was the stimulus it would provide to domestic employment. [12] For insofar as it would lead to a substitution of home produced goods for commodities previously imported, it would serve to increase employment opportunities in Great Britain. [13] Keynes's critics were generally agreed that an increase in employment through the tariff was "for him only a subsidiary gain," and that his main objective was to increase the balance of trade and relieve the pressure on the exchanges. [14] However, some, like the *London Economist*, felt that the primary objective of the tariff was to increase the level of home employment. [15] Keynes's own arguments that the tariff was largely for revenue purposes notwithstanding, the *London Economist* maintained that this measure was nothing more than a disguised form of protection.

On the other hand, there were others who felt that this could not have been Keynes's main intent. For example, Sir William Beveridge and Professor John R. Hicks contended that Keynes knew too much about the actual facts of British unemployment to make "such extravagant claims."[16] Actually, they took this position not so much because of what Keynes claimed or did not claim for his proposal, but because of their own convictions that a tariff simply could not enhance domestic employment and no one including Mr. Keynes would be foolish enough to argue otherwise. Basically, their position was that since exports must equal imports, any attempt to decrease imports in an effort to encourage the substitution of home for foreign employment would be self-defeating. Briefly stated, their argument, which constituted the keystone in the arch of free trade thinking, was that a nation's imports provide other countries the wherewithal to purchase its exports. Trade is a two-way street; hence, if a nation decides to restrict its imports, it thereby reduces the amount of purchasing power other nations have available for buying goods from it and so its own exports must necessarily decline.[17] Any advantage the nation pursuing a restrictionist policy might secure for its import competing industries would be offset by a cutback of activity in the export sector.[18] The exclusion of imports by tariffs or by restrictionist devices, the argument continues, cannot generate an increase in output and employment, but can only lead to a diversion of manpower and resources from the export to the home industries. On balance, therefore, nothing can be gained. In fact, it is argued that such "a diversion of resources is disadvantageous for the economy because it sacrifices the Law of Comparative Advantage."[19]

At issue between Keynes and his adversaries was the old argument that "imports must equal exports." Therefore, to vindicate his position, Keynes clearly had to deny the truth of this assertion. Keynes, who not too long ago had acknowledged the validity of the "imports equal exports" thesis, argued that such a neat balancing of imports and exports could obtain only in a hypothetical economic system that possesses a high degree of elasticity and an inherent capacity for stable equilibrium. However, in the real world, he argued, there is "no simple or direct relationship between the volume of imports and the volume of exports."[20] A change in the level of imports, he observed, can set off many reactions, internal and external. For example, when a nation restricts its imports through the imposition of a tariff, the effect on exports will largely depend on whether the economy was in a state of equilibrium when the cutback in imports occurred. The type of monetary policy being pursued by the country restricting its inflow of imports is also of significance. For instance, if the home economy happens to be promoting a tight money policy while all other countries continue to pursue a cheap money policy, it is not likely to experience a reduction in exports commensurate with the decline of its imports. If though, the Central Bank in the home country decides to lower its bank rate following the introduction of a restrictive policy, this action may be expected to stimulate domestic activity and thereby add to the volume of its imports. Conceivably, too, an expansive monetary policy could, by causing prices to increase, lead to a contraction of exports. However, whether prices would, indeed, rise would depend in considerable measure on the amount of surplus capacity available in the economy and how much of it could be utilized at the same degree of efficiency as the productive plant and labor previously employed.[21]

From this brief account it is clear that the effects of a reduction in imports on exports and other economic variables cannot be easily determined. In Keynes's view, the question is not answerable "merely on a priori considerations, but must be determined by applying a sound theoretical apparatus to a knowledge of many current facts, and an estimation by the practical judgment of the probabilities suggested by this application."[22] He cited instances where a reduction in imports could lead to an increase in exports as well as circumstances in which they would be decreased. But in any event, Keynes felt that it was highly improbable that a change in the value of imports would induce a like change in the value of exports.

Keynes also advanced a number of other arguments against the free trade contention that imports must equal exports. He pointed out that if this identity did, indeed, hold, there would be no need for concern with the trade balance. For if every increase in imports was accompanied by a like increment of exports, each nation could undertake an expansionary program with equanimity. No nation would have to worry about the deleterious effects an expansionary policy would have on its external balance. But this, Keynes observed, was contrary to experience.[23] Also, he noted that if imports were always equal to exports, it would make little sense to try to increase home employment by reducing costs in the import competing industries. For to the extent that imports were diminished and the ability of foreigners to buy in England correspondingly reduced, the number of unemployed in the export sector would rise by the amount of new employment in the import competing trades. But, Keynes asked, would common sense agree with the free traders? Some of Keynes's sympathizers, notably R. F. Kahn, added that if imports were necessarily equal to exports, there would be little justification for trying to reduce production costs in the export industries. For if imports were increased, exports, their higher costs notwithstanding, would similarly have to increase. But this line of reasoning, like the prior one, hardly makes sense, because it obliges consumers and producers to buy their wares in higher cost markets when, in fact, they can procure them elsewhere at lower prices.

Lastly, Keynes pointed out that there need not be an equality of imports and exports if the nation enjoying a favorable balance of trade be willing to utilize it to finance loans to foreigners. If the excess of exports over imports is used in this way, the purchasing power taken away from foreign countries through a restriction of imports will be returned to them, he argued, via an increase in the volume of loans. Therefore, Keynes concluded, so long as the improvement in the foreign balance is not used to draw gold from abroad, but is employed, instead, to increase foreign lending, there need be no adverse effect on a nation's volume of exports, as long as there occur no increases in their prices.[24]

Interestingly, Keynes's attitude toward foreign investment was completely antithetical to his former position. Whereas he had strongly opposed an increase in foreign lending back in 1923 on grounds that such investment was detrimental to the British economy, because it diverted much needed resources to abroad, he now endorsed a policy of making such foreign loans. Keynes's adversaries were quick to take cognizance of this change of heart, as noted in the following observation made by Professor Robbins:

> It is not many years ago since Keynes, with his customary Cassandra-like vehemence, was warning us to regard foreign investment as almost wholly undesirable. What queer irony of circumstance is this which in his present mood, brings him to urge, with equal vehemence, just that form of foreign investment which most sane men would agree to be without any redeeming feature.[25]

Apart from Keynes's alleged inconsistency on the question of foreign lending, the free trade camp charged that even if the volume of foreign lending were increased to fill the gap between exports and imports, the raising of tariff barriers could not possibly add to the level of home employment. Sir William H. Beveridge, one of the chief spokesmen for free trade in Britain during the early 1930s, observed that even if the foreign trade balance were to improve, it remained "unproved that an increase of lending abroad could take place without harmful contraction of lending at home." The expanded foreign lending, he argued, would simply divert savings and resources from domestic investment; hence, the higher employment in the import competing industries would be offset by the loss of employment elsewhere in the economy because of the cutback in home investment.

Beveridge based his view on the assumption that the total amount of savings available for investment is largely fixed. Therefore, an increase in foreign lending, he reasoned, must be made possible by a comparable reduction in the volume of lending available for domestic investment. Beveridge contended, in effect, that insofar as exports were sustained by increased foreign lending, this would entail a diversion of British capital abroad and the probable further cramping of home investment.

This was certainly a cogent argument and one that could be satisfactorily answered only after the appearance of *The General Theory of Employment, Interest and Money.* Utilizing the tools forged by Keynes in this work, Mrs. Joan Robinson was able to answer this difficulty by showing that a restrictive trade policy can increase the amount of savings available for both foreign and domestic investment. She pointed out that when a tariff causes an improvement in the foreign balance of trade, any ensuing increase in foreign lending can come about only on condition that the interest rate at home is lower than that prevailing abroad. But by the same token, if the interest rate at home is comparatively low, this should help stimulate domestic investment, and insofar as it leads to increased employment and income, should raise the level of savings. (In the Keynesian system, savings are a function of income and not the interest rate, as the classical economists supposed.) Thus, the increased foreign lending can be financed through the expanded volume of domestic activity and need not depend on a diversion of resources from home investment.

In supporting Keynes's contention that a decrease in imports can increase domestic employment, Mrs. Robinson noted that it was never the true orthodox view that a tariff could not bring about an improvement in employment in the short run. Classical trade, she said, simply makes a claim for the advantages of specialization, but "it cannot tell us that when one country increases its share in world employment, at the expense of reducing the output per unit of employment, its total output will be reduced" and "still less can it tell us that employment in any one country cannot be increased by increasing its balance of trade."[26]

Keynes's conversion to protection, however justified, evoked a great deal of criticism from his free trade adversaries. Professor Robbins, for example, taunted him for having abandoned "the service of high and worthy ideals in international relations,"[27] while others charged him with inconsistency. To Professor Robbins's charge Keynes retorted that it is easy to go on repeating, as the orthodox economists did, the same prescriptions "unaccompanied by any new process of cerebration."[28] He pointed out that the problem facing Great Britain was how to get out of a very tight situation. An immediate solution was required and not, as the classicists thought, a determination of the best long term policy for Great Britain to pursue under conditions of equilibrium. Free traders, he charged, did not realize that Britain's problems were different from those of the past and that, therefore, a liberal trade policy might no longer be suitable for their solution. Keynes expressed his pique and annoyance with the barbs of the traditionalists in the following expressive language:

> My critics have not taken any notice of, or shown the slightest interest in, the analysis of our present state. . . . Is it the fault of the odium theologicum attaching to Free Trade? Is it that Economics is a queer subject in a queer state? Whatever may be the reason, new paths of thought have no appeal to the fundamentalists of Free Trade. They have been forcing me to chew over again a lot of stale mutton, dragging me along a route I have known all about as long as I have known anything, which cannot, as I have discovered by many attempts, lead one to a solution of our present difficulties—a peregrination of the catacombs—with a guttering candle.[29]

Keynes readily agreed with the classical contention that a policy of free trade will best promote each nation's economic welfare, provided, however, that a condition of full employment prevails. In keeping with his earlier pronouncements, he readily acknowledged that in circumstances where a nation's manpower and capital resources are fully employed, a protectionist policy cannot add to the level of output, because of the lessened capital and labor efficiency attending such a policy. But for a country plagued with widespread industrial inactivity and labor displacement, he questioned whether a free trade policy would be as advantageous to the economy as would a restrictive trade policy, notwithstanding the higher labor and capital efficiency of free trade. Keynes did not believe that this advantage was adequate of itself to offset the benefits to total employment, the state of confidence, the budget, and the trade balance resulting from a protectionist policy. Keynes first expressed this visa in the pages of *The Times of London* when he stated,

> In ordinary circumstances, when abnormal unemployment is expected to be quite temporary, it is impossible to justify a tariff by reference to its effect on employment, For when the productive resources of the country are likely to be almost fully employed in most directions, a tariff means a diversion of output, not a net increase. I have often argued the free trade case on these lines, and would do so again in the appropriate circumstances. But at present the necessary conditions are not fulfilled. The unemployment of men and plant is so large and so widespread, has lasted so long, and looks like lasting so much longer, that I should expect a tariff to increase employment now, and for some time to come; while the advantages to business confidence, the balance of trade, and the budget are too obvious to need emphasis. Uncompromising free traders are entitled to claim that they are taking a long view, but they are on weak ground when they deny the immediate advantages[30] of a tariff.[31]

Thus, Keynes concluded that the existence of widespread unemployment of manpower and under-utilization of plant capacity vitiates the free trade argument and that a liberal trade policy can best promote a nation's economic interests only in a full-employment environment. In effect, Keynes maintained that the choice of commercial policy largely depends on the status of employment in the home economy. Given a condition of extensive labor displacement, a strong case can be made for a protectionist policy, whereas in circumstances where both full employment and external equilibrium obtain, the free trade argument comes back into its own. Significantly, Keynes provided in this contention an early intimation of his subsequent assertion in the *General Theory* that the conclusions of classical and neoclassical economics hold true only under conditions of full employment and that, therefore, theirs was the economics of a special case.

SUMMARY

In summary, Keynes recognized that if Great Britain was to solve her economic difficulties of the early 1930s, it was imperative that she undertake a consciously directed recovery program. However, the initiation of an expansion program in an economically depressed world would have serious implications for the internal and external sectors of the British economy. For to the extent that such a program would require an increase in borrowing for the financing of public works, it would place further strain on the budget and undermine business confidence.

Expansionary monetary and fiscal policies would also have adverse effects on the foreign trade balance because of their tendency to encourage imports and discourage exports. Such a deterioration of the trade balance would not only reduce opportunities for home employment, but would also upset external equilibrium, unless the volume of foreign lending could be reduced commensurately with the decline in the trade balance. But such an eventuality would not be too likely if the level of interest rates at home was less than that prevailing abroad. The resulting disequilibrium, if sufficiently prolonged, would set off a gold outflow, impair the stability of the sterling exchange, and ultimately bring about a curtailment of the expansion program.

Consequently, if Great Britain was to benefit from the promotion of an expansive domestic program, something would have to be done to correct its adverse effects on the budget and the state of confidence. Consideration would also have to be given to finding some means for safeguarding external equilibrium and the fixity of the exchange, if Great Britain was to remain on the gold standard and full confidence was to be restored in the financial leadership of London.[32]

In Keynes's estimate, the solution to all these problems was to be found in an amelioration of Britain's foreign balance of trade—an objective that he thought could be best achieved through a revenue tariff. This measure, he reasoned, would help to ease the pressure on the budget by making available from customs receipts a sizable portion of the funds required for financing a massive public-works program. By avoiding a budgetary deficit and thus eliminating the need for added taxes and by lessening the amount of foreign competition, a revenue tariff would stimulate confidence in the business community. It would also have a positive effect on employment by causing home produced goods to be substituted for foreign-made commodities. Concurrently, in the external sector a restriction of imports would make possible an improvement in the balance of trade and bring it into better balance with the volume of foreign lending. The realization of such external equilibrium would safeguard the value of the exchange and enable the Bank of England

and the government to pursue expansionist monetary and fiscal policies with equanimity.

Keynes's break with the free trade doctrine that he had so ably and eloquently defended only a few years earlier caused a considerable stir in both the financial and academic communities. His endorsement of protection was criticized as opportunistic and he was personally chided for turning his back on the lofty ideals of internationalism. But Keynes was eminently practical and when convinced that the solution of his country's difficulties was not to be found in a free trade policy, he had sufficient strength of conviction to alter his views, even if it meant leaving himself open to the charge of inconsistency. Consistency for consistency's sake had no place in his thinking; nor could he justify it in the thinking of others. To those who charged him with inconsistency, he addressed this terse retort:

> May I also register a mild complaint against the undercurrent of moral reprobation which I detect in some quarters? I seem to see the elder parrots sitting round and saying, "You can rely on us. Every day for thirty years, regardless of the weather, we have said what a lovely morning! But this is a bad bird. He says one thing one day, and something else the next."[33]

NOTES

1. J. M. Keynes, "A Gold Conference," *The New Statesman and Nation* 2, no. 29 (September 12, 1931): 300.

2. J. M. Keynes, "Proposals for a Revenue Tariff," *The New Statesman and Nation* 1, no. 2 (March 7, 1931): 54.

3. J. M. Keynes, "Further Reflections on a Revenue Tariff," *The New Statesman and Nation* 1, no. 4 (March 21, 1931).

4. J. M. Keynes, "Economic Notes on Free Trade—The Export Industries," *The New Statesman and Nation* 1, no. 4 (March 28, 1931): 175.

5. The *London Economist* noted that Keynes's embrace of protection was largely due to his conviction that Britain could not in the existing circumstances possibly improve her export position. With Britain's exports significantly reduced, Keynes felt that new opportunities would have to be developed at home for those industries which formerly serviced her overseas markets. However, if the manpower and capital formerly employed in the export sector were to be diverted to the production of goods for the home market, some restriction of imports would clearly be helpful, perhaps even necessary. According to the *London Economist*, Keynes's recommendation of a restrictive trade policy under the euphemistic title of a revenue tariff was the inevitable outcome of his pessimistic appraisal of Britain's competitive position in world markets. For a more comprehensive view of the *London Economist*'s position on Keynes's revenue tariff proposal, see "The Inconsequences of Mr. Keynes," the *London Economist* 112, no. 4568 (March 14, 1931): 549–50, "Mr. Keynes and Tariffs," the *London Economics* 112, no. 4571 (April 4, 1931): 722, and "Tariffs, Wages and Exports," the *London Economist* 112, no. 4572 (April 11, 1931): 771–72.

6. Keynes, "Economic Notes on Free Trade—The Export Industries," 175.

7. Keynes, "Proposals for a Revenue Tariff," 54.

8. "The Week," *The New Republic* 66, no. 853 (1931): 190.

9. Keynes, "Further Reflections on a Revenue Tariff," 143.

10. Keynes, "Proposals for a Revenue Tariff," 54.

11. Keynes, "Economic Notes on Free Trade—The Export Industries," 175.

12. Keynes, "Proposals for a Revenue Tariff," 54.

13. Keynes's adversaries were quick to point out that his claim that a tariff would increase employment by encouraging home produced goods to be substituted for foreign commodities was not consistent with his allegation that the tariff would increase the Treasury's receipts by 50 to 75 million pounds. It did not make sense, they pointed out, to expect to raise revenue by taxing imports and at the same time keep them from entering the country so as to stimulate home employment. To realize even the minimum 50 million pounds of revenue anticipated from this measure by Keynes, the volume of imports would have to remain virtually intact, in which case the import competing industries would receive very little encouragement. In effect, if a nation wishes to augment its revenue from tariffs, it must permit foreign goods to pass its customs gates and if it wishes to increase home employment, by substituting home produced for foreign-manufactured goods, it must obviously keep them out. But it cannot do both.

14. L. C. Robbins, "A Reply to Mr. Keynes," *The New Statesman and Nation* 1 (1931): 100.

15. "Tariffs, Wages and Exports," *London Economist* 112, no. 4572 (April 11, 1931): 771.

16. W. H. Beveridge et al., *Tariffs: The Case Examined* (London: Longmans, Green, 1932), 57, and L. C. Robbins, "Correspondence—A Revenue Tariff," *The New Statesman and Nation* 1, no. 8 (April 18, 1931): 280.

17. W. H. Beveridge, "The Case for Free Trade," *The Times of London*, March 26, 1931, 10.

18. Robbins, "Correspondence—A Revenue Tariff," 179.

19. W. H. Beveridge, *The Case for Free Trade* (*The Times of London*, March 26, 1931): 10.

20. J. M. Keynes, "Revenue Tariffs—Effects on Home Production," *The Times of London*, April 2, 1931, 6.

21. J. M. Keynes, "Economic Notes on Free Trade—The Reaction of Imports on Exports," *The New Statesman and Nation* 1, no. 7 (April 11, 1931): 242.

22. Keynes, "Economic Notes on Free Trade—The Reaction of Imports on Exports," 242.

23. J. M. Keynes, "Mr. J.M. Keynes's Rejoinder," letter to the editor, *The Times of London*, March 17, 1931, 10.

24. J. M. Keynes et al., "Addendum I," in *Report of the Committee on Finance and Industry*, Committee on Finance and Industry (Macmillan), Cmd. 3897 (London: H. M. Stationery Office, 1931), 201

25. L. C. Robbins, "A Reply to Mr. Keynes," 99.

26. J. Robinson, "Beggar-My-Neighbor Remedies for Unemployment," in *Essays in the Theory of Employment* (London: Macmillan, 1937), 212.

Note again the issue raised by Mrs. Robinson as to whether or not the loss of output resulting from the reduced labor efficiency, attending a restrictionist trade policy, can be more than offset by an increase in the amount of labor employed.

27. Robbins, "A Reply to Mr. Keynes," 100

28. J. M. Keynes, "Economic Notes on Free Trade—A Revenue Tariff and the Cost of Living," *The New Statesman and Nation* 1, no. 6 (April 4, 1931): 211.

29. Keynes, "Economic Notes on Free Trade—The Reaction of Imports on Exports," 242.

30. Note Keynes's concern with the short-run period.

31. J. M. Keynes, "The Issues for Free-Traders," letter to the editor, *The Times of London*, March 21, 1931, 8.

32. As indicated earlier, Keynes's purpose in trying to restore London to a position of financial preeminence was that this would enable Britain to extend foreign loans on a large scale and thus help to foster recovery throughout the world. Although Keynes tried largely to justify the revenue tariff on this ground, many considered it to be a wholly specious argument. His primary objective, unquestionably, was to secure an advantage for Great Britain, so that she might be able to put her own economic house in order.

33. Keynes, "Economic Notes on Free Trade—A Revenue Tariff and the Cost of Living," 211.

Chapter Eight

Keynes's Advocacy of National Autarky

As the year 1931 progressed, Great Britain's economic problems became increasingly acute. The situation became especially critical in the external sector where the balance of trade had so deteriorated that the nation was rapidly approaching debtor status. Britain's dwindling trade balance, which had been largely caused by the disparity between home and foreign production costs, was further aggravated by the prevailing world wide economic depression. Whereas foreign demand for British goods was falling off in consequence of the general cutback in economic activity, British demand for foreign foodstuffs and raw materials, being less elastic, was not declining commensurately with her exports. Also adding to Britain's external difficulties was the contraction of interest payments on her overseas investments.

To alleviate the country's balance of payments crisis, the national government proposed to undertake an economy program. By cutting back its expenditures for road construction, housing, the dole, and the salaries of public servants, the government hoped to reduce the general level of purchasing power, which, in turn, would help to curb the demand for imports and thereby ease the pressure on the trade balance.[1] Such a program, it was anticipated, would also have beneficial effects on the budget.

Keynes readily agreed that a reduction in the nation's purchasing power could induce a cutback in its imports; however, he felt that this was "an extraordinarily indirect and wasteful way of reducing imports."[2] A curtailment of purchasing power, he noted, would cause a reduction in the consumption not only of imports but of home produced goods as well. In fact, he maintained that the demand for domestically produced goods would be even more adversely affected. According to his calculations, about 80 percent of the reduction in total spending would occur at the expense of home produced goods and only 20 percent at the expense of imports.[3] In effect, to reduce the demand for imports by 1£, the consumption of home produced goods would have to be reduced by four times that amount. Thus, any significant reduction of imports would necessitate a disproportionately large reduction of home employment and income.

Being an expansionist, Keynes was naturally opposed to the national government's program. He noted that the government's approach would, by reducing expenditures, aggravate the unemployment situation. And insofar as the trade balance was concerned, he observed that "cutting the school teachers' salaries will not help us to recapture the markets of the world," for such action cannot possibly help to reduce the cost of production in the export industries.[4] Accordingly, Keynes offered his own plan for dealing with the problem of unemployment and for improving the current balance of trade. His first recommendation called for a devaluation of sterling. This, he felt, would restore British goods to their competitive position in world markets and in the process would help to stimulate home employment and improve the foreign balance. However, Keynes recognized that his own preference did not enjoy sufficient support in the country. And so, as noted earlier, he turned to a revenue tariff in the spring of 1931, as an alternative to a reduction of wages and salaries. His arguments in. favor of a tariff had a familiar ring, as noted in his following contention:

> Now the latter course (a reduction in wages and salaries), if it were to be adequate, would involve so drastic a reduction of wages and such appallingly difficult, probably insoluble, problems both of social justice and practical method that it would be crazy not to try first the effects of the alternative and much milder measure of restricting imports.
>
> It happens that this course also has other important advantages. It will not only relieve the strain on the foreign exchanges. It would also do more than any other single measure to balance the Budget; and is the only form of taxation open to us which will actually increase profits, improve employment, and raise the spirits and the confidence of the business community.[5]

In view of the many advantages associated with a tariff, it was incomprehensible to Keynes why the national government should reject this solution in preference to an economy program whose effect would be "to reduce the standard of life of as many people as are within their reach in the hope that some small portion of the reductions of standards will be at the expense of imports."[6] To prefer this costly alternative to a direct restriction of imports simply did not make sense to him. However, ensuing developments made it unnecessary for Keynes to become further embroiled in controversy with the government, for in late September Great Britain went off the gold standard and devaluation of the pound became an accomplished fact.

The demise of the gold standard, though a surprise, was due to many deep-seated causes. Among some of the more significant factors were the disparity between British and foreign production costs; the worldwide deflation; the gold hoarding practices of the United States and France; and the abnormal international transfer of funds, especially as required by reparations and war debts.[7] Proximately, however, Britain's abandonment of the gold standard was caused by the wave of distrust that engulfed the pound after the banking crisis that occurred in Central Europe that summer.

The crisis was touched off in midsummer with the collapse of the highly regarded Austrian Creditanstalt Bank. This development created considerable uneasiness in the banking community and led to a widespread withdrawal of funds from Central Europe. This loss of confidence plunged the Darmstadter und National bank into difficulties of great magnitude and on July 13 it, too, was forced to suspend payments. To preclude a complete collapse of the German banking system and the reichsmark, the government placed an embargo on all external payments. This action had a serious impact on London because it immobilized a considerable portion of a number of its banks' assets.[8]

In the meantime, pressure on the pound was mounting and the outflow of gold continued unabated. To stem the loss of gold, the Bank of England utilized its supply of foreign exchange reserves, but the amount of resources on hand was hardly adequate for the task. As a result, the British authorities were forced in the closing days of July to enlist the assistance of the Bank of France and the U.S. Federal Reserve System. An agreement was concluded among these parties on July 31. According to its terms, France and the United States agreed to make available 50 million pounds to the Bank of England. [9]

Reinforced with these reserves, the British monetary authorities were able to re-enter the foreign exchange market in support of sterling.[10] At first, they thought that the psychological effects resulting from the negotiation of the French-American Loan would be enough to stem a further run on the Bank of England's reserves. Unhappily, the authorities underestimated the severity of their problem and the gold outflow continued. Under the circumstances, the French-American credit proved to be grossly inadequate and so within a matter of a few weeks another advance of 30 million pounds had to be arranged with the French and American Central Bank authorities. But still the drain continued. Only the possession by the Bank of England of hundreds of millions of pounds could have saved sterling from its inevitable fate,[11] and so, on September 21, 1931, the authorities had no alternative but to suspend gold payments.

This unexpected turn of events had a profound impact on Keynes's commercial policy views. In the altered circumstances, his proposal for protection lost it a sense of urgency. Tariffs were no longer needed to mitigate

Britain's external difficulties, because at the new lower gold value of sterling the prices of her goods were again among the cheapest in the world. Accordingly, within a week after Great Britain's departure from the gold standard, Keynes wrote a letter to *The Times of London* urging that consideration of the general tariff that he had recently advocated be postponed for the time being.[12] The important consideration for the present, he averred, was the currency question. Attention should be given to the probable future level of sterling in relation to gold and how many other countries ware likely to follow Great Britain's lead in going off the gold standard. Keynes also suggested that consideration be given to the possibility of formulating a sound international currency policy to take the place of gold—one that would help to "rebuild the financial supremacy of London, on a firm basis." Until these questions could be resolved, he felt that it would not be possible to determine whether or not Great Britain should turn to a protectionist policy.

Although Keynes did not by any means shut the door on the tariff question, it is not at all surprising that he should modify his position on this issue. After all, he had long been in favor of devaluation as a means of dealing with Great Britain's external problems. The only reason, it will be recalled, why he did not press this alternative more strenuously than he did was that it did not enjoy the widespread support of the financial community, the political parties, and the general public. But in the altered circumstances of the early fall of 1931 all this had changed. Britain now stood to gain far more from devaluation than from a general tariff. Whereas a tariff could influence only the level of imports, the devaluation of the pound would encourage exports as well as discourage imports. In short, it would have two salutary effects on the balance of trade instead of one. Also of note is the fact that devaluation would assist the balance of trade without any need for a reduction of money incomes and at the same time provide a spur to home employment. Keynes summarized the advantages attending the devaluation of sterling in the following appraisal, which appeared in the pages of the *Sunday Express* on September 27, 1931, a day before his letter was published in *The Times of London*, asking the government and the British public to defer consideration of the tariff question until all of the ramifications of the *de facto* devaluation could be properly evaluated.

> For if the sterling exchange is depreciated by, say, 25 percent, this does as much to restrict our imports as a tariff of that amount; but whereas a tariff could not help our exports and might hurt them, the depreciation of sterling affords them a bounty of the same 25 percent by which it aids the home producer against imports.
>
> In many lines of tirade the British manufacturer today must be the cheapest producer in the world in terms of gold. We gain these advantages without a cut of wages and without industrial strife. We gain them in a way which is strictly fair to every section of the community, without any serious effects on the cost

of living. For less than a quarter of our total consumption is represented by imports; so that sterling would have to depreciate by much more than 25 percent before I should expect the coat of living to rise by as much as 10 percent. This would cause hardships to no one, for it would only put things back where they were two years ago. Meanwhile, there will be a great stimulus to employment. [13]

Keynes's ambivalence on the tariff issue illustrates the extent to which his thinking on foreign trade policy was made subservient to domestic economic considerations. In the beginning of his career, the priority he assigned to domestic considerations was evident only in his monetary thinking. Now, it extended to commercial policy as well. During the time that Great Britain was without any practical means for dealing with her internal and external economic difficulties, Keynes marshaled all his intellectual powers to develop a water-tight case for protection. But with devaluation a reality and the hope for a more favorable solution to Britain's problems in the offing Keynes was quick to endorse it and temporarily, at least, set aside his own case for protection.

To those not familiar with the workings of his mind, Keynes's new posture might appear somewhat awkward, and yet, it was not. Being always concerned primarily with promoting the national advantage, and particularly that of Great Britain, it was entirely consistent for Keynes to favor a postponement of any action on the tariff issue and, instead, lend his support to devaluation. For the advantages accruing to Great Britain from a depreciated currency would exceed those resulting from a tariff. Over the course of his life, John Maynard Keynes may have been dissonant in both theory and practice, but this was so because only in this way could he remain consistent in the one thing that really mattered—the furtherance of the domestic welfare.

In the period immediately following Great Britain's abandonment of the gold standard, Keynes had little else to add to the question of free versus restricted foreign trade. In an article titled "The Prospects of the Sterling Exchanges," which appeared in the *Yale Review* in March 1932, Keynes suggested that the only alternative open to debtor countries for achieving external equilibrium was to restrict their imports from creditor countries such as the United States and France. This he thought they could most effectively accomplish by abandoning gold or severely restricting its use, as noted in his following observation:

This alternative—and, as I have said there is no other door left open—is for the rest of the world to get on as best it can without buying the exports of those countries such as France and the United States, which have an unbalanced credit position. The abandonment of the gold standard by a large group of countries and its restricted operations by others form an unavoidable means,

adopted far from deliberately or even consciously, for destroying those unbalanced creditor positions by undermining the trade balance of the creditors. The
creditors by leaving no other means of payment have, in effect, demanded that
the debtors shall find some way of destroying these creditors' own trade balance. [14]

Keynes also made some reference to the foreign trade question in his
Means to Prosperity, which appeared in 1933. This volume consisted largely
of several articles that he had originally prepared for *The Times of London*
and the *New Statesman and Nation*. Although arguments may be cited in this
work both for and against free trade, on balance it appears that he was more
receptive to a liberal trade policy at this time than he had been two years
earlier, as noted in the following comment:

Currency depreciation and tariffs were weapons that Great Britain had in hand
until recently as a means of self-protection. A moment came when we were
compelled to use them, and they have served us well. But competitive currency depreciations and competitive tariffs, and more artificial means of improving an individual country's foreign balance such as exchange restrictions, import prohibitions, and quotas, help no one and injure each, if they are applied
all round. Admittedly, Keynes does in this observation express strong reservations about the widespread use of restrictive measures, but do his words pres-
age a return to the brand of orthodox free trade he championed in the early
1920s? [15]

This modification of Keynes's views was conditioned, no doubt, by the
steady, if not dramatic, improvement of Britain's trade balance after the
disastrous experience of 1931. It is also significant to note that Keynes's
more receptive attitude toward free trade reflected a major recommendation
he made to the World Economic Conference that was to convene in London
in June 1933 for the purpose of seeking a solution to the world's economic
problems. In that recommendation he urged worldwide cooperation in the
undertaking of an expansive loan expenditure program as the best means for
fostering recovery.

The Conference opened on a hopeful note; however, that optimism was
soon dashed when the President of the United States, Franklin D. Roosevelt,
advised the conferees that he was opposed to any scheme of international
cooperation based on restoration of a rigid international standard. He made it
clear that he favored a conscious management of the standard that, in keeping
with Keynes's own earlier pronouncements, would assign prior preference to
the attainment of a dollar with stable purchasing power and to other domestic
considerations. The president's pronouncement torpedoed the proceedings
and the Conference terminated without accomplishing anything.

Although Keynes had hoped that the World Conference could find some
way of alleviating the international slump, he could not fault the President's

point of view, because he himself would have reacted the same way. Keynes, it will be remembered, had long supported a currency system that would be managed with a view toward achieving a stable internal price level rather than a fixed rate of exchange. Accordingly, he applauded Mr. Roosevelt's action in the following complimentary terms in the pages of the *Daily Mail*:

> It is a long time since a statesman cut through the cobwebs as boldly as the President of the United States. . . . He has told us where he stands, and he invited the Conference to proceed with substantial business. But he is prepared to act alone if necessary; and he is strong enough to do so. . . . The President's a message has an importance that transcends its origins. It is, in substance, a challenge to us to decide whether we propose to tread the old, unfortunate ways, or to explore new paths; paths new to statesmen and bankers, but not new to thought. For they lead to the managed currency of the future, the examination of which has been the prime topic of post-war economics. [16]

Disheartened by the failure of the World Economic Conference to act favorably on his proposal for a worldwide expansion program, Keynes then directed his efforts to salvaging whatever he could from the wreckage. Foiled in his endeavor to promote recover on a worldwide basis, he decided to experiment on a less grandiose scale. Accordingly, he suggested that Great Britain put his recommendations to the test on a purely national scale. But to insure the success of this experiment, he felt that all relationships with the outside world would have to be severed, and so he was forced once again to move closer toward protectionism. This he did unflinchingly and unequivocally in two articles he wrote shortly after the demise of the Conference. [17]

In restating his position on the question of commercial policy, Keynes asserted that he would not dispute the fundamental truths of free trade now any more than he had in 1923. However, he was quick to add that his "background of economic theory" was now somewhat different from what it had been at that time, and so, he would not charge Mr. Baldwin, as he did then, with being "a victim of the protectionist fallacy in its crudest form," [18] for believing that a tariff could relieve the British unemployment situation. But more important, Keynes attributed his change of attitude to the fact that the conditions of the present were different from those of the pre-war period.

Keynes further contended that many of the arguments presented on behalf of free trade by its supporters during the nineteenth century were no longer applicable during the 1930s. In arguing the free trade case, they contended that such a policy would employ the world's manpower and resources to their greatest advantage, thereby maximizing the total wealth of all nations; advance the cause of freedom; promote personal initiative; serve as a bulwark against the forces of privilege, monopoly, and obsolescence; and assure peace, concord, and economic justice among nations. Of all these arguments, Keynes was most critical of the contention that free trade was promotive of international amity and tranquility. He found it difficult to understand how the struggle for international markets, the penetration of economic boundaries by the resources and influence of foreign capitalists, and the dependence of domestic well-being on the ever changing economic policies of foreign governments could possibly serve the cause of international peace and harmony.

In Keynes's judgment, economic internationalism leads to strife rather than to international accord. To maximize international specialization and the geographical diffusion of capital, nations must protect their foreign interests, capture new markets, and generally pursue imperialistic economic policies. But these activities, argues Keynes, are hardly likely to engender good feeling and understanding throughout the world. Another factor, in Keynes's estimate, that makes for a great deal of international enmity is the separation between the ownership and management of capital. This divorce is bad enough within a country, but raises even more disturbing issues when it transcends national boundaries. Generally, the foreign investor lacks knowledge and responsibility toward what he owns. His primary preoccupation is that his resources he invested in that area where he can realize the highest rate of return. He is not too concerned with the effects his capital transfers are likely to have on the well-being of the countries from which he withdraws his funds. But such an attitude, observed Keynes, can hardly be deemed to be conducive to cordial international relations. Because of the strains and enmities caused by economic internationalism, Keynes favored, instead, a policy of economic isolationism, which he supported in these terms:

> I sympathize, therefore, with those who would minimize, rather than those who would maximize, economic entanglements between nations. Ideas, knowledge, art hospitality, travel—these are the things which should of their nature be international. But let goods be homespun wherever it is reasonably and conveniently possible; and, above all, let finance be primarily national. [19]

Thus, if nations could become more self-reliant, the cause of peace, Keynes felt, would be greatly enhanced.

Another free trade argument with which Keynes took exception was the principle of comparative cost. Although valid in the economic setting of the nineteenth century, he felt that the theory had lost much of its significance in the existing circumstances. He observed that in earlier times the prevalence of wide differences in the degree of industrialization in various areas of the world had made possible many opportunities for national specialization. However, Keynes did not believe that the advantages presently forthcoming from the international division of labor were at all comparable to those of the past, because there now remained little difference between national efficiencies. Unlike the pre-war period, mass production processes could now be performed in most countries and climates with equal efficiency, and for this reason he seriously questioned one of the most cogent argument for free trade, as witnessed in his following contention:

> But I am not persuaded that the economic advantages of the international division of labour today are at all comparable with what they were. I must not be understood to carry my argument beyond a certain point. A considerable degree of international specialization is necessary in a rational world in all cases where it is dictated by wide differences of climate, natural resources, native aptitudes, level of culture and density of population. But over an increasingly wide range of industrial products, and perhaps of agricultural products, also, I become doubtful whether the economic cost of national self-sufficiency is great enough to outweigh the other advantages of gradually bringing the producer and the consumer within the ambit of the same national, economic and financial organization. Experience accumulates to prove that most modern mass-production processes can be performed in most countries and climates with almost equal efficiency.[20]

Arguing further against the applicability of the comparative cost principle in the economic environment of the 1930s, Keynes noted that as a nation's wealth increases, primary and manufactured goods play a diminishing role in the standard of living as compared to residential construction, personal services, and other sheltered items that do not enter the channels of foreign commerce. In other words, as living standards improve, an increasing proportion of the goods making up that standard of life must of necessity be produced at home. Therefore, Keynes concluded that even if some small increase were to occur in the cost of producing at home many of those goods previously imported, the national standard of living would not be appreciably affected. Moreover, even if the material standard were to deteriorate somewhat because of the higher costs of import substitutes, this would be more than offset by the other advantages forthcoming from self-sufficiency. In short, national autarky, though it might cost something, was still preferable to economic internationalism.

In addition to the above arguments, Keynes maintained that a policy of limited international economic involvement was made necessary by the failure of capitalism, which he described in these caustic terms:

> The decadent international but individualistic capitalism, in the hands of which we found ourselves after the war, is not a success. It is not intelligent, it is not beautiful, it is not just, it is not virtuous—and it doesn't deliver the goods.[21]

Keynes observed that because of capitalism's inability to deal with the great social and economic issues of the times, nations such as Russia, Germany, Italy, and even Ireland had been compelled to introduce political economic systems that departed radically from the capitalistic model. The United

States and Great Britain, though largely adhering to the traditional political economic arrangements, were also seeking a new form of organization. Keynes cautioned, however, that if Great Britain was to achieve an economic system ideally suited to its needs, a considerable amount of testing would be required. To guarantee the success of these experiments, Keynes felt it was absolutely essential that the British economy be free of those world forces that tended to establish a pattern of uniform equilibrium in accordance with the so called principles of laissez-faire capitalism. Keynes maintained that, during the experimental period, it was imperative that the British retain mastery over their own fate and remain as free as they could from the interferences of the outside world.[22] The realization of such economic isolation, he thought, would not only enable Great Britain to conduct her experiments independently, but also make her task easier insofar as they could be carried on without excessive economic cost.

Turning to a consideration of the type of system Great Britain should implement, Keynes felt that it should retain "as much private judgment and initiative as possible." Private enterprise, he insisted, should continue to occupy a dominant place in the economy; however, retention of this role for private capital, he cautioned, was contingent on a sizable reduction in the rate of interest. In fact, he opined that the interest rate might have to be reduced to zero within the next thirty years. To insure this reduction of money costs, Keynes suggested a separation of the British capital market from that of the rest of the world.[23] Keynes felt that should Great Britain reject this course of action and revert, instead, to a policy of international financial and economic involvement, she would inflict great harm on herself. Economic internationalism, embracing the free movement of capital and of loanable funds as well as the unrestricted movement of goods, he said, could condemn Britain for a generation to come to a much lower level of economic well-being than could be achieved under an alternative system.[24]

Another feature of the economic system proposed by Keynes for Great Britain was increased governmental participation in the economy. The whole of economic activity, he asserted, should not be determined exclusively by the test of the accountant's profit, because such a criterion does not permit a nation to exploit its economic potentialities to the fullest. From a profit standpoint, the crucial consideration is not whether resources, manpower, and technique are available for undertaking a particular project—for example, slum clearance—but only whether such a program will be financially worthwhile. Thus, quips Keynes, "we have to remain poor because it does not 'pay' to be rich." To eliminate this burdensome loss of wealth to the nation, Keynes advocated a modification of the state's view toward the undertaking of many socially advantageous, though not necessarily profitable, economic projects. This should not be interpreted to mean, however, that Keynes would do away completely with the profit test, for he readily recognized that there are many sectors of the private economy for which it is eminently suited.

The state's participation in economic affairs, as outlined by Keynes, would not be confined to the domestic economy. He also envisaged for the state an activist role in the external sector. In fact, he pointed out that if the economic functions of the state were to be expanded, a policy would have to be formulated as to the type and quantity of goods to be exchanged abroad. But if the character of Great Britain's foreign trade was to be determined by state action, then free trade, as understood by the orthodox economists, could no longer be said to exist.

SUMMARY

To sum up, Keynes's position on the question of free versus restricted trade as of the middle of 1933 was clear and unequivocal. Whereas he had shown some vacillation on this issue in the pages of his *Means to Prosperity*, he was now unmistakably committed to a policy of protection.

The conditions of the twentieth century, Keynes noted, were different from those of the past; hence, many of the arguments in support of free trade, albeit valid for the earlier period, were no longer applicable. Turning to specifics, Keynes opposed free trade, because, contrary to the claims of its proponents, such a policy served only to engender international enmity. Secondly, he took exception to free trade, because he did not believe that the advantages of the international division of labor in the present circumstances were at all comparable with those of the period prior to World War I. This he attributed to the widespread introduction of mass-production techniques throughout the world. Thirdly, Keynes argued that the existence of an efficient worldwide capitalism, as assumed by the economic internationalism of the nineteenth century, no longer obtained in the 1930s, and so, a new form of political economic organization would have to be devised to fill the void. To insure the success of this effort, Keynes felt that Britain would have to minimize its trade and financial contacts with the rest of the world. By following a course of economic isolation, Britain could then initiate an expansive monetary policy designed to reduce the interest rate, and assign increased economic responsibility to the public sector without fear of the disequilibrating effects such policies might otherwise have on both the internal and external sectors of the economy.

NOTES

1. J. M. Keynes, "Some Consequences of the Economy Report," *The New Statesman and Nation* 2, no. 25 (August 15, 1931): 189.
2. J. M. Keynes, *Essays in Persuasion* (New York: Harcourt, Brace, 1932), 281.

3. Keynes, *Essays in Persuasion*, 282.

4. Keynes, *Essays in Persuasion*, 166.

5. Keynes, *Essays in Persuasion*, 283–84.

6. Keynes, *Essays in Persuasion*, 285.

7. P. Einzig, *The Tragedy of the Pound* (London: Kegan Paul, French, Trubner, 1932), 9.

8. P. Einzig, *The Comedy of the Pound* (London: Kegan Paul, French Trubner, 1933), 17.

9. Einzig, *The Comedy of the Pound*, 19.

10. For a short time after the conclusion of this agreement the Bank of England withdrew its support of sterling and on August 3 even permitted its value to fall below the gold export point. In the light of subsequent developments the decision to allow sterling to depreciate proved to be a tactical mistake because it caused a further loss of confidence in the pound.

11. In the course of the crisis, the Bank of England paid out £200,000,000 in gold or its equivalent. This sum represented about one-half of the total foreign claims on London. (See Keynes, *Essays in Persuasion*, 289.)

12. J. M. Keynes, "The Tariff Question," letter to the editor, *The Times of London*, September 29, 1931, 15.

13. *The Sunday Express*, September 27, 1931.

14. J. M. Keynes, "The Prospects of the Sterling Exchanges," *The Yale Review*, March 1932, 446.

15. J. M. Keynes, *The Means to Prosperity* (New York: Harcourt, Brace, 1933): 20–21.

16. R. F. Harrod, *The Life of John Maynard Keynes* (London: Macmillan and Company, 1951): 455.

17. J. M. Keynes, "National Self Sufficiency," *The Yale Review* 22, no. 4 (June 1933). This article also appeared under the same title in *The New Statesman and Nation* 6, no. 124 (July 8, 1933). See also Keynes's "National Self-Sufficiency—II," *The New Statesman and Nation* 6, no. 125 (July 15, 1933).

18. J. M. Keynes, "Free Trade for England," *The New Republic* 37, no. 472 (December 19, 1923): 87.

19. Keynes, "National Self-Sufficiency," 37.

20. Keynes, "National Self-Sufficiency," 37

21. Keynes, "National Self-Sufficiency—II," 65.

22. Keynes, "National Self-Sufficiency—II," 65.

23. "The Gospel of Self-Sufficiency," the *London Economist* 117, no. 4691 (July 22, 1933), 171.

24. Keynes, "National Self-Sufficiency—II," 65.

The General Theory of Employment, Interest and Money and Its Relevance for Keynes's Foreign Trade Views

This part of the study will try to show how Keynes's *General Theory*, which dealt largely with a closed economy, had important implications for Keynes's foreign trade views for a nation operating in an open economy. In addition, it will examine Keynes's writings on foreign trade issues as they related to Great Britain in the pre-war period and how they caused him to veer further away from the tenets of free trade.

Inasmuch as the *General Theory* deals largely with a closed economy, Keynes did not have much to say directly about a nation's dealings in an open economy. Nevertheless, his break with classical economics on the issue of employment had very significant trade implications for a nation enjoying full employment as opposed to one operating below that level.

Because classical economics was deemed to be the economics of a special case, holding only when the economy is in a state of full employment, it follows that many of its doctrines are relevant only when the condition of full employment has been satisfied. Would this mean, therefore, that Keynes would subscribe to free trade only if the prerequisite of full employment were first met? Certainly, that inference seems to be justified by a number of observations he made on the issue in the pages of the *General Theory*.

Keynes's reflection on the concept of a favorable balance of trade provides another interesting perspective on his foreign trade views. A favorable balance of trade, wherein the value of exports exceeds the value of imports, represents foreign investment. Like domestic investment, foreign investment constitutes an offset to savings and thereby adds to the level of aggregate demand. This offset is especially critical for a mature economy, just as Great Britain was in the late 1930s, where the propensity to consume is falling and the propensity to save is rising.

Although Keynes did not openly suggest that a nation pursue restrictive trade policies to achieve a favorable balance of trade, he certainly appreciated its benefits and did say that it is reasonable for the government to be preoccupied with its trade balance. Nevertheless, it is difficult to determine whether or not Keynes would have favored state intervention to achieve that end. At best, it demonstrates once again his ambivalence on economic matters, an issue to which reference was made at the very outset of this study.

Although not directly related to the main theme of the *General Theory*, Keynes, for whatever reason, digressed to a discussion of the "underground economists" and the foreign trade views of the Mercantilists. Although Keynes does not openly endorse the use of tariffs, quotas, and other barriers to trade associated with Mercantilism, he is more inclined to favor their views rather than those of the free traders. Fundamentally, the difference between the two devolves around the role that the balance of payments plays in their systems.

Whereas the classicists would use the interest rate to equilibrate the trade balance, the Mercantilists would manage the trade balance to influence the interest rate. In the Keynesian system, the interest rate was of critical importance, because of its significance for the determination of the level of investment, which, in turn, determined the level of employment. If, then, the management of the trade balance is of such major importance, then it may be reasonably assumed that Keynes would favor some form of intervention in the flow of imports and exports.

Therefore, given his concern for investment and its importance for the determination of employment, it is understandable why Keynes gravitated more toward the Mercantilist position of restrictive or managed trade than toward the free trade doctrine of the classicists. Even though he may not have explicitly endorsed the use of tariffs, quotas, and other crude "beggar thy neighbor" restraints on international trade, Keynes's sympathies were clearly in favor of the Mercantilists.

In the years following the publication of the *General Theory*, Great Britain's economic situation at home and abroad showed little, if any, improvement. In that depressed environment, Keynes gave up hope for any international cooperation and became increasingly insular in his thinking. Nations, he felt, should become more self-sufficient. World conditions had changed. Trade among nations was no longer as critical as it had been in the prior century. A large part of consumption was now made up of services that could only be rendered at home. The Law of Comparative Advantage had lost some of its relevance because many goods could now be produced with the same efficiency all over the world.

To the extent that trade was necessary, because of factors such as differences in climate and the location of resources, it should be better planned or managed. Accordingly, he distanced himself from multilateral international trade and urged, instead, greater reliance on bilateralism and the use of barter arrangements. Indeed, Keynes had come a long way from his stalwart defense of multilateral free trade immediately after World War I to his disavowal of it just prior to World War II.

Chapter Nine

Keynes's Views on Foreign Trade during the Period of the General Theory of Employment, Interest, and Money

As of mid 1933, the evidence suggests that despite his vacillation in *The Means to Prosperity*, Keynes was still inclined toward protectionism. His position after that date is not so clear. Was it because he had little else to say on the subject or, too, was it because he became too preoccupied with the preparation of *The General Theory of Employment Interest and Money*?[1] To find some clue as to what his position was on the issue, one must turn to a consideration of that work.

The *General Theory* deals largely with a closed economy. Although it does not deal extensively with issues relating to an open economy—for example, fixed versus flexible exchange rates, trade balances, the transmission of fluctuations from one county to another, restricted trade, and the role of foreign investment—the *General Theory* does touch these and other issues such as Mercantilism at least tangentially. And from these observations it may be possible to gain some insight as to his position on free versus restricted trade.

One important inference that can be drawn on the issue comes from Keynes's dissatisfaction with the classical assumption of full employment His argument is that full employment is a condition that obtains only in special circumstances; therefore, classical economics is the economics of a special case. Consequently, it is erroneous to apply its doctrines to all conditions, especially in periods of less than full employment. If that is the case, then in Keynes's view "the unqualified advantages of laissez-faire in respect of foreign trade become questionable."[2]

On the other hand, Keynes acknowledges that given a high level of employment and income, the orthodox arguments in favor of international specialization and free trade are difficult to refute. He points out that "if our central controls succeed in establishing an aggregate volume of output corresponding to full employment as nearly as is practicable, the classical theory comes into its own from this point onwards."[3]

The inference to be drawn from Keynes's assertion is unambiguous. If full employment can be achieved, then the classical doctrines that include free trade come into play. This means, then, that full employment constitutes a necessary condition or prerequisite for the acceptance of free trade, as evidenced by Keynes's own words:

> If nations can learn to provide themselves with full employment by their domestic policy, there need be no important economic forces calculated to set the interest of one country against that of its neighbors. There would still be room for the international division of labor and for international lending inappropriate conditions. . . . International trade would cease to be what it is, namely, a desperate expedient to maintain employment at home by forcing sales on foreign markets and restricting purchases, which, if successful will merely shift the problem of unemployment to the neighbor which is worsted in the struggle, but a willing and unimpeded exchange of goods and services of mutual advantage.[4]

Clearly, Keynes's endorsement of free trade was not without qualification. It depended on the status of domestic employment. He was careful to distinguish between a condition of full and less than full employment in terms of opportunity cost. Under full employment, the issue is not one of finding employment for idle workers and resources, but how to find the best possible employment for each worker and resource.[5] By contrast under a condition of less than full employment, the issue is not how to utilize these resources in the best manner possible, but how to engage them at all.[6] Thus, the opportunity cost analysis, though valid under conditions of full employment, would not be equally valid under conditions of widespread unemployment. As a result, the free trade argument, which is consistent with the opportunity cost analysis, the division of labor, and the principle of comparative advantage, loses much of its relevance in a state of depressed economic activity.

There is an essential difference in the nature of the problems facing a fully employed and a less-than-fully employed economy. Therefore, policies that are suited for one may not be suited for the other.[7] In the former, maximum productivity or efficiency is the norm, while in the latter, maximum output and employment should be the criterion.[8]

As noted earlier, maximum productivity and efficiency can be achieved through the specialization of labor and the free exchange of goods and services. Maximum output on the other hand may at times be more readily achieved through an increase in investment, whether domestic or foreign, that is, a favorable trade balance.[9] In a condition of less than full employment, it is entirely possible for a nation to increase its level of home employment by diverting demand from foreign to home produced goods.[10]

Although it is true that a restricted trade policy frustrates the optimum international division of labor and results in a loss of productivity, it is also true that such a policy could promote a higher level of employment and income in a country experiencing widespread economic distress. The increase in domestic output and employment caused by a restrictive trade policy could more than offset the loss of efficiency attending the international division of labor. From this perspective, it would appear to be counterproductive for a nation to economize in the use of labor only to have it go to waste in unemployment. In sum, if unemployment is severe, a protectionist policy may well be more advantageous, whereas if the amount of labor displaced is not too great, a free trade policy would be more beneficial.

In analyzing Keynes's theory of employment, one cannot help but appreciate the pivotal importance of investment in the determination of employment and income. As noted by Keynes even prior to the publication of the *General Theory*,

> Employment can only increase *pari passu* with an increase in investment; unless, indeed there is a change in the propensity to consume. For since consumers will spend less than the increase in the aggregate supply price when employment is increased, the increased employment will prove unprofitable unless there is an increase in investment to fill the gap.[11]

The key to high levels of employment is to be found in an ever increasing volume of investment, more so for a wealthy than for a poor country. The more affluent the country, the greater the margin between consumption and its potential production and, therefore, the greater the urgency for finding adequate investment projects. Nevertheless, whether we are dealing with an advanced or expanding economy, the problem facing both of them is the same. Owing to the fixed psychological propensity of people to save, suitable investment projects must be found to offset those savings.

But if adequate investment projects cannot be found at home in the production of durable goods, construction activity, and the manufacture of goods for inventory, what alternative, apart from government spending, would such an economy have to escape the prospect of chronic under-full employment?

An effective alternative for countries that have a sizable volume of international trade would be an increase in foreign investment, that is, a favorable balance of trade on income account with the rest of the world.[12] This form of investment would provide the same offset to saving as would domestic investment.[13]

Foreign investment constitutes an excess of exports over imports. If exports cannot be increased above imports, then an alternative would be to reduce imports through the medium of restrictive trade policies. In addition to restricting imports by means of tariffs and quotas, it is possible to achieve the same objective through exchange depreciation or a general wage reduction, the latter to which Keynes was opposed.[14]

To the extent that a restrictive trade policy causes an increase in demand for domestically produced goods without adding to the amount available for domestic consumption, a favorable balance of trade narrows the gap between total output and that part consumed domestically. In effect, the trade balance or foreign investment operates in the same way as domestic investment, because it provides "a national outlet for domestic savings."[15]

The role of foreign investment is neatly summarized by Professor J. H. G. Pierson in the following terms:

> Given a nation's volume of savings, offsets to that savings must be found. Economists tell us that we need a volume of investment and other non-consumption offsets to saving equal in magnitude to the volume of savings forthcoming at a full employment level of national income, and that we are not likely to come anywhere near attaining such a volume of investment through the unaided operation of natural forces; and that foreign investment is a peculiarly strategic kind of investment for purposes of closing the gap.[16]

Although Professor Pierson does not indicate how that margin of foreign investment is to be obtained, the fact that "unaided" natural forces cannot close the gap strongly suggests that it may be necessary to resort to some form of restrictive trade to realize it.

From the standpoint of a single country, there is no gainsaying that an improvement in its trade balance is just as effective a means of bolstering employment and income as an increase in domestic capital formation. Present day China with its large trade surpluses provides a good case in point. But in pursuing such policies, nations should be aware of the fallacy of composition and division, that is to say, what applies to one of the parts does not necessarily apply to the whole.

An increase in one country's trade surplus can only come at the expense of one or more other trading partners. An improvement in the trade balance of a particular country makes possible an increase in its employment only by reducing employment in other countries. We are dealing with a constant sum game. For the world as a whole the overall level of employment remains the same. Clearly, not all countries can hope to achieve at one and the same time a favorable balance of trade as a means of increasing employment.

The above to the contrary notwithstanding, the fact remains that a country with a large trade deficit need not try to gain a trade surplus at the expense of its trading partners, but could, by reducing its imports and balancing its foreign accounts, add to its level of employment without unfairly exporting unemployment to abroad. Nevertheless, a far better course of action would be for all nations to increase their domestic investment. Only in this way could employment be increased for the entire world.

In view of the critical role played by investment in Keynes's theory of employment and because a favorable trade balance is synonymous with investment, one may reasonably ask, "How much emphasis did .Keynes place on foreign investment and how disposed was he to augment a country's trade balance through a restriction of foreign trade ?"

He offers no hard answer to these questions except to say that a nation's well-being depends on home or foreign investment, which between them make up aggregate investment. This lack of preference may be discerned from the following statements, which appear toward the end of the *General Theory*:

> When a country is growing in wealth somewhat rapidly the further progress of this happy state of affairs is liable to be interrupted in conditions of laissez faire, by the insufficiency of the inducements to new investment. . . . They may be found either in home investment or in foreign investment which between them, make up aggregate investment. [17]

But then to add to the uncertainty of his position, he adds the following:

> In a society where there is no question of direct investment under the aegis of public authority, the economic objectives, with which it is reasonable for the government to be preoccupied, are the domestic rate of interest and the balance of trade. [18]

While Keynes provides an answer as to how domestic investment can be advanced, that is to say, through a lowering of the interest rate, he fails to provide any specific advice in the second citation as to how the government should handle the balance of trade. Clearly, it should be increased if conditions warrant, but just how is this to come about? One could argue that since a restriction of imports is one way for increasing the trade balance, such a measure would be entirely consistent with Keynes's point of view. Whether he would favor a tariff or a quota to achieve this end cannot be directly inferred from this particular passage. Nevertheless, a case can be made for supporting such a thesis. Professor Lloyd Metzler, for example, notes that the classical argument against a favorable balance of trade as a permanent policy stands or falls with the classical assumption of full employment. And since Keynes rejected the notion that full employment always exists, he was bound to accept the idea that a reduction of imports through tariffs would have a definite influence on the level of employment. For, given a condition of widespread unemployment, a restriction of imports will, by adding to the volume of total investment and therefore, to the level of aggregate demand, increase the amount of home employment.[19]

In the *General Theory*, Keynes, for unknown reasons, delves into a number of topics that are not directly related to the development of his theory of employment. They include his discussion on Mercantilism and his reference to members of the economic "underground," for example, Silvio Gesell, as he characterizes them. Our interest, though, will be restricted to his reflections on Mercantilism.

As in other parts of the *General Theory*, Keynes, in his observations on the Mercantilists, remains ambivalent on the issue of free trade. Arguments can be marshaled on both sides of the issue. At the very outset, he claims that, contrary to his earlier position on the issue,[20] a protectionist trade policy can increase the level of domestic employment. Continuing in this vein, Keynes notes that in an economy with a gold standard, the government should be concerned with the balance of trade because it can control the level of investment through it. In those instances wherein the authorities have no control over the level of interest or other inducements to home investment, "measures to increase the favorable balance of trade" are appropriate.

Again, Keynes does not specify what those measures should be. They could, of course, include export subsidies or a restriction of imports through tariffs, quotas, and other restrictive measures. In any case, they do constitute an interference with the free flow of goods and services; hence, it would not be an overstatement to say that he was sympathetic toward some form of intervention.

Keynes's support for restricted trade goes beyond its relevance for investment. He points out that a favorable trade balance has a positive effect not only for investment but also for the level of interest as well. In a country on the gold standard, the interest rate, *ceteris paribus*, will be determined by the quantity of the precious metal. Therefore, a favorable balance, by increasing the money supply, will stimulate not only foreign but also domestic investment through a lower level of interest. Keynes summarizes his argument for the conscious control of the trade balance in the following terms:

> Thus, as it happens, a preoccupation on the part of authorities with a favourable balance of trade served both purposes; and was, furthermore, the only available means of promoting them. At a time when the authorities had no direct control over the domestic rate of interest or the other inducements to home investment, measures to increase the favourable balance of trade were the only direct means at their disposal for increasing foreign investment; and at the same time, the effect of a favourable balance of trade on the influx of the

precious metals was their only indirect means of reducing the domestic rate of interest and so increasing the inducement to home investment. [21]

But right after having provided this endorsement for the exercise of control over the balance of trade, Keynes tempers it by stating that the reader should not reach "a premature conclusion as to the practical policy" to which his argument might lead one. There are strong strictures, he states, unless they can be justified on special grounds. He goes on to say that the advantages of the division of labor are substantial even though classical economics may have overstated their value. In his own words, he states:

> There are strong presumptions of a general character against trade restrictions unless they can be justified on special grounds. The advantages of the international division of labour are real and substantial, even though the classical school greatly overstressed them. [22]

What, then, is one to make of this seeming retraction?

Actually, Keynes does not shut the door on restricted trade in all cases, because he does leave room for it on "special grounds." He does not identify those special grounds, but one can reasonably assume that a condition of widespread unemployment could qualify for such an exception. If that interpretation of his position is correct, then given a condition of severe unemployment a strong case can be made for restricted trade. But if this condition be replaced by full employment, then the free trade doctrine gains currency once again.

To add to his seeming indecision on foreign trade in his comments on Mercantilism, Keynes returns once again to explain his reservations about the laissez-faire doctrine of free trade. The reason, he states, why he has difficulty with the classical argument is owing to "the inadequacy of the theoretical foundation on which it rests." Specifically, he takes exception to the classical view that "the rate of interest and the volume of investment are self-adjusting at the optimum level."[23] As a result, there is no need to be concerned with the trade balance. By contrast, the Mercantilists realized that the interest rate and the volume of investment are not self-equilibrating at the best possible level; hence, their manipulation of the trade balance to equate them at a high level was justified in Keynes's estimate.

In sum, whereas the Mercantilists employed the trade balance to influence the interest rate, the orthodox economists used the interest rate to effect the trade balance. In light of his concern with employment, Keynes, quite understandably, faulted the orthodox economists, because by using the bank rate to ensure external equilibrium, they wholly ruled out "the objective of maintaining a domestic rate of interest consistent with full employment."[24]

The question that remains then is, "how are the Mercantilists to adjust their trade balance?" Clearly it is reasonable to assume that they would have to manage it through restrictive means. But if a protectionist policy is correct in those instances wherein the interest rate and the volume of investment are not self-adjusting at an optimum level, then Keynes cannot give a blanket endorsement to the classicists' argument for free trade in all circumstances. At best, he can subscribe to their policy of free trade only when the interest rate and volume of investment equate at full employment—the point at which the classical doctrine becomes operative once again.

As between the Mercantilists and the orthodox economists, Keynes was more partial toward the former. Insofar as dealing with "the economic system as a whole and with securing the optimum employment of the system's entire resources,"[25] he thought that the methods of the Mercantilists were more practical than those of the classicists. He was impressed by the Mercantilists' attempts to maintain the level of employment by disposing of a surplus of goods through foreign trade. This, of course, would entail the need for an excess of exports over imports, for if the flow of goods were equal to the outflow of goods, the effort would be self-defeating.

Keynes believed that the early economic thinkers of the sixteenth and seventeenth centuries were justified in seeking a favorable balance of trade, because of the tendency for the propensity to save to exceed the inducement to invest.[26] The problem of unemployment that confronted the Mercantilists was the same as the one Keynes was trying to solve during the inter-war years. Small wonder, therefore, why he was more partial toward them.

In the years between the publication of the *General Theory* and the outbreak of World War II, Keynes had little else to say about the issue of foreign trade. His literary output diminished during this period, especially after having experienced a heart attack in the summer of 1937. Nevertheless, Keynes did, in his limited pronouncements make it clear that he had not returned to orthodox free trade. He continued to believe that international considerations should be subordinated to the needs of the domestic economy—for example, high employment—and not the other way around.[27]

During this period, he seemed to draw away from the use of tariffs, quotas, and the customary measures for regulating foreign trade. Instead, his position seemed to be more aligned to what may be described as planned or managed trade, but certainly not free trade. Keynes's move to planned trade was not as sudden as it might appear, because he had been moving in this direction as early as 1930 in his *Treatise on Money*.[28]

Although Keynes published no major work after 1936 and the outbreak of World War II in 1939, his advocacy of planned trade can be discerned from a number of articles and letters that appeared in *The Times of London* during that interval.

The economic recovery of Great Britain in early 1937 provides a good illustration of how Keynes's planned trade would work. Basically, it would be flexible and work in the same manner as fiscal policy. It would operate in a countercyclical way. During economic downturns, a country should check imports and undertake other restrictive measures to assist the balance of trade. During a period of recovery, on the other hand, trade would be liberalized and the trade balance allowed to fall to a deficit position.[29]

In effect, just as it is appropriate to vary the level of expenditures and taxes over the course of the business cycle so, too, it would be helpful to regulate the flow of imports and exports over that time frame. Commercial policy would be used as a complement to fiscal policy to control the movements of the business cycle. It appears that this is precisely what he had in mind in one of his comments in *The Times of London*:

> These. (fiscal and commercial policies) I urge are the methods which will best serve to protect us from the excesses of the boom, and at the same time, put us in good trim to ward off the cumulative dangers of the slump when the reaction comes, as come it will surely will.[30]

In another article that appeared in *The Times of London* on October 7, 1938, Keynes added another element to his scheme of planned foreign trade, namely, barter.[31] Surprisingly, the rationale for this measure did not derive from any specific development in the foreign sector, but from what was happening to labor and capital productivity during the depths of the Great Depression.

Keynes points out that the large increases in labor productivity, both in the United States and Great Britain, unaccompanied by a corresponding increase in demand, would further aggravate the problem of unemployment in both countries. In addition, the rapid advances in technology and capital efficiency meant that less investment would have to be made in monetary terms to sustain the current level of expenditures. Investment requirements could be financed out of depreciation reserves without having to tap current net savings. This would only serve to widen the gap between investment and the country's propensity to save.

Under these circumstances, it would be very improbable that full employment could be achieved without abnormally large loan expenditure programs by the government. This problem of unemployment, Keynes thought, had to be attacked on a number of fronts. For one thing, in order to keep Great Britain's trade balance from becoming a source of disinvestment and an additional source of unemployment, he urged that an appropriate mechanism be set up to balance Britain's exports and imports. Interestingly, he did not suggest that this balance be achieved through an increase in tariffs, but by barter, as the following comment attests:

> In the circumstances of the moment, I suggest that the balance of trade position and the net disinvestment in this country's foreign assets which is probably going on also needs particular attention—not, indeed, by aggravation of tariffs

but by a new, and now necessary, machinery for linking up exports with
imports, so as to make sure that those from whom we buy spend a reasonable
proportion of the proceeds in corresponding purchases from us. We can no
longer afford to leave the barter aspect of foreign trade to look after itself.[32]

With imports and exports in balance, the effect on the domestic economy
would at worst be neutral. In fact, such a balance could even turn out to have
a positive effect on the economy. As Professor Roy Harrod, Keynes's biogra-
pher, pointed out, there is a strong possibility that an increased demand for
exports, even though offset by an increase in the volume of imports, could
stimulate the level of home employment, if the increase in exports requires
an increase in capital formation.[33]

Keynes's advocacy of a bilateral approach to international trade was relevant not only to the trade balance, but also for the successful carrying out of
the government's loan expenditure programs.[34] An increase in public expenditures, say, would lead to an increase in personal income of which some
proportion would be used for the purchase of imports. Through this transmission effect, however unintended, other countries would be the beneficiaries
of the increase in home expenditures, unless offset by an increase in exports
to them. To deal with these unintended consequences, Keynes believed that
the trade balance could be safeguarded only through a conscious linking of
imports and exports. Again, writing in *The Times of London* in the spring of
1939, just months before the outbreak of World War II, he reaffirmed the
need for planned or managed trade in the following terms:

> The handling of foreign trade cannot be left to individual enterprise unaided.
> For individuals have no machinery for the linking of imports to exports which
> is now essential for our financial strength. This is an urgent problem of im-
> mense difficulty—not less so because the solution is so contrary to our tradi-
> tions and preferences.[35]

As an additional measure for maintaining control over the balance of
payments, Keynes urged the tightening of the embargo on the transfer of
capital funds to overseas by British citizens. (This was not a wartime measure, because although the clouds of war were gathering over Europe, hostilities had not yet broken out.)

By restricting the movement of these funds, Keynes felt that the whole of
the country's liquid capital resources could be held in reserve to meet adverse trade balances as well as assist the Treasury in financing its loan
expenditure program without regard to external considerations. For these
reasons, concluded Keynes, "it is a small measure of sacrifice to ask from
owners of capital that they should refrain from running away."[36]

SUMMARY

A reading of *The General Theory of Employment, Interest and Money* does not provide a clear and absolute answer as to whether Keynes was a free trader or a protectionist. The answer to that question cannot be stated categorically, but must instead be conditional. It all depends. But on what does it depend?

Basically, Keynes's position on the issue depends on the state of employment in the economy. On this issue, very importantly, he contended that classical economics represented the economics of a special case, that of full employment. Accordingly, if full employment could be assured, Keynes would unhesitatingly subscribe to free trade; if not, then the tenets and policy recommendations of classical economics would not hold. In those circumstances, for example, widespread unemployment, he would favor a restrictive trade policy.

If a country is at full employment, then the opportunity cost argument calls for greater efficiency, a division of labor, and free trade. On the other hand, if a country is faced with high unemployment, it makes little sense to seek greater efficiency while creating greater waste through the displacement of more workers by the importation of foreign produced goods. In those circumstances, the objective should be to increase output and income, especially if the economic benefits of restricted trade exceed those of free trade.

The fact that Keynes's attitude toward foreign trade varied, depending on the state of the domestic economy, does not mean that he was inconsistent. Given a condition of full employment, free trade would be in order; otherwise, a restrictive trade policy might be more appropriate. From the earliest phase of his career, Keynes's concern was with what best served the interests of the domestic economy, for example, stable prices, insulation from external fluctuations, the maintenance of high employment, and so on. From that standpoint, it cannot be said that he was inconsistent in his commercial policy. His position on the issue all depended on the state of the domestic economy.

In his comments on the Mercantilists, Keynes, again, does not reveal a clear and unambiguous answer as to where he stood on the issue of free trade and protectionism. Nevertheless, he appeared to be more closely aligned to the Mercantilist than to the classical position on the issue.

As noted, Keynes's break with the classical economists was due to their deficiencies on the theory of employment. Their disagreement on foreign trade derived essentially from the same source. Keynes argued that he was not opposed to the classicists' position on foreign trade because it is based on laissez-faire, but because of "the inadequacy of the theoretical foundations" on which it rests.

In regard to the point of disagreement, the classicists believed that the rate of interest and the volume of investment (key elements in Keynes's theory of employment) were self-correcting at high levels of employment. The Mercantilists, on the other hand, did not believe that the interest rate and the volume of investment were self-equilibrating at the best possible level and so thought that it was appropriate to manipulate the trade balance in such a way as to equate the interest rate with the level of investment at a high level of activity.

In sum, the classicists would adjust the interest rate to affect the trade balance, but Keynes was opposed to this approach, because it was more important to use the interest rate for insuring full employment than for adjusting the trade balance. The Mercantilists, by contrast, used the trade balance to influence the rate of interest, which is critical for the determination of domestic investment and the level of employment.

Inasmuch as Keynes was more disposed to intervene in the economy than were the classicists, who believed that adjustments should be left to the free market, it is not surprising that he was more sympathetic to the Mercantilist than to the classical position on the issue of free versus protected trade.

In tracking Keynes's position on foreign trade between the publication of the *General Theory* in 1936 and the outbreak of World War II in 1939, one does not find any evidence that he reverted back to a policy of orthodox free trade. Admittedly, he does not, when attempting to equate imports and exports, suggest the use of tariffs, quotas, or other crude "beggar thy neighbor" instruments. But this does not mean that he returned to the ranks of the free traders.

In fact, during this period he abandoned the cause of multilateral trade and embraced instead a system of planned or managed trade. He would balance Britain's trade account not through the adjustment of internal prices and the free ebb and flow of imports and exports, but through bilateral agreements and barter arrangements. Perhaps even more contrary to the tenets of free trade was his recommendation that capital transfers abroad should be regulated by the government. In his view, that capital should be used to cover balance of payments deficits and made available to finance the Treasury's loan expenditure programs

There is no gainsaying that during this period just prior to the onset of World War II Keynes continued to distance himself from free trade and move ever closer to planned trade. His separation from free trade may not have been as dramatic as it was in 1931 when he openly favored a tariff on British imports. In 1939, his restriction on imports was more subtle and less severe, but a restriction nonetheless. In his reference to the need to balance imports and exports, he depended, as noted, primarily on bilateral agreements, barter, and the control of capital. But suppose those measures did not work; would he have fallen back to the use of tariffs and quotas?

The answer is not clear, for he makes no specific mention of these instruments. Although Keynes may have remained silent on the use of these more restrictive measures, his pronouncements during the pre-war period made it quite clear that he preferred a system of planned over free trade. Admittedly, Keynes may have employed a less harsh set of tools for controlling the trade balance; however, in the end his objective remained the same, namely, the alignment of Britain's foreign trade with the best interests of the domestic economy. Effectively, his position for an open economy was the same as for a closed economy—how best to promote a full and stable level of home employment.

NOTES

1. J. M. Keynes, *The General Theory of Employment, Interest and Money* (New York: Harcourt Brace, 1936).

2. Keynes, *The General Theory of Employment, Interest and Money*, 21.

3. Keynes, *The General Theory of Employment, Interest and Money*, 378.

4. Keynes, *The General Theory of Employment, Interest and Money*, 382–83.

5. R. Stevens, *The New Economics and World Peace* (Philadelphia: The Pacifist Research Bureau, 1944), 3.

6. N. S. Buchanan and F. A. Lutz, *Rebuilding the World Economy* (New York: The Twentieth Century Fund, 1947), 57.

7. A. E. Hansen, *Recovery or Stagnation ?* (New York: W.W. Norton and Company, 1938), 16–18.

8. D. Dillard, *The Economics of John Maynard Keynes* (New York: Prentice Hall, 1948), 315.

9. J. Robinson, *Essays in the Theory of Employment* (London: Macmillan, 1937), 186.

10. This notion was certainly not a novel one. John A. Hobson in his *International Trade* noted, "If we once admit that there exists a larger margin or excess of productive capacity which is proved to exist in most trades during periods of slackness or depression, we begin to comprehend the true underlying source of the plausibility of protection." J. A. Hobson, *International Trade* (London: Methuen, 1904), 155.

11. J. M. Keynes, "A Self-Adjusting System," *The New Republic*, February 2, 1935, 36.

12. Present-day China represents a good case in point. With consumption low relative to income, the government offsets those resulting savings through foreign investment.

13. J. Robinson, *Introduction to the Theory of Employment* (London: Macmillan, 1937), 98–99.

14. For a full consideration of the effects that these measures have on a country's balance of trade and on the level of employment, see Mrs. Joan Robinson's *Essays in the Theory of Employment*, 211

15. A. Maffry, "Foreign Trade in the Postwar Economy," *The Survey of Current Business* (November 1944): 11.

16. J. H. G. Pierson, *Full Employment and Free Enterprise* (Washington, D.C.: Public Affairs Press, 1947), 90.

17. Keynes, *The General Theory of Employment, Interest and Money*, 335.

18. Keynes, *The General Theory of Employment, Interest and Money*, 335.

19. L. A. Metzler, "The Theory of International Trade," in *A Survey of Contemporary Economics*, ed. H. S. Ellis (Philadelphia: Blakiston, 1948), 250–51.

20. Keynes was referring to his position in 1923 when he stated, "If there is one thing that Protection cannot do, it is to cure Unemployment." J. M. Keynes, "Free Trade," *The Nation and the Athenaeum* 34, no. 8 (November 24, 1923): 302–3.

21. Keynes, *The General Theory of Employment, Interest and Money*, 336.

22. Keynes, *The General Theory of Employment, Interest and Money*, 338–39.

23. Keynes, *The General Theory of Employment, Interest and Money*, 339.

24. Keynes, *The General Theory of Employment, Interest and Money*, 339.

25. Keynes, *The General Theory of Employment, Interest and Money*, 340.

26. Keynes, *The General Theory of Employment, Interest and Money*, 346–48.

27. S. Harris, *John Maynard Keynes, Economist and Policy Maker* (New York: Charles Scribner's Sons, 1955), 187.

28. According to Professor Harrod, Keynes reconciled himself to a policy of planned trade after 1933. That would have occurred at about the same time that Keynes came out in favor of national self-sufficiency. See R. F. Harrod, *The Life of John Maynard Keynes* (London: Macmillan, 1951), 568.

29. J. M. Keynes, "How to Avoid a Slump II—Dear Money," *The Times of London*, January 13, 1937, 13.

30. Keynes, "How to Avoid a Slump II—Dear Money," 14.

31. J. M. Keynes, "Foreign Trade—The Barter Aspect," *The Times of London*, October 7, 1938, 10.

32. Keynes, "Foreign Trade—The Barter Aspect," 10.

33. Harrod, *The Life of John Maynard Keynes*, 10.

34. J. M. Keynes, "Crisis Finance—I—Employment and the Budget," *The Times of London*, April 17, 1939, 13–14.

35. Keynes, "Crisis Finance—I—Employment and the Budget," 13–14.

36. If it is assumed that the volume of current savings cannot escape abroad, because of government restrictions, then this amount of savings is necessarily available to the Treasury and private investors. Should it be further assumed that there is no trade deficit, then the country's income will be equal to public plus private expenditures and the difference between the country's aggregate income and what individuals spend is equal to savings and, therefore, available for paying taxes and making loans to the Treasury.

IV

Keynes's Views on Foreign Trade during and after World War II

This part of the study provides an account of Keynes's activities during and after World War II in the service of the British Government.

During the war, Keynes was in the service of the British Treasury. His attention was largely focused on the economic problems that would face Great Britain after the war. Of particular concern was the large balance of trade difficulties she would confront after the cessation of hostilities.

At first, Keynes felt that Britain should retain in the post-war period the system of international trade developed during the war with its heavy reliance on the control of capital movements, blocked accounts, and bilateral agreements. However, the extension of these measures in the post-war period was not possible, because in accepting Lend-Lease Aid from the Americans, she committed to the elimination of discriminatory practices in international trade after the war.

Given this constraint, Keynes tried to develop in his Clearing Union Proposal a plan that would address Britain's needs and yet be responsive to American demands. The proposal was based on the bancor, an international currency defined in, but not redeemable in gold. Actually, the bancor took the form of a line of credit assigned to each member state to supplement its own reserves. Basically, the union would act much like an international bank, overseeing the transfer of these credits from country to country.

The Americans, though, under the leadership of Harry Dexter White, who represented the U.S. Treasury Department, developed their own plan, the International Monetary Fund (IMF), for the expansion of multilateral free trade in the post-war period. The difference between it and the Clearing Union was that each nation would contribute a certain amount of its own currency to the IMF instead of being awarded a credit valued in terms of bancor. These currencies would not be loaned out, but bought or sold by each of the member nations in the IMF.

On other aspects of the plans, both allowed for flexible exchange rates, control of capital movements, and discretion over a country's trade balance. Nevertheless, a nation's autonomy would be circumscribed at least to some extent, because certain actions required the approval of the governing body.

In the subsequent deliberations at Bretton Woods in 1944, the IMF was selected as the model for the post-war expansion of multilateral trade. The reasons were that the IMF posed a lesser danger to inflation and the concept of the bancor was too novel for most conferees.

Whether the statesman took over from the economist, as the *London Economist* questioned at the time, Keynes, notwithstanding the rejection of his own plan, did endorse the IMF. But in doing so, and in later accepting the terms of the Anglo-American Loan Agreement, which he helped to negotiate in Washington, D.C., after the end of the war, the question is, "Did the concessions Keynes have to make restore his standing as a free trader or did he still remain beyond the pale of orthodoxy?"

The answer is that he did not return to doctrinaire free trade, but neither did he embrace protectionism if that meant a reliance on tariffs, quotas, and other "beggar thy neighbor" policies. Notwithstanding his reservations about free trade, Keynes believed that there was still much that was valuable in the classical argument. However, he did not think that the classical medicine, as he put it, could work by itself and that we could depend on it. The medicine would be painful, he thought, if it could not be supplemented by expedients such as exchange flexibility and import controls. He would, therefore, combine the best of the two extremes: freedom and control. And so, in embracing managed trade, Keynes ended up advocating the same conscious direction for a country in an open economy as one for a closed economy in his *The General Theory of Employment, Interest and Money*.

Chapter Ten

Keynes and the Currency Proposals for the Expansion of Multilateral International Trade Following the End of World War II

A BRIEF REVIEW OF THE CURRENCY PROPOSALS

The Clearing Union

During the autumn of 1941, Keynes, who was now in the service of the British Treasury, turned his attention to the international economic problems that would face Great Britain in the post-war period. Of particular concern to him was the large balance of trade difficulties she would inherit after the cessation of hostilities.

Initially, he felt that Britain should retain in the post-war period the system of international trade developed during the war emergency, viz., tight controls, blocked accounts, and bilateral agreements.[1] But however necessary such an arrangement may have been in Britain's interest, it could not hold after the war, because in accepting Lend-Lease Aid from the United States, she committed to "the elimination of all forms of discriminatory treatment in international commerce and the reduction of tariffs and other trade barriers."[2]

The challenge facing Keynes was "How could Britain resolve her post-war problems and at the same time satisfy the United States' demands?" To answer that question, Keynes and his colleagues at the Treasury developed the Clearing Union Proposal—a plan for greater international monetary cooperation.[3] Although Keynes had to abandon the bilateral approach he had espoused just prior to the war, his basic position respecting the priority of domestic over international considerations did not change. He believed that greater monetary cooperation among nations need not compromise their authority in the determination of domestic policies.

Although Keynes had doubts at the outset about a return to an open non-discriminatory system in the area of commercial policy, he moved forward with the development of the plan. In his view, much of the rise in protectionism during the inter-war period was due in large measure to the lack of adequate reserves among nations.[4] To relieve this pressure, Keynes suggested that the reserves of each participating country be supplemented by a right to borrow an assigned amount[5] from an International Clearing Union.

These reserves would not be in the form of national currencies, but in the form of bancor, an international bank money.[6] The bancor would be defined by the governing board in terms of gold and subject to change from time to time. Although it could not be redeemed in gold, it would be accepted as the equivalent of gold by all members of the union in settling their accounts.[7]

Given the gold value of the bancor, nations would define the initial values of their own currencies in terms of bancor. Countries could not change the value of their currencies beyond a certain amount without the consent of the Governing Board.[8] This provision would help to insure some degree of stability in the short run, but flexibility over the longer term. The Clearing Union would not have a Fund of fixed assets. Instead, overdraft facilities would be made available to each participating country. Each member would be assigned a quota or line of credit stated in bancor, which it might receive from the Clearing Union.[9] In exchange for this line of credit, each member country would accept the obligation to accumulate credit balances the extent to which debtor nations would utilize their overdraft privileges at the union.[10] Considered in the aggregate, this simply means that the creditor nations as a group would extend credits to the debtor nations as a group.

Basically, the plan was based on the same principle that supports a closed banking system, namely, the necessary equality of credits and debits. At the outset, the total quota was estimated at about 35 billion dollars.[11] It would, however, be subject to change from time to time, depending on the aggregate value of international trade.

Under the bancor plan, each participating member would look on its quota in the union as a reserve of international currency similar to the gold reserves that it held under the gold standard.[12] An increase in a country's credit balance would be comparable to an increase in gold reserves, and an increase in a country's debit balance would be comparable to a loss of gold.

However, unlike the importation of gold, an improvement in a country's credit balance would not involve a withdrawal of purchasing power from circulation.[13] For those credits would be available for extending loans to those countries that needed them. This is comparable to what happens in the banking system. An individual who deposits part of his or her income in a commercial bank does not cause any inconvenience to others, because the funds are available to them for borrowing. By contrast, under the gold standard, the precious metal could be added to a country's physical reserves and withdrawn from circulation.

Despite the ease with which nations could add to their debit and credit balances, the Clearing Union recognized that they could not grow without limit; some constraints would have to be imposed on them. Consider the case of a debtor nation that has exhausted its quota. As much as Keynes was opposed to interfering with a nation's discretion in economic matters, some restraint had to be placed on those nations attempting to live beyond their means. How, then, would the union deal not only with chronic debtors, but with creditor nations as well?

In the case of a debtor country, the union would allow it to increase its debit balance by an amount equal to one-quarter of its quota without any penalty. However, any amount in excess of that limit would be subject to a penalty of 1 to 2 percent. Under no circumstance could a debtor nation run its debit balance to an amount in excess of its quota.[14] Other measures for dealing with a country's chronic deficits included the devaluation of its currency, the imposition of controls on the outward movement of capital, and the surrender of some proportion of its gold and liquid reserves, and the introduction of any internal measures deemed appropriate for the restoration of equilibrium.[15]

Keynes did not place all the responsibility for the world's trading difficulties on the improvidence of debtor countries. Creditor nations were also part of the problem. By withdrawing international money from circulation and hoarding it, instead of returning it to the international spending stream through the purchase of goods for home consumption, those creditor nations exerted a strong deflationary pressure on all other countries.[16]

It is only in recent times, Keynes noted, that we have come to realize more fully that employment and income can be maintained only through the expenditure of income previously earned on goods and services.[17] The inference to be drawn from this observation, quite clearly, is that the world had come to heed the message of the *General Theory*. Its lesson was just as cogent for an open as well as for a closed economy.

But how can countries with large credit balances be encouraged to disgorge them? This is not an easy task, because creditor countries are less likely to accede to outside interference than are debtor countries. Also, it should be noted that, unlike debit balances, there are no limitations on the size of credit balances. They can be constrained only to the extent that debit balances can be lowered. But a more direct means for reducing those credit balances is required.[18] One approach would be to impose penalties on large excessive balances.[19] For example, the union provided that a nation with a credit balance in excess of one-quarter of its assigned quota would be subject to a penalty of 1 percent on that amount plus another 1 percent on that part of its credit balance in excess of one-half of its quota.

In addition to the levying of penalties on their excessive credit balances, members would be obliged to discuss with the governing board appropriate measures to restore equilibrium to their trade accounts. They would include the possibility of domestic credit expansion; exchange appreciation; the reduction of trade barriers; and the extension of international development loans. In the end, though, the creditor country reserved the right to accept or reject those recommendations.

The imposition of some responsibility on creditor nations to assist debtor members to restore their external equilibrium was consistent with Keynes's abhorrence of deflation and his advocacy, instead, of expansionary policies from the time of his recommendations in the *Manchester Guardian Commercial Supplements* after World War I to his urging a worldwide expansion program in his *The Means to Prosperity*. To balance their accounts, debtor nations would have to increase their exports, reduce their imports, or engage in a combination of the two. Given his dislike for deflation, Keynes would have preferred an expansion of exports. But in order to achieve that end, creditor nations would have had to be willing to expand their purchases of goods and services from those members with deficit balances.

Keynes was convinced that it would be far more harmful for debtor nations to pursue deflationary policies in order to restore balance in their trade accounts than it would be for creditor countries to increase their purchases of goods from them. [20]

One of the more surprising features of Keynes's Clearing Union Proposal was its connection to gold. Certainly, it did not appear to be consistent with his past views on the yellow metal. Why, then, this seeming rehabilitation of the precious metal? First, gold still possessed a strong psychological value. [21] Given the popularity of gold, Keynes realized that no international currency would be acceptable unless it made some provision for gold. [22]

Although Keynes did make some allowance for gold, the metal would not perform the function that it did under the traditional international gold standard. Admittedly, gold might be exchanged for bancor, but there was no provision in the plan for the free convertibility of bancor into gold. If that were the case, gold reserves would have had to be maintained against bancor balances and the Clearing Union would then be the same as the international gold standard. Quite simply, gold was employed in the plan only as a measure for defining the value of the bancor; it was not intended to perform the same function that it did under the traditional gold standard.

Inasmuch as the Clearing Union was concerned with current trade transactions, it did not deal with capital movements. Nevertheless, Keynes believed that each nation should, according to its needs, establish some form of capital control authority to oversee the inward and outward movements of capital. Its main responsibilities would be to distinguish legitimate long term loans of creditor nations from those of debtor nations, which serve to create international disequilibrium and to control all types of short term speculative movements. But the method and degree of control over capital movements should be left to the discretion of each member country and not to the union.[23]

The International Monetary Fund

Although Keynes's Clearing Union Proposal for a multilateral international trading system had considerable merit, it was turned down at the Bretton Woods deliberations in favor of the one presented by the U.S. Treasury expert Harry Dexter White. Keynes's proposal was largely rejected for two reasons: First, it was believed by the Americans that under the bancor plan the liability of the United States might become grossly excessive. Second, the notion of an international institution creating international credit and lending it on overdraft to the Central Banks of those countries with trade deficits was too novel a concept for most of the conferees.[24]

The basic difference between the two proposals rested on their treatment of reserves.[25] The Keynes plan suggested that each country's monetary reserves be supplemented by drawing rights in the form of bancor, an international currency, from the Clearing Union. The White plan recommended that an international Fund be established to which each member would contribute a quota of its own currency plus gold. These quotas would be paid in advance.[26]

Each country's quota would be determined by an index representing its gold stocks, level of national income, and fluctuations in its balance of trade. On the basis of these calculations, the total value of all quotas contributed to the Fund would amount to $8.8 billion. Of this amount, $2.75 billion would be contributed by the United States and $1.35 billion by the United Kingdom.[27]

Whereas the total value of quotas was fixed under the IMF plan, the Clearing Union could create its own reserves through the expansion of debit and credit balances. Because the Clearing Union did not have to depend on any prior contribution from its members, but could, instead, create its own international bank money, it was potentially more expansive than the IMF. For this reason, as noted earlier, the Americans feared that the Keynes plan provided a greater threat to inflation.

Should a "credit balance" country accumulate claims on other members of the system, they would be exercised against monetary assets actually on deposit in the Fund.[28] Countries with a debit balance would draw on their reserve of foreign currencies, exchanging their money for whatever foreign exchange they might need.[29] This acquisition of another country's currency would be through an out and out purchase. It would not be through a loan, because the Fund was not intended to be a lending institution as the Clearing Union would have been. Therefore, instead of redeeming a loan of foreign currency, the deficit country would simply repurchase its own currency with other national currencies or gold whenever it was able to do so.[30]

Under the White plan, a country could not purchase other countries' currencies without limit. First of all, a member might not be able to buy a national currency declared to be in short supply by the Fund.[31] In general, the Fund's holding of a deficit country's currency could not exceed 75 percent of that country's quota. Under no circumstance could the Fund's supply of a given country's paper currency exceed 200 percent of its quota.[32]

In addition, the Fund tried to discourage deficit countries from availing themselves too freely of its facilities by imposing penalty charges on the amount of their excess purchases of other countries' currencies. The interest service charge on those excess amounts was 0.5 percent during the first year and increased by an additional 0.5 percent for each subsequent year. Whenever the Fund's supply of a member's currency reached a point where the service charge reached 4 percent, the member and the Fund would have to consider measures for decreasing that excess supply. Fundamentally, the deficit country would either have to increase exports or reduce imports through such measures as price and cost reductions, depreciation of the currency, subsidies to exports, and exchange control.[33]

The Fund's preferred measure was exchange depreciation,[34] as spelled out in article IV, section 6 of the IMF proposal.[35] Under the terms of this latter clause, a deficit country could propose a change in the par value of its currency if that change was expected to correct a fundamental disequilibrium. If the proposed change, together with all prior changes, did not exceed 10 percent of the original par value, a member could make the change without objection. Changes in excess of 10 percent would still be allowed if the Fund was convinced that it was needed to correct a fundamental disequilibrium.

Like the Clearing Union, the International Monetary Fund proposal also dealt with countries that ran up surpluses in their trade accounts. A member would become a surplus country when the Fund's holding of its currency fell below the amount that was originally contributed to it.[36] This surplus position would become critical when "the demand for a member's currency seriously threatens the Fund's ability to supply that currency."[37]

To replenish the Fund's supply of a "scarce" currency, the authorities could ask the country with a surplus to exchange its currency for gold or, too, ask for a loan on mutually agreeable terms. Should the Fund fail to increase its supply of a particular currency, it could then declare that currency "scarce" and thereupon apportion its existing supply according to the relative needs of its members, general economic conditions, and any other special considerations.[38]

In addition, the Fund might authorize its members to limit the freedom of exchange in the "scarce" currency. The type of exchange control to be used would be left to each member's discretion. The arrangement would not be permanent nor would it be more restrictive than necessary to balance the demand and supply of the "scarce" currency.

The designation of a country's currency as "scarce" and subject to exchange control would have serious implications for a surplus country. For that would mean that its goods would be subject to discrimination in foreign markets. The only way to avoid that disadvantage would be for the surplus country to make more of its currency available to other countries by buying more from them. That would not only ease the pressure on it, but also help deficit countries to deal with their balance of payment problems. In effect, the use of the "scarce" currency clause would not only help debtor countries, but also place some urgency on surplus countries to help maintain general international equilibrium.[39]

The foregoing account provides some of the major differences between the Clearing Union and the IMF proposals. But despite these and other differences, the plans had the same objective. For its part, the Clearing Union was designed to promote a multilateral clearing system devoid of exchange restrictions, whereas the IMF hoped to promote "orderly exchange arrangements" and "to assist in the establishment of a multilateral system of payments in respect of current transactions between members and in the elimination of foreign exchange restrictions which hamper the growth of world trade."[40]

Given this brief account of the essential features of the two currency proposals, our task in the next section is to determine in what way, if any, Keynes's endorsement of both plans altered his thinking on the issue of free versus restricted trade. Did it cause him to lean more toward the one or the other or, too, did it cause him to move toward a third course?

A COMPARISON OF KEYNES'S FOREIGN TRADE VIEWS WITH THE PROVISIONS OF THE CURRENCY PROPOSALS

On the basis of the foregoing account, albeit brief, of the main provisions of the Clearing Union and International Monetary Fund proposals, one is prompted to ask: "How did Keynes's endorsement of those plans square with his own pre-war position on foreign trade?" Did he move closer to orthodox free trade or did he remain committed to more restrictive trade, which included such measures as flexible exchange rates, control over capital flows, avoidance of deflation, freedom from external fluctuations, the right to exercise control over the balance of trade and the flow of imports and exports, and freedom from a rigid international monetary standard such as gold?

Inasmuch as Keynes was the chief architect of the Clearing Union Proposal, his endorsement of it is understandable, but how does his subsequent acceptance of the IMF proposal drafted by the Americans square with his pre-war position on foreign trade? Did he move closer to orthodox free trade or did he remain committed to more restrictive trade including such measures as flexible exchange rates, freedom to set domestic interest rates, control over capital flows, avoidance of deflation, freedom from external fluctuations, the right of a country to exercise control over the balance of trade, and freedom from a rigid international monetary standard such as gold.

Given the constraints he had to face in developing the Clearing Union Proposal and the difficult bargaining position facing the British in negotiating the terms of the International Monetary Fund at Bretton Woods, Keynes, for reasons of political necessity, had to modify his thinking on foreign trade, even though he had doubts about the feasibility of returning to an open non-discriminatory system of free trade.[41] Clearly, under the terms set by the Americans, he had to modify his position on foreign trade, most especially by moving away from bilateral and barter trading arrangements. But in making these and other concessions to the Americans, Keynes did not in the process revert back to orthodox free trade. But neither could he be characterized as a protectionist urging the use of tariffs, quotas, and other crude instruments to regulate the flow of trade. Actually, many of the provisions developed in the Clearing Union Proposal and conditions to which he subscribed in the IMF were consistent with his pre-war views on the need for a more restricted or managed trading system.

Between the *General Theory* and the outbreak of World War II, Keynes had become increasingly insular in his views on foreign trade. First, he moved ever closer to national autarky and made foreign considerations subservient to those of the domestic economy. Having lost confidence in the expansion of international trade, he turned to bilateral and barter arrangements. To preserve national autarky or self-determination, he favored, as previously noted, control over capital movements, avoidance of deflation, an autonomous instead of an internationally determined interest rate better suited to meet the needs of home employment, and opposition to gold standard.

Although the British were obliged by the Americans to move to an expansion of multilateral unrestricted international trade, they were still able to negotiate agreements which reflected much of Keynes's pre-war thinking. Admittedly, Britain and Keynes had to surrender their position on bilateral trade and barter agreements, but much else remained on which they could agree.

One of the most, if not the most, important issue between Keynes and the currency proposals was the question of national autonomy. The fact that the

Keynes of the Clearing Union and Bretton Woods era drew closer to the need for international monetary cooperation should not be interpreted to mean that he was abandoning his support for national self-determination and the priority of domestic over foreign considerations. Although he had to make some concessions to the Americans, his pre-war position on foreign trade remained little changed. This perspective is well supported by Professor Seymour Harris, a distinguished Keynesian scholar, in the following term:

> Above all, he now said and reiterated that Great Britain would not subject its economy to controls from without; that a country pursuing prudent policies at home must not be embarrassed by strains originating abroad; (and) that domestic policies of each country are the primary concern. [42]

In advancing his own Credit Union plan and in later subscribing to the terms of the IMF, Keynes remained committed to the principle that each country should be free to pursue its own domestic agenda without fear of interference from outside forces. For example, one of the reasons he assigned large quotas to each member of the Clearing Union was to provide them a wider degree of maneuverability in managing their foreign trade. The larger the quota, the more extended the period over which it could make the necessary adjustments. [43]

The original provision of the Fund Agreement in article IV, section 5 also upheld this principle of self-determination. In large measure, this provision was made in deference to the British. Keynes firmly believed that in accepting the "manifold and substantial benefits " of the IMF, Great Britain would not have to surrender anything that was vital for managing her own domestic affairs as she deemed fit. [44] According to Professor A. E. Robinson, "Sovereignty was retained in the one matter where it was absolutely necessary— the right to follow an internal economic policy consistent with full employment." [45] If that is the case, then the goal of full employment trumps all other considerations, including matters relating to foreign trade.

One reason, among others, why Keynes was consistent in drafting the Clearing Union Proposal and later subscribing to Harry Dexter White's IMF proposal was that they both allowed for some flexibility in each country's foreign exchange rate.

Under a fixed-rate regime, each country must keep its wages and other costs of production in conformity with those of its trading partners. As a result, that country may not be completely free to pursue monetary and other policies to promote full employment and other domestic objectives. Because of the constraint to march in lockstep with other members of a fixed exchange rate regime, it loses its autonomy and surrenders the means for achieving what is best for the domestic economy.

By contrast, under a flexible exchange rate system, there is no need for a country to relate its costs, prices, and interest rates to those of other countries, as in a fixed exchange rate system. If prices, costs, and interest rates deviate from those of its trading partners, the adjustment will be made in the external value of its currency. In short, the external value of the currency adjusts to the internal value—not the other way around. Thus, a flexible exchange rate system would enable a country to pursue independently whatever domestic and fiscal policies best suit its needs.

Both the Clearing Union and the IMF recognized this advantage. The Clearing Union allowed members, subject to approval by the Governing Board, to alter the value of their exchange rates as required by the state of their foreign trade. This provision in the bancor plan and in the IMF was completely consistent with Keynes's desire for short term stability and long term flexibility—a position he advocated in his *Tract on Monetary Reform* in the aftermath of World War I. [46]

The IMF, too, made ample provision in article IV of the Bretton Woods Agreement for the alteration of a member's exchange rate, so that it may "conform to whatever *de facto* internal value results from domestic policies, which themselves shall be immune from criticism from the Fund." [47] As in the case of the Clearing Union Proposal, members were subject to certain prerequisites, for example, a condition of fundamental disequilibrium, before they could alter the value of their currencies. Therefore, the IMF arrangement was very much consistent with Keynes's long held view that a country's exchange rate should, for purposes of facilitating trade, be stable in the short run, but flexible in the long run. [48]

If nations were to have control over their exchange rates, balance of payments, and interest rates, in keeping with Keynes's pre-war position on foreign trade, they would have to have authority to regulate their capital flows.

Such authority could be justified on a number of grounds. Certainly, such control would help to mitigate speculative capital flows in anticipation of a revaluation of the exchange rate or, too, other hot money flows not in the best interests of the domestic economy. To be effective, changes in exchange rates must be combined with the control of capital movements as suggested by the Bretton Woods Agreement. When those two instruments are so joined, they are hardly less efficient than foreign exchange control and decidedly more effective than quotas or tariffs. [49] Controls over capital flows are also necessary to assure the success of a country's monetary and or fiscal policy. An expansive program in one country could lead to an increase in imports from other countries not offset by a corresponding increase in exports. The purpose of controlling capital transfers in these circumstances would be to limit the spillover effects and to reduce the loss of jobs abroad.

If nations were to have control over their foreign exchange rates, balance of payments, and interest rates, they would necessarily have to have authority to regulate their capital flows. All of these conditions were in keeping with Keynes's pre-war thinking on foreign trade.

Both the Clearing Union and IMF proposals made provision for the control of capital flows and were consistent with Keynes's views on other important matters as well. That Keynes was satisfied with the provisions in the Clearing Union may be taken as a foregone conclusion, but as far as the IMF is concerned, his reactions are as follows:

> Let me take first . . . our power to control the domestic rate of interest so as to secure cheap money. Not merely as a feature of the transition, but as a permanent arrangement, the plan accords to every member government the explicit right to control all capital movements. What used to be heresy is now endorsed as orthodox It follows that our right to control the domestic market is secured on firmer foundations than before, and is formally accepted as a proper part of a good inter-national arrangement. [50]

A principle long sought by Keynes during the inter-war period was the right of each country to manage the domestic rate of interest for its own best economic interests. Writing in 1935, just prior to the publication of his *General Theory*, he stated, "It is essential that they (the interest rate and the volume of credit) should be employed in future with exclusive regard to internal conditions and, in particular, the state of employment."[51] He reaffirmed his position during the Bretton Woods period when, in an address to the House of Lords in May 1944, he stated that "we intend to retain control of our domestic rate of interest, so that we can keep it as low as suits our own purposes, without interference from the ebb and flow of international capital movements or flights of hot money."[52]

The Clearing Union and the IMF proposals both acknowledged the right of their member states to determine independently their own domestic interest rates. Both plans accorded them the prerogative to control international capital movements. The Clearing Union advocated setting up control machinery to distinguish between "long term loans of creditor countries, which help to maintain equilibrium and of controlling short term speculative movements or flights of capital."[53] Similar provision was made by the IMF under article VI, section 3 of the Fund Agreement, which stated that "members may exercise such controls as are necessary to regulate international capital movements."[54]

Inflation and deflation both have serious consequences, but of the two Keynes thought that deflation was the worse of the two evils. He was of this persuasion from the very outset of his career, as may be confirmed in a series of articles he prepared for the *Manchester Guardian Commercial Supplements* shortly after the end of World War I. Deflation feeds on itself, for if a firm anticipates a further lowering of prices, it may well conclude that future prices will be lower than current costs. As a result, it will either cut back production or not produce at all.

Inasmuch as both plans were desirous of expanding the volume of multilateral international trade, deflation, clearly, was not an acceptable option. Nevertheless, both plans recognized that nations experiencing balance of trade problems might well be disposed to pursuing deflationary policies by restricting imports and trying to stimulate exports by reducing costs and prices. If successful, this approach would shift some of the burden to creditor nations for helping to solve the balance of payments problems facing debtor nations. But how could creditor nations be induced to cooperate with debtor nations in reducing their deficits?

Both plans would try to enlist the involvement of creditor nations through the imposition of sanctions on them. The bancor plan would try to stimulate expansion in the creditor nations by exacting a penalty on their excess balances at the union. In addition, nations with excess balances at the union were encouraged to reduce the volume of those balances through an appreciation of their foreign exchange rates and a liberalization of their trade practices.[55] The IMF would also try to reduce the need for deflation among debtor nations by pressuring creditor nations to pursue expansionary policies. That it hoped to achieve through its exercise of the "scarce currency clause" to which reference was made earlier. If the Fund were to find it difficult to supply the currency of a particular country, it could declare it "scarce" and then ration whatever supply it had available. Once that declaration was made, member states could be authorized by the Fund "temporarily to impose limitations on the freedom of exchange operations in the 'scarce' currency."[56] The imposition of such exchange controls would permit all members to discriminate against the goods of the creditor county whose currency was deemed to be "scarce."

Keynes was quite positive on the "scarce" currency clause, for it "puts the creditor country on the spot so acutely that in the view of us all the creditor country cannot simply afford to let such a situation arise."[57] The placing of more responsibility on creditor countries, Keynes noted, would help to eliminate one of the main causes of the type of deflation that occurred in the interwar period, namely, "the draining of reserves out of the rest of the world to pay a country which was obstinately lending and exporting on a scale immensely greater than it was lending and importing."[58]

That Keynes, the Clearing Union, and the IMF proposals found common ground on the issue of deflation is not surprising. Such a condition, from Keynes's point of view, was inconsistent with high and stable levels of employment. From the proposals' perspective, countries should not try to balance their foreign accounts by pursuing deflationary policies, because that would be at odds with their objective of promoting the expansion of multilateral international trade.

It has been noted that Keynes moved closer to international cooperation and endorsement of the currency proposals, because it might now be possible in the early 1940s to apply Keynesian economics on an international as well as on a national scale.[59] This view by Professor Harrod seems to have been confirmed by Keynes's own belief that only in recent times was it realized more fully that employment and income can only be maintained through the expenditure of income previously earned on goods and services produced in the process.[60] This, of course, is just as true in the foreign as in the domestic sector of the economy.

To the extent that the proposals in the Clearing Union and IMF could insure a larger and more balanced volume of trade, they could, Keynes believed, promote higher and more stable levels of employment. The increased volume of trade would, *sui generis*, add to aggregate demand, while more balanced trade would reduce the level of foreign disinvestment and add further to a country's overall demand.

Therefore, to the extent that greater international cooperation could lead to an expansion of demand, this outcome would be consistent not only with the requirements of the *General Theory*, but also with Keynes's long held conviction that the way to solve the world's economic problems was through a well-coordinated expansionary program along the lines recommended at the World Economic Conference and in his *Means to Prosperity* in 1933. Whether the question was deflation or expansion, there was no issue between Keynes and the currency proposals, because the latter were simply catching up to his own long held position on these issues.

Keynes's views on the role of gold in the currency proposals were somewhat less consistent with his pre-war position. The reasons for this modification were more political than economic. Notwithstanding his own misgivings, he realized that gold still had a psychological value and it would be futile to expect countries with large holdings of the metal, for example, the United States and Great Britain, to demonetize their gold stocks.[61]

In acceding to the gold provisions in the Clearing Union and IMF plans, Keynes was not espousing a return to the traditional gold standard. For in the Clearing Union proposal, gold would be used only to define the value of the bancor. Gold would not flow freely from hand to hand, but enjoy only a "one-way convertibility." Nations could exchange gold for bancor, but not the other way around. The IMF also used gold for defining the value of national currencies as a means for settling international accounts. Unlike the orthodox gold standard, however, it did not tie a nation's currency rigidly to a given amount of gold and, therefore, to a fixed exchange rate system.

Despite these concessions, Keynes did not believe that either plan mandated a return to the traditional gold standard. The essence of the gold standard rests in something altogether different, he insisted, as noted in the following:

> If I have any authority to pronounce on what is and what is not the essence of and meaning of a gold standard, I should say that this plan (the IMF) is the exact opposite of it . . . . The gold standard, as I understand it, means a system under which the external value of a national currency is rigidly fixed to a fixed quantity of gold which can only honorably be broken under *force majeure* and it involves a financial policy which compels the internal value of the domestic currency to conform to this external value as fixed in terms gold. On the other hand, the use of gold merely as a convenient common denominator by means of which the relative values of national currencies—these being free to change—are expressed from time to time, is obviously quite another matter.[62]

On the basis of Keynes's definition of the gold standard, neither plan would so qualify. Indeed, both of them would accord with Keynes's view that a nation's exchange rate should be flexible and not fixed, as would be the case under the gold standard. A nation's currency should conform to its internal value—not the other way around. On this essential point, there was no difference between Keynes and the two plans.

SUMMARY

A review of Keynes's proposal for the Clearing Union and his subsequent endorsement of the IMF plan reveal that, although he had to make certain concessions for political reasons, there is little to suggest that his pre-war position on foreign trade underwent any radical transformation. Keynes was well aware of the need for Britain to retain in the post-war period a system of international trade that it had developed prior to the war—a system of tight controls, blocked accounts, and bilateral bargains.[63] But however expedient an extension of that arrangement may have been for Britain in the post-war world, it was precluded by the Mutual Aid Agreement,[64] which mandated more open and less discriminatory trade. That was the political reality. Constrained by the terms of the Lend-Lease Agreement, Keynes did his best to meet the American demands, while at the same time retaining as much of the pre-war system that had evolved in Great Britain prior to the war.

Given the political realities of the time, Keynes had to distance himself from some of the more restrictive practices he had favored. Nevertheless, much of the theoretical foundation he had developed between the end of World War I and the start of World War II was reflected in both currency proposals.

On key issues, Keynes was able to find common ground with both proposals. These issues included flexible exchange rates, the determination of domestic interest rates, the control of capital movements, the avoidance of deflation, the promotion of expansive policies, rejection of the orthodox gold standard, and the priority of internal over external needs.

On the issue of exchange rates, Keynes and both currency proposals agreed that they should be flexible and not rigidly set for all time. This did not mean that rates should fluctuate from minute to minute or even from day to day. There was something to be gained from this arrangement. For the stability of rates over the short run provides certainty and is helpful for the flow of commerce. On the other hand, the flexibility of rates over the longer period is better suited for addressing domestic structural issues and longer-term balance of payment problems.

Very importantly, both plans respected a nation's right to set its own interest rate. This was especially important for Keynes, because the interest rate determined the level of investment and should be set, therefore, at whatever rate would guarantee full employment.

The control of a nation's capital flow had special significance for both Keynes and the currency proposals. For those movements could affect a country's exchange rate and, of course, the balance of payments. These flows also play a significant role in the determination of domestic and foreign investment. Because of its pivotal role in all these areas, both proposals, which were consistent with Keynes's views, authorized member states in their respective plans to set up their own mechanisms to control capital flows, especially those of a speculative or hot money character.

Inasmuch as the objective of the currency plans was the expansion of a non-discriminatory multilateral trading system, they both called for expansive monetary policies in all member states. Clearly, there could be no difference between Keynes and the two plans on this issue, because for Keynes full employment could be achieved and maintained only through an increase in demand, as called for in the *General Theory*.

That both Keynes and the currency proposals should agree on the need to avoid deflation is self-evident. For the currency proposals, deflation would run counter to the objective of increasing the volume of trade. For Keynes, deflation would lead to reduced output, employment, and income—the very issues he was trying to resolve in the *General Theory* and other publications prior to World War II.

On the issue of national autonomy, the question was, "Should each nation pursue its own best domestic interests or should those concerns be determined by balance of payments, interest rates, capital flows, and other external forces?" Keynes's position was unequivocal. The first priority should be the realization of high and stable levels of employment. Unless this condition is satisfied, the advantages of foreign trade cannot be realized. Both proposals, though they sought to promote greater economic cooperation, recognized the principle of self-determination and the priority of domestic over external considerations. This they did by incorporating into their respective

structures various mechanisms, for example, flexible exchange rates, autonomously determined interest rates for attaining full employment, and balance
in their foreign accounts without fear of external interference.

A reading of the currency proposals reveals that while their purpose was
to expand non-discriminatory multilateral trade, this did not imply a return to
the principles of orthodox free trade. The Bretton Woods Agreement explicitly recognized that the new rules, while trying to minimize their adverse
effects on international trade, would leave governments free to follow autonomous economic policies.[65] From Keynes's perspective, "they lay down by
international agreement the essence of the new doctrine, far removed from
the old orthodoxy."[66] The inference to be drawn is quite clear—domestic
concerns take precedence over external ones even if that means a break with
the tenets of classical free trade.

From his perspective, Keynes thought that the deliberations at Bretton
Woods were consistent with his thinking on a number of trade principles,
including flexible exchange rates, an autonomous interest rate policy, freedom from foreign induced deflation, rejection of the orthodox gold standard,
and the need to deal with unemployment. In an address to the House of
Lords, here is what he had to say:

> Have those responsible for the monetary proposals been sufficiently careful to
> preserve those principles from the possibility of interference? I hope your
> lordships will trust me not to have turned by back on all that I have fought for.
> To establish those three principles which I have just stated has been my main
> task for the last twenty years. . . . I have spent my strength to persuade my
> countrymen and the world at large to change their traditional doctrines and, by
> taking better thought to remove the curse of unemployment. Was it not I . . .
> who wrote that 'Gold is a barbarous rule'? Am I so faithless, so forgetful, so
> senile that, just at the very moment of the triumph of these ideas . . . I go off to
> help forge new chains to hold us fast in the old dungeon? I trust, my Lords,
> that you will not believe it.[67]

In light of the foregoing comparison of Keynes's views on foreign trade
vis-à-vis the trade provisions set forth in the two currency proposals, there is
no evidence to suggest that the Keynes of the war and post–World War II
years reverted back to free trade. Although he had to distance himself, because of American pressure, from the trading model Britain had employed
during the war, he did remain true to many of the principles to which he had
subscribed earlier in his career, as noted in the above quotation. While it is
true that he did on a number of occasions acknowledge the advantages of free
trade, those concessions were never absolute. Those benefits were always
qualified. The classical medicine could not work by itself and had to be
supplemented by the kinds of reform he had advocated over the years. Very
importantly, free trade could not come into its own without first satisfying

the prerequisite of full employment, and the other conditions that were specified in his model of planned or managed trade. At the end of Bretton Woods, Keynes could be described as neither a free trader nor an out and out protectionist; it all depended on the state of a country's level of employment and its state of well-being.

NOTES

1. R. F. Harrod, *The Life of John Maynard Keynes* (London: Macmillan, 1951), 525.

2. Article VII of the Mutual Aid Agreement, February 2, 1942, in *The New Economics*, ed. S. Harris (New York: Alfred A. Knopf, 1947), 259.

3. J. M. Keynes, "Proposals for an International Clearing Union," in *The New Economics*, ed. S. Harris (New York: A. A. Knopf, 1947), 343–58.

4. J. M. Keynes, "The International Clearing Union," speech delivered to the House of Lords, London, May 13, 1943, in *The New Economics*, ed. S. Harris (New York: Alfred A. Knopf, 1947), 359–68.

5. R. G. Hawtrey, *Bretton Woods for Better or Worse* (London: Longmans, Green, 1945), 26.

6. D. H. Robertson, "The Postwar Monetary Plans," *The Economic Journal* 53 (December 1943): 353.

7. A. W. Crawford, *World Currency Stabilization Proposals* (Washington, D.C.: Finance Dept., Chamber of Commerce of the U.S., 1944), 10.

8. Keynes, "Proposals for an International Clearing Union," 327.

9. Crawford, *World Currency Stabilization Proposals*, 8.

10. R. G. Hawtrey, *The Balance of Payments and the Standard of Living* (London: Oxford University Press, 1950), 91.

11. Keynes, "Proposals for an International Clearing Union," 360.

12. F. A. Lutz, "International Monetary Mechanism—the Keynes and White Proposals," *Essays in International Finance* no. 1 (Princeton: International Finance Section, Princeton University, July 1943), 4.

13. Lutz, "International Monetary Mechanism," 7.

14. Keynes, *Proposals for an International Clearing Union*, 331.

15. Keynes, *Proposals for an International Clearing Union*, 330.

16. J. Robinson, "The International Currency Proposals," in *The New Economics*, ed. S. Harris (New York: A. A. Knopf, 1947), 352.

17. Keynes, "The International Clearing Union," 362.

18. J Robinson, "The International Currency Proposals," 344.

19. This provision had shades of present-day Major League Baseball's rule whereby financially successful teams with payrolls above a certain limit are obliged to pay a salary cap tax. Interestingly, too, Professor F. A. Lutz suggested that this proposal to tax the excess balances of creditor nations was an attempt to implement the suggestion of Silvio Gesell, who was cited in the *General Theory*, to tax balances in the field of international finance.

20. A. Smithies, "Reflections on the Work and Influence of John M. Keynes," *The Quarterly Journal of Economics* 65 (1951): 592.

21. Both the United States and Great Britain were opposed to the demonetizing of their gold stocks; see J. H. Willians, "International Monetary Plans," *Foreign Affairs* 23 (October 1944): 43.

22. Lutz, "International Monetary Mechanism," 8.

23. Keynes, *Proposals for an International Clearing Union*, 336.

24. See J. H. Williams, "International Monetary Plans," *Foreign Affairs* 23 (1944): 43; also see, "The Joint Currency Schemes," the *London Economist* 146, no. 5253 (April 29, 1844): 560–61.

25. For a point-by-point comparison of the Keynes and White proposals, see J. Robinson, "The International Currency Proposals," 342–58.

26. Hawtrey, *Bretton Woods for Better or Worse*, 3.

27. Robinson, "The International Currency Proposals," 345.

28. A. Hansen, "International Monetary and Financial Problems," New York Council on Foreign Relations, 1944, 14.

29. Hawtrey, *Bretton Woods for Better or Worse*, 34.

30. A. G. Hart, *Money, Debt and Economic Activity* (New York: Prentice Hall, 1948), 405.

31. U.S. Department of State, *Articles of Agreement of the International Monetary Fund* (Washington D. C.: U.S. Government Printing Office, 1945), 6.

32. U.S. Department of State, *Articles of Agreement of the International Monetary Fund*, 7–8.

33. Halm, *Monetary Theory* (Philadelphia: Blakiston, 1946), 27.

34. Halm, *Monetary Theory*, 277.

35. U.S. State Department, *Articles of Agreement of the International Monetary Fund*, 4–5.

36. Halm, *Monetary Theory*, 277.

37. U.S. State Department, *Articles of Agreement of the International Monetary Fund*, 11.

38. U.S. State Department, *Articles of Agreement of the International Monetary Fund*, 11.

39. A. Robinson, "John M. Keynes," *The Economic Journal* 57 (1947): 1–68.

40. U.S. Department of State, *Articles of Agreement of the International Monetary Fund*, 1.

41. Harrod, *The Life of John Maynard Keynes*, 531.

42. S. Harris, "International Economics: Introduction," in *The New Economics*, ed. S. Harris (New York: A. A. Knopf, 1947): 259.

43. Hahn, *Monetary Theory*, 270.

44. Keynes, "The International Monetary Fund," 374.

45. Robinson, "John M. Keynes," 55.

46. Robinson, "John M. Keynes," 54, and A. Smithies, "Reflections on the Work and Influence of John M. Keynes," 592.

47. Keynes, "The International Monetary Fund," 376.

48. According to Professor Gottfried Haberler, a completely flexible exchange rate system does not automatically restore equilibrium. For example, when a country pursues an expansive policy, imports will decrease because of their higher relative prices and exports will increase so that the two will come into balance. But this is a simplification of the problem, because it fails to consider such factors as demand, supply, and income elasticity. The expectation of depreciated currency also fails to consider the possibility that speculative capital movements could be induced with every expected change in the exchange rate, thereby introducing another element of instability into the balance of payments. See G. Haberler, "Some Factors Affecting the Future of International Trade and International Economic Policy," in *Economic Reconstruction*, ed. S. Harris (New York: McGraw Hill, 1945), 331–33. Also see A. Lerner, "Economic Liberalism in the Postwar World," in *Postwar Economic Problems*, ed. S. Harris (New York: McGraw Hill, 1943), 133–34.

49. N. S. Buchanan and F. A. Lutz, *Rebuilding the World Economy* (New York: The Twentieth Century Fund, 1947), 241.

50. Keynes, "The International Monetary Fund," 375.

51. "The Future of the Foreign Exchanges," *Lloyd's Bank Monthly*, October 1935, 53.

52. Keynes, "The International Monetary Fund," 374.

53. British Treasury, *Proposals for an International Clearing Union*, reprinted in *The New Economics*, ed. S. Harris (New York: A. A. Knopf, 1947), 337.

54. U.S. Department of State, *Articles of Agreement of the International Monetary Fund*, 10.

55. T. Balogh, "The International Aspects of Full Employment," in *The Economics of Full Employment—Six Studies in Applied Economics* (Oxford: Basil Blackwell, 1945), 165.

56. U.S. Department of State, *Articles of Agreement of the International Monetary Fund*, 11.

57. Harrod, *The Life of John Maynard Keynes*, 571.

58. Keynes, "The International Monetary Fund," 373.

59. Harrod, *The Life of John Maynard Keynes*, 525–26.

60. "Proposals for an International Monetary Union," 362.

61. J. H. Williams, "International Monetary Plans," *Foreign Affairs* 23 (1944): 43.

62. Keynes, "The International Monetary Fund," 375–76.

63. Harrod, *The Life of John Maynard Keynes*, 525.

64. In accepting Lend-Lease Assistance from the United States under the terms of the Mutual Aid Agreement (February 2, 1942), Britain agreed to "the elimination of all forms of discriminatory treatment in international commerce and the reduction of tariffs and other barriers."

65. Buchanan and Lutz, *Rebuilding the World Economy*, 280.

66. Keynes, "The International Monetary Fund," 376.

67. Keynes, "The International Monetary Fund," 374–75.

Chapter Eleven

Keynes and the Anglo-American Loan

During World War II, Keynes served as a financial advisor to Great Britain's Treasury. Throughout most of that time, he was largely preoccupied with the country's post-war problems. Therefore, when American Lend-Lease Assistance was abruptly terminated after Victory over Japan in August 1945, there were few people better able to deal with the crisis than John Maynard Keynes.

Inspired by his previous success in dealing with the Americans at Bretton Woods, Keynes thought that a free gift of £1,550,000 or, too an interest-free loan from the Americans was entirely possible. However, he warned the Labour Cabinet that was now in office that whatever aid the Americans were prepared to grant would come with "strings attached." [1]

Accordingly, Keynes was sent to Washington as the head of a delegation to determine what credit arrangement could be worked out to deal with the emergency. Negotiations opened on September 11, 1945, and were concluded in early December of that same year. The Agreement [2] was approved by Parliament in that same month, but Congress did not ratify it until July 1946.

The principal feature of the Agreement was, of course, the American loan, which amounted to a line of credit of $3.75 billion to be drawn on between July, 1946 and the end of 1951. The loan was to be repaid in fifty annual installments and carried an interest rate of 2 percent. [3]

In consideration of this loan, Great Britain, as Keynes had predicted, would have to subscribe to a number of conditions. From the U.S. standpoint, the loan was designed to accomplish more than to assist Great Britain to convert to a peacetime economy. One of the many objectives sought by the Americans in making this assistance available was the early establishment of a multilateral system of trade and exchange. But before such a system could be established, the British would have to satisfy a number of conditions.

The first of these was the dissolution of the Sterling Area "dollar pool," which had been set up during the war. Under its terms, all dollar and gold earnings realized by the members of the group—which consisted of Egypt, the Anglo-Egyptian Sudan, Iraq, Iceland, and the Faroe Islands—were pooled and allocated according to their needs for prosecuting the war. [4]

Exchange transactions among members of the group were subject to little restriction; however, transactions with countries outside the area were rigidly regulated to conserve dollar and gold earnings. Such an arrangement was justified during the war, but to extend it into peacetime would run counter to the worldwide multilateral trading system the Americans were trying to develop. Before such a system could be established, therefore, all dollar and sterling receipts realized by the Sterling Area countries from their current transactions would have to be freely converted into any other currency. Britain was obliged to complete arrangements for this convertibility within one year following the completion of the Agreement.

Although Keynes preferred to postpone the date, he conceded that convertibility was in Britain's best interests in the long run. If London was to retain her position in the international banking community, it was essential that sterling be made convertible. [5] He also recognized that Britain, with her dependence on investment income and sensitivity to international capital movements, could not prosper in the post-war world without acceding to this change.

Another very important condition imposed by the loan agreement was that Britain would have to terminate exchange controls on all current transactions with the United States after July 1946 and with all other countries by July 1947. Thereafter, she would reintroduce foreign exchange controls on dollar payments only during such times as the dollar was declared to be "scarce" by the IMF. Even with this latter provision, the British made a very large concession to the Americans. However, the British did not have to surrender as much as it first appeared. For this was largely counterbalanced by the provision contained in the Agreement on import restrictions. To insure that the British would not squander the loan "in an orgy of reckless importing," article II of the Agreement [6] provided that the United Kingdom could retain its system of import licensing. [7]

In effect, this meant that instead of controlling the exchange dealings themselves, the British could achieve the same results of foreign exchange control without having to resort to it. [8] Thus, although the British did have to forego the use of foreign exchange restrictions, their loss of authority over the balance of payments was not as great as it might first appear. For the concession still left Keynes and the British outside the realm of orthodox free trade.

A number of additional stipulations set forth in the Financial Agreement bear noting. First, a number of procedures were outlined for the settlement of sterling balances accumulated by the sterling area and other countries up to the time of the understanding.[9] Secondly, it directed that the United Kingdom should not use any part of the proceeds forthcoming from the loan to repay its short term debts to other countries. And lastly, it ordered that any sterling balances released or otherwise available for current payment should, within one year after the effective date of the agreement, "be freely available for current transactions in any currency area without discrimination."[10]

In addition to their acceptance of the Financial Agreement, whose terms have been briefly cited, the British were obliged to satisfy a number of other prerequisites before being granted the loan. In matters of international exchange and investment, the United Kingdom was required to subscribe to both the IMF and the International Bank for Reconstruction and Development. In the sphere of commercial policy, it was asked to accept the principles of the proposed International Trade Organization.

Although the Anglo-American Loan was the main agendum, the Washington meeting also took up the matter of commercial policy. Keynes was not directly involved in those negotiations. Instead, Britain was represented by Sir Percivale Liesching and Professor Lionel Robbins. The results of those discussions were reported in the *Proposals for Consideration by an International Conference on Trade and Employment* and released at the same time as the Financial Agreement in December 1945

One of the major recommendations made by the proposals was the International Trade Organization. As an additional condition for receiving the American Loan, Britain was obliged to accept the principles set forth in that proposed organization.

On the basis of this brief summary of the Anglo-American Loan, one may ask: "How pleased were the British and Keynes with the outcome of their Washington meeting?" Realistically, it is difficult to assess what their true feelings were because they were not on an equal footing with the Americans. They were not playing on a level field. The Americans were intent on using the Loan Agreement as a wedge for creating a non-discriminatory multilateral trading system. The British, on the other hand, came to Washington in desperate need of financial assistance. They had to make concessions they otherwise would not have made. Nevertheless, by article VII of the Mutual Aid Agreement they had already agreed to eliminate all forms of trade discrimination and to reduce tariffs and other barriers to trade.[11]

Compared with the Bretton Woods Plan there is no question that the financial clauses of the loan accelerated Great Britain's movement toward a multilateral trade system.[12] It would be foolhardy to argue that the British, in accepting the terms of the *Financial Agreement between the Government of the United States and the United Kingdom* and subscribing to the *Proposals*

for Consideration by an International Conference on Trade and Employment
were still able to maintain their autonomy.

Despite Britain's weak bargaining position, the Washington Agreements, especially the one relating to the loan, did reserve some degree of autonomy for the country. For example, although it is true that Britain relinquished an important instrument over her balance of payments when she consented to the removal of exchange controls by 1947, she did not lose complete control over her external economic affairs. This, of course, satisfied one of Keynes's longstanding concerns, namely, that foreign trade considerations should not take precedence over domestic needs.

As noted earlier, Britain was still permitted to retain quantitative import restrictions as a means of safeguarding equilibrium in her international accounts. Moreover, she could still avail herself of a number of instruments provided by the IMF, including the variation of exchange rates and the employment of discriminatory measures against countries whose currencies were declared to be "scarce" by the IMF for maintaining control over her balance of payments. Therefore, although the British did make certain concessions to the Americans, the Financial Agreement was not totally inconsistent with Keynes's views on foreign trade policy.

The British acceptance of the ITO as one of the conditions of the loan is another matter. One of the objectives of that organization, in keeping with the terms of the Atlantic Charter and section VII of the Mutual Trade Agreement,[13] called for a substantial reduction of tariffs and the elimination of tariff preferences. Although Keynes endorsed this and other commercial policy measures, he did not believe that they would interfere with Britain's domestic objectives[14] nor with her authority to control her foreign commerce.[15] Because of the significance of this contention, it is best to have Keynes explain his position in his own words in an address he gave to the House of Lords:

> In working out the Commercial Policy Paper. . . I believe that your representatives have been successful in maintaining the principles and objects which are best suited to the predicament of this country. The plans do not wander from the international terrain and they are consistent with widely different conceptions of domestic policy. . . . It is not true, for example, to say that state trading and bulk purchasing are interfered with. Nor is it true to say that the planning of the volume of our exports and imports, so as to preserve equilibrium in the international balance of payments, is prejudiced. Exactly the contrary is the case. Both currency and the commercial proposals are derived to favor the maintenance of equilibrium by expressly permitting various protective devices when they are required to maintain equilibrium and by forbidding them[16] when they are not required.[17]

Keynes's contention that the proposed International Trade Organization recognized the need for leaving governments free to pursue autonomous economic policies is validated by the high priority it attaches to the promotion of domestic full employment and the authority it grants nations to manage their balance of payments. Similarly, the broader *Proposals for Consideration by an International Conference on Trade and Employment*, of which the ITO is a part, acknowledges that the maintenance of high and stable levels of employment is a necessary condition for the expansion of international trade and for the promotion of liberal international agreements in the fields of commercial policy, monetary stabilization, and investment. [18]

The *Proposals* are unequivocal in directing each signatory nation to "take action designed to achieve and maintain full employment within its own jurisdiction, through measures appropriate to its political and economic institutions." [19] To insure such authority, the *Proposals* further provide that "members confronted with an adverse balance of payments should be entitled to impose quantitative import restrictions as an aid to the restoration of equilibrium in the balance of payments." [20]

Clearly, the agreements hammered out in Washington, D.C., provided that nations should not be precluded by purely external forces from pursing domestic policies designed to insure full employment. Ironically, the conferees realized that multilateral trade could flourish only by placing certain restrictions on it.

Although the British had to accede to certain American demands because of their weaker bargaining position, the fact of the matter is that those concessions did not contravene Keynes's basic position on the preeminence of national autonomy. Neither was he obliged to alter his position on the need for restrictive trade measures as a means for insuring that autonomy.

Notwithstanding the fact that Keynes was a staunch advocate of national autonomy and therefore compelled to favor some degree of restriction over foreign trade, it would be erroneous to characterize him as an absolute protectionist. A qualification is in order. Theoretically, if nations could maintain high and stable levels of employment, classical economics would come back into its own and the doctrine of free trade would again have relevance for him. Given a condition of full employment, the need would not be for an increase in output from levels below a nation's productive capacity, but for greater efficiency and labor productivity through specialization and the international division of labor.

If all nations pursued expansionist policies simultaneously, the pressure that would otherwise impact a single country's trade balance from an expansive monetary or fiscal policy would be greatly attenuated. Keynes had emphasized such a need for simultaneity as early as 1933 and again in 1936. Writing in *The Means to Prosperity* in 1933, he argued that "we should attach great importance to the simultaneity of the movement towards increased expenditures. For the pressure on its foreign balance which each country fears as the result of increasing its own loan expenditures will cancel out if other countries are pursuing the same policy at the same time."[21] He reaffirmed this recommendation in the *General Theory* by noting that it was the simultaneous undertaking of expansionary policies that will restore economic health over the world whether gauged by the level of employment or the volume of international trade.[22]

The lesson to be learned from the foregoing is quite clear. The more successful nations are in promoting full employment, the less frequently will they have to resort to restrictive trade, and the more often, therefore, "the classical medicine" can do its work. It is precisely because the currency and commercial plans recognized the prior right of each nation to safeguard its own equilibrium that Keynes held out such high hopes for their success in leading the world to a system of more liberal trade. Consider what he had to say in defense of those currency and commercial proposals that resulted from the Washington meeting:

> The outstanding characteristic of the plans is that they represent the first elaborate and comprehensive attempt to combine the advantages of a freedom of commerce with safeguards against the disastrous consequences of a laissez-faire system that pays no direct regard to the preservation of equilibrium and merely relies on the eventual working out of blind forces.[23]

This assertion clearly underscores the fact that Keynes did not have faith in the ability of Adam Smith's "invisible hand" to insure the greatest good in all circumstances; hence, the need for the kind of intervention he was endorsing.

Certain differences aside, both the currency and commercial proposals were in line with Keynes's pre-war position. Both reflected the type of international trading system he had hoped to implement during the inter-war years. The main features of that system included high levels of employment; freedom from a rigid international monetary standard such as gold; flexible exchange rates; the right of each nation to pursue an autonomous monetary policy; freedom from externally induced fluctuations; and the right to exercise control over the balance of payments through the regulation of capital movements and the flow of imports and exports—the very principles acknowledged by Bretton Woods and the Washington Agreement.

Despite the fact that both the financial and trade proposals that came out of the Washington meeting reflected much of Keynes's pre-war thinking on foreign trade, he appeared at times to be ambivalent on the issue. The reason, quite simply, is that notwithstanding his misgivings with the free trade doctrine of classical economics, he was also well aware of its advantages. On the other hand, he felt that free trade could not be left free to operate without taking into account its ramifications for a country's level of employment and its balance of trade. His hope, quite clearly, was to harness in some way both the benefits of free trade and full employment under one system.

SUMMARY

Our conclusion is that at the end of his life Keynes could not categorically be classified as either a protectionist or a free trader. Fundamentally, he was in favor of a managed multilateral international trading system. This was entirely consistent with his view in the *General Theory*, where his major concern was with the level of employment. Because the classical school erred in its assumption of full employment, much of what was based on it—for example, free trade—came into question.

In Keynes's view, if a condition of full and stable employment could be assured, then much of the free trade argument would come back into play. For many of the problems it deals with—for example, comparative advantage, the role of relative prices, the shifts required between production for home and foreign markets, the forces of international competition, and so on—are valid subjects of theoretical inquiry and political interest.

In addition to its flawed assumption of full employment, Keynes was not comfortable with the way free trade might impact a nation's trade balance. For example, a nation on free trade might find that its pursuit of an expansive fiscal policy to increase employment could well create a disequilibrium in its balance of trade due to an increase in imports, a decrease in exports, and an outflow of capital funds.

To protect itself from such an imbalance that could, if sufficiently protracted, threaten its internal expansion, a nation should be free of interference from outside forces. The fact that both the *Financial Agreement between the Governments of the United States and the United Kingdom and the Proposals for Consideration by an International Conference of Trade and Employment* recognized that high levels of employment and the right of countries to manage their balances of payments, as prerequisites for the development of a multilateral free trading system, were in large measure consistent with Keynes's pre-war thinking on foreign trade.

The following passage, which is taken from the last article he wrote before his death and which appeared posthumously in the *Economic Journal*, provides a fair assessment of his thinking following Bretton Woods and the Washington meetings:

> I must not be misunderstood. I do not suppose that the classical medicine will work by itself or that we can depend on it. We need quicker and less painful aids of which exchange variation and overall import controls are the most important. But in the long run these expedients will work better and we shall

need them less if the classical medicine is also at work. And if we reject the medicine from our system altogether, we may just drift from expedient to expedient and never get really fit again. The great virtue of the Bretton Woods and Washington proposals, taken in conjunction, is that they marry the use of the necessary expedients to the wholesome long-run doctrine. It is for this reason that, speaking in the House of Lords, I claimed that: 'Here is an attempt to use what we have learnt from modern experience and modern analysis, not to defeat, but to implement the wisdom of Adam Smith.'[24]

Ideally, Keynes wished to combine both the advantages of free trade and protection in a single system. If countries could achieve high and stable levels of employment, as a prerequisite, then the advantages of free trade would follow. This state of affairs, he thought, could best be accomplished by allowing free trade to function over the long run, provided, once again, that restrictive trade policies could be employed whenever expedient, to protect the home economy from short term disruptions that usually characterize an open free trade system.

It is difficult to understand how this fusion would work. Would free trade be the underlying system with exceptions made for restrictive measures when needed, or would free trade simply be a long term desideratum to be achieved over the course of time? Apart from this issue was the larger question as to whether Keynes, in accepting many of the American proposals, retreated from his earlier position on restricted trade and moved back to free trade. As the *London Economist* framed the question: "Did Keynes the statesman take charge of Keynes the economist?"[25]

Did Keynes really change his views? Perhaps he did and perhaps he didn't. To help answer that question was the reason for undertaking this study.

NOTES

1. According to Professor Harrod, those "strings" were not new, but nothing more than a reaffirmation of the policy to which Britain had pledged herself in article VII of the Mutual Aid Agreement. See R.F. Harrod, *The Life of John Maynard Keynes* (London: Macmillan, 1951), 605.

2. British White Paper, OMD 6708, *Financial Agreement Between the Governments of the United States and the United Kingdom*, December 1945.

3. *Financial Agreement Between the Governments of the United States and the United Kingdom*.

4. Political and Economic Planning, *Britain and World Trade* (London: Political and Economic Planning, 1947), 70

5. J. M. Keynes, "The Anglo-American Financial Arrangements," speech delivered before the House of Lords, December 18, 1945, reprinted in *The New Economics*, ed. S. Harris (New York: Alfred A. Knopf, 1947), 392.

6. N. S. Buchanan and F. A. Lutz, *Rebuilding the World Economy* (New York: The Twentieth Century Fund, 1947), 123.

7. Political and Economic Planning, *Britain and World Trade*, 70.

8. Buchanan and Lutz, *Rebuilding the World Economy*, 1251.

9. Professor Harrod states that as of June 30, 1945, those balances amounted to 3,356 million British pounds.

10. *Financial Agreement Between the Governments of the United States and the United Kingdom*, op. cit., p. 394.

11. A. Robinson, "John M. Keynes," *The Economic Journal* 107 (1947): 56.

12. Political and Economic Planning, *Britain and World Trade*, 72–73.

13. *Proposals for Consideration by an International Conference on Trade and Employment*, Washington, D.C., reproduced in N. S. Buchanan and F. A. Lutz, *Rebuilding the World Economy* (New York: The Twentieth Century Fund, 1947), 397–414.

14. S. Harris, "International Economics: Introduction," in *The New Economics*, ed. S. Harris (New York: Alfred A. Knopf, 1947), 262.

15. Keynes, "The Anglo-American Financial Arrangements," 392–93.

16. For example, a country pursuing an expansionist policy can use those instruments when it is trying to balance its foreign accounts. However, it is not justified in doing so if its purpose is to create a surplus or add to it. See R. Nurkse, "Domestic and International Equilibrium," in *The New Economics*, ed. S. Harris (New York: Alfred A. Knopf, 1947), 274.

17. Keynes, "The Anglo-American Financial Arrangements," 393.

18. *Proposals for Consideration by an International Conference on Trade and Employment*, 396–97.

19. *Proposals for Consideration by an International Conference on Trade and Employment*, 397.

20. *Proposals for Consideration by an International Conference on Trade and Employment*, 401.

21. J. M. Keynes, *The Means to Prosperity* (New York: Harcourt, Brace, 1933), 24.

22. J. M. Keynes, *The General Theory of Employment, Interest and Money* (New York: Harcourt, Brace, 1936), 281–85.

23. Keynes, "The Anglo-American Financial Arrangements," 393.

24. "The Balance of Payments of the United States," *The Economic Journal* 56, no. 222 (June 1946): 186.

25. "John Maynard Keynes," the *London Economist* 150, no. 5357 (April 27, 1946): 657–58.

Chapter Twelve

Summary and Conclusions

Over the course of his life, John Maynard Keynes often abandoned ideas previously developed and at times even contradicted his previous thought. This inconsistency is especially true in the field of international economics, where he alternated between the extremes of free trade and protectionism and planned trade in between. Indeed, it is not possible to identify his position on this issue without reference to a specific date or phase of his illustrious career. The one thing that is certain is that his views on foreign trade were conditioned by the needs of the domestic economy, most notably high and stable levels of employment and the protection of the domestic economy from disturbances from abroad.

Specifically, it was this conflict between internal and external needs that caused him to part company with the pre-1914 gold standard. A review of his opposition to the gold standard is instructive, because the reasons for his opposition to it help to explain his later misgivings about the doctrine of free trade. Fundamentally, Keynes was opposed to the pre-1914 gold standard because it often achieved external balance at the expense of the domestic economy in term of employment, wages, prices, and loss of capital. Secondly, a country could not pursue an autonomous monetary policy attuned to its own needs. Rather, it had to march in lockstep with all other countries on the standard. To maintain a fixed exchange rate, all countries on the standard had to have the same interest rate and relative prices. If a country's relative prices rose because of differences in wages and other costs, they would have to be brought back into line through deflationary measures, including an increase in the amount of labor displacement.

Keynes was opposed to this forced uniformity because circumstances and needs differ from nation to nation. A country experiencing unemployment should be able to lower domestic interest rates, but may be unable to do so because of an outflow of capital and the need to protect the value of its fixed rate of exchange. Keynes was opposed to this one-size-fits-all approach. By analogy, he pointed out that "if the force of gravity was materially different in different countries, the same might apply to the standard of weight as it does to the gold standard."[1]

If gold was to play any role in a nation's currency, Keynes preferred that it be managed and should attain external equilibrium with a minimum of internal disruption. Such a standard would allow for the variation of the Central Bank's gold buying and selling prices, the centralization of gold reserves, the divorce of the gold reserve from the note issue, and control of capital movements. These measures would add to the monetary authority's gold reserves and thereby better enable it to deal with a country's balance of payment deficits. This would relieve the pressure on countries to make internal adjustments for interest rates, relative prices, employment, and income.

It bears noting that Keynes's preference for a managed as opposed to the pre-1914 gold standard suggests a bias in favor of the management of economic affairs rather than to leave them to the play of the free market. Another corollary that follows from Keynes's view of the gold standard is that when the United Kingdom experienced economic difficulties in the late 1920s and early 1930s, he understood full well that participation in an open foreign trade system, like membership in the gold standard system, could interfere with a nation's attainment of internal equilibrium.

Despite reservations about the gold standard, Keynes was entirely orthodox in his thinking about commercial policy for some time after World War I. But as Great Britain found it increasingly difficult to achieve internal equilibrium after her return to the gold standard in 1925, he became less confident that she could resolve her domestic and foreign problems by continuing to adhere to a free trade policy

Keynes first gave indication of this change of attitude in the pages of his *Treatise on Money*, a work that he largely thought out in the depressed British environment of the late 1920s. In it, Keynes expressed considerable concern about the disparity between the volume of foreign lending and the size of the foreign balance. The latter was not keeping pace with the former because of the higher British production costs and the existence of tariff barriers abroad. To rectify the problem, Keynes suggested that it would be well to increase the size of the foreign trade balance by "applying usefully some method of establishing differential prices for home and foreign goods."[2]

Although Keynes's advocacy of a tariff in the *Treatise* was couched in rather "elaborate theoretical language," his defense of protection before the Macmillan Committee in 1930 was far less artful. To cope with Great Britain's economic slump, he suggested that the government undertake a widespread expansion program. However, the promotion of a cheap money policy by Britain in a depressed world environment would create a condition of external disequilibrium, for it would increase her volume of lending abroad, while reducing the size of her trade surplus through an increase in its imports and a decrease in its exports. In effect, much of the benefit from the stimulus would go abroad. Moreover, should this imbalance be sufficiently prolonged, it would bring the domestic monetary expansion to an end.

To eliminate such a prospect, Keynes urged in the special appendix to the Macmillan Report that the British foreign balance be protected through the imposition of tariffs on imports and the granting of subsidies to exports. This meant, therefore, that if any adjustment had to be made in the foreign account, the incidence of that correction should be made to fall on the external and not on the internal sector of the economy. And so, as in the case of the gold standard, Keynes, in deciding the proper commercial policy, favored that course that would best serve the interests of the domestic economy.

In the spring of 1931, Keynes came out even more strongly for a protectionist policy by urging a revenue tariff for Great Britain. Such a measure, he noted, would bolster business confidence, relieve pressure on the budget, increase the surplus on the foreign trade balance, and reduce the level of domestic unemployment.

However, his support for this measure was short lived, because on September 21, 1931, just a few months later, Great Britain abandoned the gold standard. As a result of this development, Keynes asked that consideration of his tariff proposal be postponed. And well he might, for Britain stood to gain far more from the devaluation of the pound that attended her divorce from gold than from a revenue tariff. But did this *volte face*, at least in spirit, make him any less a protectionist?

Did this turn of events cause Keynes to return to the ranks of the free traders? One would have thought so, because no longer fettered by a fixed exchange rate, Britain would no longer have to adjust wage rates, relative prices, and interest rates on the basis of a common standard. Moreover, the cheaper pound would make imports more costly and exports less expensive.

For a time after September 21, 1931, it appears from what he had said in *The Means to Prosperity* in 1933 about the disadvantages of currency depreciation and tariffs that he did become more sympathetic toward free trade. But this change of heart, if that was the case, was of short duration. For following the demise of the World Conference, which failed to embrace his proposal for a worldwide expansion, Keynes became disenchanted with international cooperation, turned inward, and became increasingly insular in his thinking.

For one who had made so many contributions to international affairs, it is difficult to understand what precipitated his disenchantment. Could it have been his disappointment over the rejection of his proposal by the World Conference? That does not seem to be the case. For if one were to take him at his word, the reasons he cited for his change of direction were due to the changed circumstances in the world after World War I, the greater role of services in consumption, the narrowing of differences in the production of goods, and the lessened relevance of comparative advantage in areas other than those due to geography and climate. In light of these developments, Keynes thought that, apart from differences of climate, the location of natural resources, and the like, the need for foreign trade had been reduced and nations should become more self-sufficient. These were, indeed, powerful arguments for a lesser degree of economic involvement among nations. In any event, Keynes became disillusioned with the existing open system and all its problems. He was prepared to move toward national autarky with its more closed economic arrangements.

In *The General Theory of Employment, Interest and Money*, Keynes, disenchanted as he was with international cooperation, confined himself largely to domestic issues. His main concern in that work was, of course, the problem of unemployment. Despite his movement away from international trade and finance, the *General Theory* does have a number of implications for the foreign sector of a nation's economy.

The most important of these is that the orthodox doctrine of free trade, like other aspects of classical economic theory, can be valid only under conditions of full employment. Given an environment of less than full employment of manpower and other resources, the free trade doctrine that is predicated on the opportunity cost analysis becomes open to question. In those circumstances, the comparative cost principle loses some of its significance, for the alternative to employing manpower and other resources at less than optimal efficiency, which would be the case under a protectionist policy, would be not to employ them at all. In effect, it would not make much sense to economize in the use of labor on the one hand only to have it go to waste on the other.

Moreover, despite the fact that a protective trade policy would reduce productivity, it might, by expanding employment opportunities in the import competing industries, create a need for more domestic investment. In the end, this added investment could lead to a higher level of output, income, and employment than would a policy of free trade in a state of depressed activity. Therefore, because protectionism is more likely to increase the level of home employment and income, especially in a nation that has a large import surplus, the advantages of adhering to a free trade policy in conditions of widespread labor and capital displacement may be seriously questioned.

Considered from the standpoint of a single country experiencing underemployment equilibrium, a protectionist trade policy could be an effective means for increasing the level of home employment. The improvement of the foreign trade balance that such a policy makes possible is synonymous with an increase in investment that is, of course, a prime driver of economic activity.

Parenthetically, in following the above reasoning, one should be cautioned not to fall victim to the fallacy of composition and division, that is, what applies to one part of an entity does not necessarily apply to the whole. For example, a country with a large trade deficit would gain from a restrictive trade policy, if all others followed more liberal policies. But that might not be the case if all countries followed the same protectionist policies. Nevertheless, a nation with a large trade deficit need not aspire to a trade surplus, but could, by simply reducing its imports and balancing its foreign trade accounts, add to its level of output, employment, and income. Even so, the fact remains that the better alternative would be for all nations to pursue expansive policies concurrently. For, indeed, a rising tide lifts all boats.

In the years following the publication of the *General Theory*, Keynes provided much more insight as to his views on foreign trade. The one thing for certain is that he did not revert back to orthodox free trade. As a matter of fact, he moved even farther away from that doctrine, so much so that he abandoned all hope of monetary let alone commercial cooperation among nations. In an important letter to the *The Times of London* in the fall of 1938, he put forth the idea that the proper solution for Great Britain's international economic problems rested in bilateral trade. This represented the culmination of his movement toward planned or managed trade—an objective he had first tried to achieve after the breakdown of the World Conference

The outbreak of World War II did not cause Keynes to alter his view on the need for planned trade in the post-war world. However, toward the end of 1941 some change started to occur in his thinking on the question of post-war international cooperation. This modification was caused in large measure by the generous Lend-Lease assistance provided by the United States to Great Britain in the Mutual Aid Agreement. It was also influenced by the Agreement's stipulation that the British participate in a multilateral international trading system the Americans were planning for the post-war era. Although Keynes may have moved away from bilateral to more multilateral trade, he remained steadfast on the commercial aspects of foreign trade and the requirement that external considerations not interfere with domestic employment and other needs.

Constrained though he was by the British commitment to a post-war multilateral international trading system, Keynes, in formulating his Clearing Union Proposal and later endorsing the International Monetary Fund, remained committed to the principle that a nation's external activity should not frustrate the attainment of full employment or other domestic objectives. The reason Keynes could remain consistent in very large measure with his pre-war position on foreign trade is that both proposals mirrored many of his own views.

Notwithstanding his movement away from bilateral trade, Keynes could not be characterized as a free trader in the traditional sense. Basically, the reason is that at times the promotion of programs designed to achieve full employment and membership in an open free trade system may be incompatible. And because Keynes gave preference to the solution of unemployment and other internal issues over external considerations, he could no more sanction a policy of doctrinaire free trade then than he could in the 1930s.

Fundamentally, Keynes could not revert to his free trade position of the early 1920s because of his assumption that the economy tends to equilibrate at a level of less than full employment. If full employment were in place, as assumed by classical economics, free trade would come into its own. But given a condition of widespread labor displacement, restricted trade might do more to increase the level of output, employment, and income than would an open-trade policy. In addition, a free trade policy might not be as effective in neutralizing transmission and spillover effects as restricted trade might be.

Therefore, just as his postulate of less than full employment caused Keynes to part company with the classicists in the field of general economic theory, so, too, it was this same claim that caused him to take exception with their endorsement of free trade for all levels of employment.

Although Keynes could not completely subscribe to the tenets of free trade, even while endorsing the currency proposals, neither could he be classified as an absolute protectionist. For he still believed that there was much to commend the classical position on trade, if it could be modified. His contention was that if full employment could be assured, all else in classical economics, including free trade, would follow.

Ideally, therefore, Keynes sought to combine the advantages of free trade and protection into a single system. Such a fusion of the two, he believed, would permit fundamental free trade forces to restore any disturbed equilibrium in the long run and restrictive measures such as import and exchange rate controls to provide protection against short-run disequilibria, which free trade is unable to deal with effectively.[3] Whether such a scheme would actually work out in practice is entirely problematic.

The above to the contrary notwithstanding, the one thing that is certain is that over the course of his lifetime. Keynes fought consistently and with notable success to liberate the domestic economy from the depressing effects of external forces. Fundamentally, he sought to extend the lessons learned in the closed economy of the *General Theory* to the wider world by making foreign trade and commercial policy dependent on the needs of the domestic economy and the state of its employment. In conclusion, the evidence marshaled by this study clearly shows that Keynes's views on foreign trade were subservient to the needs of the domestic economy so that in the end foreign trade became the handmaiden of full employment.

NOTES

1. J. M. Keynes, *A Treatise on Money*, vol. II (London: Macmillan, 1930), 332.
2. Keynes, *A Treatise on Money*, vol. II, 189.
3. J. M. Keynes, "The Balance of Payments of the United States," *The Economic Journal* 56, no. 222 (June 1946): 186.

Bibliography

BOOKS AND PAMPHLETS BY JOHN M. KEYNES

Keynes, J. M. *Indian Currency and Finance*. London: Macmillan, 1913.
————. *The Economic Consequences of the Peace*. New York: Harcourt, Brace and Howe, 1920.
————. *Monetary Reform*. New York: Harcourt, Brace, 1924. (The English edition is titled *A Tract on Monetary Reform*.)
————. *The Economic Consequences of Sterling Parity*. New York: Harcourt, Brace, 1925. (The English edition is titled *The Economic Consequences of Mr. Churchill*.)
————. *A Treatise on Money*, volume 1, *The Pure Theory of Money*. London: Macmillan, 1930.
————. *A Treatise on Money*, volume 2, *The Applied Theory of Money*. London: Macmillan, 1930.
————. *Essays in Persuasion*. New York: Harcourt, Brace, 1932.
————. *Essays in Biography*. London: Macmillan, 1933.
————. *The Means to Prosperity*. New York: Harcourt, Brace, 1933.
————. *The General Theory of Employment, Interest and Money*. New York: Harcourt, Brace, 1936.
————. *How to Pay for the War*. New York: Harcourt, Brace, 1940.
Keynes, J. M., and H. D. Henderson. *Can Lloyd George Do It? An Examination of the Liberal Pledge*. London: The Nation and Athenaeum, 1929.

PERIODICAL ARTICLES BY JOHN M. KEYNES

Keynes, J. M. "Recent Economic Events in India." *The Economic Journal* 19, no. 73 (March 1909): 51–67.
————. "Report upon the Operations of the Paper Currency Department of the Government of India during the Year 1910–11." *The Economic Journal* 22, no. 85 (March 1912): 145–47.
————. "Currency in 1912." *The Economic Journal* 24, no. 93 (March 1914): 152–57.
————. "The City of London and the Bank of England, August, 1914." *The Quarterly Journal of Economics* 29, no. 1 (November 1914): 48–71.
————. "The Prospects of Money, November, 1914." *The Economic Journal* 24, no. 95 (December 1914): 610–34.

182 Bibliography

———. "War and the Financial System, August, 1914." *The Economic Journal* 24, no. 95 (December 1914): 460–86.

———. "The Forward Market in Foreign Exchanges." *Manchester Guardian Reconstruction Supplement* (April 20, 1922): 11–15.

———. "The Stabilization of the European Exchanges—I." *Manchester Guardian Reconstruction Supplement* (April 20, 1922): 3–5.

———. "The Theory of the Exchanges and Purchasing Power Parity." *Manchester Guardian Reconstruction Supplement* (April 20, 1922): 6–8.

———. "The Reconstruction of Europe: A General Introduction." *Manchester Guardian Reconstruction Supplement* (May 18, 1922): 66–67.

———. "The Genoa Conference." *Manchester Guardian Reconstruction Supplement* 3 (June 15, 1922): 132–33.

———. "The Consequences to Society of Changes in the Value of Money." *Manchester Guardian Reconstruction Supplement* 5 (July 27, 1922): 321–28.

———. "Inflation as a Method of Taration." *Manchester Guardian Reconstruction Supplement* 5 (July 27, 1922): 268–69.

———. "Is a Settlement of the Reparation Question Possible Now?" *Manchester Guardian Reconstruction Supplement* 8 (September 28, 1922): 462–64.

———. "Speculation in the Mark and Germany's Balances Abroad." *Manchester Guardian Reconstruction Supplement* 8 (September 28, 1922): 480–82.

———. "The Stabilization of the European Exchanges—II." *Manchester Guardian Reconstruction Supplement* 11 (December 7, 1922): 658–61.

———. "The Stabilization of the European Exchanges—A Plan for Genoa." *Manchester Guardian Supplement* (April 20, 1922): 3.

———. "The Underlying Principles." *Manchester Guardian Reconstruction Supplement* 12 (January 4, 1923): 717–18.

———. "Professor Jevons on the Indian Exchange." *The Economic Journal* 33, no. 129 (March 1923): 60–65.

———. "Is Credit Abundant?" *The Nation and the Athenaeum* 33, no. 14 (July 7, 1923): 470.

———. "Bank Rate at Four Per Cent." *The Nation and the Athenaeum* 33, no. 15 (July 14, 1923): 502.

———. "Bank Rate and Stability of Prices—A Reply to Critics." *The Nation and the Athenaeum* 33, no. 16 (July 21, 1923): 530.

———. "The Measure of Deflation." *The Nation and the Athenaeum* 33, no. 17 (July 28, 1923): 558.

———. "Mr. Baldwin's Task." *The New Republic* 35, no. 452 (August 1, 1923): 252–53.

———. "The American Debt." *The Nation and the Athenaeum* 33, no. 18 (August 4, 1923): 566–67.

———. "Currency Policy and Unemployment." *The Nation and the Athenaeum* 33, no. 19 (August 11, 1923): 611–12.

———. "Free Trade." *The Nation and the Athenaeum* 34, no. 8 (November 24, 1923): 302–3.

———. "Free Trade and Unemployment." *The Nation and the Athenaeum* 34, no. 9 (December 1, 1923): 335–36.

———. "Free Trade for England." *The New Republic* 37, no. 472 (December 19, 1923): 86–87.

———. "A Reply to Sir William Beveridge." *The Economic Journal* 33, no. 131 (December 1923): 476–86.

———. "Gold in 1923." *The Nation and the Athenaeum* 34, no. 18 (February 2, 1924): 623–24.

———. "The Prospects of Gold." *The Nation and the Athenaeum* 34, no. 20 (February 16, 1924): 692–93.

———. "Gold in 1923." *The New Republic* 38, no. 482 (February 27, 1924): 10–11.

———. "The Prospects of Gold." *The New Republic* 28, no. 484 (March 12, 1924): 66–67.

———. "The Franc." *The Nation and the Athenaeum* 34, no. 24 (March 15, 1924): 823–24.

———. "The Franc." *The New Republic* 38, no. 486 (March 26, 1924): 120–21.

———. "Does Unemployment Need a Drastic Remedy?" *The Nation and the Athenaeum* 35, no. 8 (May 24, 1924): 235–36.

———. "A Drastic Remedy for Unemployment." *The Nation and the Athenaeum* 35, no. 10 (June 7, 1924): 311–12.

———. "Public and Private Enterprise." *The Nation and the Athenaeum* 35, no. 12 (June 21, 1924): 374–75.

———. "The Policy of the Bank of England." *The Nation and the Athenaeum* 35, no. 16 (July 19, 1924): 500–501.

———. "Foreign Investment and National Advantage—An Address to the Liberal Summer School at Oxford." *The Nation and the Athenaeum* 35, no. 19 (August 2, 1924): 584–87.

———. "The Return Towards Gold." *The Nation and the Athenaeum* 36, no. 21 (February 21, 1925): 707–9.

———. "The Bank Rate." *The Nation and the Athenaeum* 36, no. 23 (March 7, 1925): 790–92.

———. "The Return Towards Gold." *The New Republic* 42, no. 537 (March 18, 1925): 92–94.

———. "The Problem of the Gold Standard." *The Nation and the Athenaeum* 36, no. 25 (March 21, 1925): 866–70.

———. "Is Sterling Overvalued?" *The Nation and the Athenaeum* 37, no. 1 (April 4, 1925): 28–30.

———. "Is Sterling Overvalued—II?" *The Nation and the Athenaeum* 37, no. 3 (April 18, 1925): 86.

———. "The Gold Standard." *The Nation and the Athenaeum* 37, no. 5 (May 2, 1925): 129–30.

———. "Is the Pound Overvalued?" *The New Republic* 42, no. 544 (May 6, 1925): 286–87.

———. "The Gold Standard—A Correction." *The Nation and the Athenaeum* 37, no. 6 (May 9, 1925): 169–70.

———. "England's Gold Standard." *The New Republic* 42, no. 546 (May 20, 1925): 339–40.

———. "The Arithmetic of the Sterling Exchange." *The Nation and the Athenaeum* 37, no. 11 (June 13, 1925): 338.

———. "The Committee on the Currency." *The Economic Journal* 35, no. 138 (June 1925): 299–304.

———. "The Gold Standard Act, 1925." *The Economic Journal* 35, no. 138 (June 1925): 312–13.

———. "Am I a Liberal—I?" *The Nation and the Athenaeum* 37, no. 19 (August 8, 1925): 563–64.

———. "Am I a Liberal—II?" *The Nation and the Athenaeum* 37, no. 20 (August 15, 1925): 587–88.

———. "Great Britain's Cross of Gold." *The New Republic* 44, no. 563 (September 16, 1925): 88–90.

———. "The French Franc." *The Nation and the Athenaeum* 38, no. 15 (January 9, 1926): 515–17.

———. "The French Franc—A Reply." *The Nation and the Athenaeum* 38, no. 16 (January 16, 1926): 544–45.

———. "Some Facts and Last Reflections about the Franc." *The Nation and the Athenaeum* 38, no. 18 (January 30, 1926): 603–4.

———. "Coal: A Suggestion." *The Nation and the Athenaeum* 39, no. 4 (April 24, 1926): 91–92.

———. "Back to the Coal Problem." *The Nation and the Athenaeum* 39, no. 16 (May 15, 1926): 159.

———. "The First Fruits of the British Gold Standard." *The New Republic* 47, no. 600 (June 2, 1926): 54–55.

———. "The First Fruits of the Gold Standard." *The Nation and the Athenaeum* 39, no. 12 (June 26, 1926): 344–45.

———. "The Franc Once More." *The Nation and the Athenaeum* 39, no. 15 (July 17, 1926): 435–36.

———. "The Future of the Franc." *The New Republic* 47, no. 610 (August 11, 1926): 328–29.

———. "The End of Laissez-Faire—I." *The New Republic* 48, no. 612 (August 25, 1926): 13–15.

————. "The End of Laissez-Faire—II." *The New Republic* 48, no. 613 (September 1, 1926): 37–41.

————. "The Autumn Prospects for Sterling." *The Nation and the Athenaeum* 40, no. 3 (October 23, 1926): 104–5.

————. "The Position of the Lancashire Cotton Trade." *The Nation and the Athenaeum* 40, no. 6 (November 13, 1926): 209–10.

————. "Will England Restrict Foreign Investments?" *The New Republic* 49, no. 626 (December 1, 1926): 34–36.

————. "Mr. McKenna on Monetary policy." *The Nation and the Athenaeum* 40, no. 19 (February 12, 1927): 651–53.

————. "The Colwyn Report on National Debt and Taxation." *The Economic Journal* 37, no. 146 (June 1927): 198–212.

————. "The British Balance of Trade, 1925–1927." *The Economic Journal* 37, no. 148 (December 1927): 551–65.

————. "Note on the British Balance of Trade." *The Economic Journal* 38, no. 149 (March 1928): 146–47.

————. "The Stabilization of the Franc." *The Nation the Athenaeum* 43, no. 13 (June 30, 1928): 416–17.

————. "The Amalgamation of the British Note Issues." *The Economic Journal* 38, no. 150 (June 1928): 321–28.

————. "Is There Enough Gold?" *The Nation and the Athenaeum* 44, no. 16 (January 19, 1929): 545–46.

————. "The Bank Rate—Five and a Half Per Cent." *The Nation and the Athenaeum* 44, no. 20 (February 16, 1929): 679–80.

————. "The German Transfer Problem." *The Economic Journal* 39, no. 153 (March 1929): 1–7.

————. "The Treasury Contribution to the White Paper." *The Nation and the Athenaeum* 45, no. 7 (May 18, 1929): 227–28.

————. "The Question of High Wages." *Political Quarterly* 1, no. 1 (January 1930): 110–24.

————. "British Industry, Unemployment and High Wages." *Barron's The National Financial Weekly* 10, no. 12 (March 24, 1930): 22–23.

————. "The Industrial Crisis." *The Nation and the Athenaeum* 47, no. 6 (May 10, 1930): 163–64.

————. "Economic Possibilities for Our Grandchildren—I." *The Nation and the Athenaeum* 48, no. 2 (October 11, 1930): 36–37.

————. "Economic Possibilities for Our Grandchildren—II." *The Nation and the Athenaeum* 48, no. 3 (October 18, 1930): 96–98.

————. "The Great Slump of 1930—I." *The Nation and the Athenaeum* 48, no. 12 (December 20, 1930): 402.

————. "The Great Slump of 1930—II." *The Nation and the Athenaeum* 48, no. 13 (December 27, 1930): 427–28.

————. "Proposals for a Revenue Tariff." *The New Statesman and Nation* 1, no. 2 (March 7, 1931): 53–54.

————. "Further Reflections on a Revenue Tariff." *The New Statesman and Nation* 1, no. 4 (March 21, 1931): 142–43.

————. "Economic Notes on Free Trade—The Export Industries." *The New Statesman and Nation* 1, no. 5 (March 28, 1931): 175–76.

————. "Economic Notes on Free Trade—A Revenue Tariff and the Cost of Living." *The New Statesman and Nation* 1, no. 6 (April 4, 1931): 211.

————. "Revenue Tariff for Great Britain." *The New Republic* 66, no. 853 (April 8, 1931): 196–97.

————. "Economic Notes on Free Trade—The Reaction of Imports on Exports." *The New Statesman and Nation* 1, no. 7 (April 11, 1931): 242–43.

————. "Some Consequences of the Economy Report." *The New Statesman and Nation* 2, no. 25 (August 15, 1931): 189–90.

———. "A Gold Conference." *The New Statesman and Nation* 2, no. 29 (September 12, 1931): 300–301.

———. "The Budget." *The New Statesman and Nation* 2, no. 30 (September 19, 1931): 329.

———. "Mr. Keynes' Theory of Money: A Rejoinder." *The Economic Journal* 41, no. 163 (September 1931): 412–23.

———. "A Reply to Dr. Hayek: The Pure Theory of Money." *Economica* 11, no. 34 (November 1931): 387–597.

———. "The Prospects of the Sterling Exchanges." *The Yale Review* 21, no. 3 (March 1932): 433–47.

———. "Reflections on the Sterling Exchange." *Lloyds Bank Monthly Review* 3, no. 26 (April 1932): 143–60.

———. "The World's Economic Outlook." *The Atlantic Monthly* 149, no. 5 (May 1932): 521–26.

———. "The Monetary Policy of the Labour Government—I." *The New Statesman and Nation* 4, no. 82 (September 17, 1932): 306–7.

———. "The Monetary Policy of the Labour Government—II." *The New .Statesman and Nation* 4, no. 82 (September 24, 1932): 338–39.

———. "A Note on the Long-Term Rate of Interest in Relation to the Conversion Scheme." *The Economic Journal* 42, no. 167 (September 1932): 415–23.

———. "The World Economic Conference, 1933." *The New Statesman and Nation* 4, no. 96 (December 24, 1932): 825–26.

———. "A Programme for Unemployment." *The New Statesman and Nation* 5, no. 102 (February 4, 1933): 121–22.

———. "The Multiplier." *The New Statesman and Nation* 5, no. 110 (April 1, 1933): 405–7.

———. "National Self-Sufficiency." *The Yale Review* 22, no. 4 (June 1933): 755–69.

———. "National Self-Sufficiency—I." *The New Statesman and Nation* 6, no. 124 (July 8, 1933): 36–37.

———. "National Self-Sufficiency—II." *The New Statesman and Nation* 6, no. 125 (July 15, 1933): 65–67.

———. "Mr. Keynes' Control Scheme." *American Economic Review* 23, no. 4 (December 1933): 675.

———. "President Roosevelt's Gold Policy." *The New Statesman and Nation* 7, no. 152 (January 20, 1934): 76–77.

———. "A Self-Adjusting Economic System?" *The New Republic* 82, no. 1054 (February 20, 1935): 35–37.

———. "The Report of the Bank for International Settlements, 1934–1935." *The Economic Journal* 45, no. 179 (September 1935): 594–97.

———. "The Future of the Foreign Exchanges." *Lloyd's Bank Monthly Review* 6, no. 68 (October 1935): 527–35.

———. "The Supply of Gold." *The Economic Journal* 46, no. 183 (September 1936): 412–18.

———. "The General Theory of Employment." *The Quarterly Journal of Economics* 51, no. 2 (February 1937): 209–23.

———. "Alternative Theories of the Rate of Interest." *The Economic Journal* 47, no. 186 (June 1937): 240–52.

———. "The 'Ex Ante' Theory of the Rate of Interest." *The Economic Journal* 47, no. 188 (December 1937): 663–69.

———. "Mr. Keynes' Consumption Functions Reply." *The Quarterly Journal of Economics* 52, no. 4 (August 1938): 709–12.

———. "The Policy of Government Storage of Foodstuffs and Raw Materials." *The Economic Journal* 48, no. 191 (September 1938): 449–60.

———. "Relative Movements of Real Wages and Output." *The Economic Journal* 49, no. 193 (March 1939): 34–51.

———. "The Concept of National Income." *The Economic Journal* 50, no. 197 (March 1940): 60–65.

———. "The Objective of International Price Stability." *The Economic Journal* 53, nos. 210–11 (June–September 1943): 185–87.

————. "The Balance of Payments of the United States." *The Economic Journal* 56, no. 222 (June 1946): 172–87.

NEWSPAPER ARTICLES, LECTURES, AND SPEECHES
BY JOHN M. KEYNES

Keynes, J. M. "Monetary Policy—Relation of Price Levels." *The Times of London*, September 4, 1925, 20.

————. "The Issues for Free-Traders." Letter to the Editor. *The Times of London*, March 21, 1931, 8.

————. "Mr. J. M. Keynes' Rejoinder." Letter to the Editor. *The Times of London*, March 27, 1931, 10.

————. "Revenue Tariffs—Effects on Home Production." Letter to the Editor. *The Times of London*, April 2, 1931, 6.

————. "The Tariff Question." Letter to the Editor. *The Times of London*, September 29, 1931, 15.

————. "An Economic Analysis of Unemployment." In *Unemployment as a World Problem*, edited by Q. Wright. Chicago: University of Chicago Press, 1931, 3–42.

————. "Halley-Stewart Lecture (1931)." *The World's Economic Crisis and the Way of Escape*. New York: The Century Company, 1932, 55–75.

————. "Mr. Keynes' Programme." Letter to the Editor. *The Economist* 116, no. 4674 (March 25, 1933): 642.

————. "Public Works." Letter to the Editor. *The Times of London*, July 28, 1933, 10.

————. "Mr. Roosevelt's Experiments." *The Times of London*, January 2, 1934, 11–12.

————. "From Keynes to Roosevelts Our Recovery Plan Assayed." *The New York Times*, December 31, 1934, p. 2, sec. VIII.

————. "How to Avoid a Slump—I: The Problem of the Steady Level." *The Times of London*, January 12, 1937, 13–14.

————. "How to Avoid a Slump—II: Dear Money." *The Times of London*, January 13, 1937, 13–14.

————. "How to Avoid a Slump—III Opportunities of Policy." *The Times of London*, January 14, 1937, 13–14.

————. "The Boom and the Budget." Letter to the Editor. *The Economist* 126, no. 4875 (January 30, 1937): 240.

————. "Bankers, Boom and Budget." Letter to the Editor. *The Economist* 126, no. 4877 (February 13, 1937): 359.

————. "The Gold Problem." Letter to the Editor. *The Times of London*, June 10, 1937, 17.

————. "Public Works—Improvisation or Planning?" Letter to the Editor. *The Times of London*, January 3, 1938, 13.

————. "Interest Rates and the Treasury." Letter to the Editor. *The Economist* 130, no. 4932 (March 5, 1938): 499–500.

————. "Foreign Trade—The Barter Aspect." Letter to the Editor. *The Times of London*, October 7, 1938, 10.

————. "Crisis Finance—I: Employment and the Budget." *The Times of London*, April 17, 1939, 13–14.

————. "Crisis Finance—II: The Supply of Savings." *The Times of London*, April 18, 1939, 15–16.

————. "Borrowing by the State—I: High Interest and Low." *The Times of London*, July 24, 1939, 13–14.

————. "Borrowing by the State—II: A Programme of Method." *The Times of London*, July 25, 1939, 13–14.

————. "Bretton Woods." Letter to the Editor. *The Economist* 147, no. 5268 (August 12, 1944): 215.

―――. "The Anglo-American Financial Arrangements." Speech delivered before the House of Lords, December 18, 1945. In *The New Economics*, edited by S. Harris. New York: Alfred A. Knopf, 1947, 380–95.

―――. "The International Clearing Union." Speech delivered before the House of Lords, May 18, 1943. In *The New Economics*, edited by S. Harris. New York: Alfred A. Knopf, 1947, 359–68.

―――. "The International Monetary Fund." Speech delivered before the House of Lords, May 23, 1944. In *The New Economics*, edited by S. Harris. New York: Alfred A. Knopf, 1947, 369–79.

GENERAL PERIODICAL ARTICLES

Ackerman, Clement: "The Economic Consequences of the Peace." *Pacific Review* 1 (1920): 93–108.

Adarkar, B. P., and D. Gosh. "Mr. Keynes' Theory of Interest." *The Indian Journal of Commerce* 21 (1941): 285–300.

Adler, Hans J. "U.S. Import Demand During the Interwar Period." *American Economic Review* 35 (1945): 418–27.

Anderson, Karl L. "Protection and the Historical Situation: Australia." *The Quarterly Journal of Economics* 53 (1938): 86–104.

Balogh, T. "Some Theoretical Aspects of the Gold Problem." *Economica* 4 (1937): 274–94.

―――. "League of Nations on Post-War Foreign Trade." *The Economic Journal* 54 (1944): 256–61.

―――. "The American Loan." *The Economist* 150 (1946): 12.

―――. "The Balance of Payments and Domestic Economic Policy." *Bulletin of the Oxford University Institute of Statistics* 13 (1951): 55–64.

―――. "International Equilibrium and U.S. Private Investment." *Bulletin of the Oxford University Institute of Statistics* 13 (1951): 247–55.

Balogh, T., and P. P. Streeten. "The Inappropriateness of Simple Elasticity Concepts in the Analysis of International Trade." *The Bulletin of the Oxford University Institute of Statistics* 13 (1951): 65–77.

The Banker. "Death of a Genius." *The Banker* 78 (1946): 74–80.

Benham, F. "The Terns of Trade." *Economica* 7 (1940): 360–76.

―――. "The Muddle of the Thirties." *Economica* 12 (1945): 1–9.

Beveridge, W. H. "The Case for Free Trade." *The Times of London*, March 26, 1931, 10.

―――. "An Analysis of Unemployment." *Economica* 3 (1936): 357–86.

Bloomfield, A. I. "Postwar Control of International Capital Movements." *American Economic Review* 36 (1946): 687–709.

Burns, A. F. "Keynesian Economics Once Again." *The Review of Economic Statistics* 29 (1947): 256–67.

Burrows, H. R. "J. M. Keynes—Part I—His Life and Thought." *The South African Journal of Economics* 20 (1952): 149–64.

―――. "J. M. Keynes—Part II—His Theory." *The South African Journal of Economics* 2 (1952): 242–60.

Champernowne, D. G. "Unemployment, Basic and Monetary: The Classical Analysis and the Keynesian." *The Review of Economic Studies* 3 (1936): 201–16.

Chang, T.C. "The British Demand for Imports in the Inter-War Period." *The Economic Journal* 56 (1946): 188–207.

Clark, C. "Determination of the Multiplier from National Income Statistics." *The Economic Journal* 48 (1938): 435–48.

Condliffe, J. B. "The Value of International Trade." *Economica* 5 (1938): 123–37.

―――. "Exchange Stabilization and International Trade." *The Review of Economic Statistics* 26 (1944): 166–69.

Curtis, M. "Foreign Trade and Employment." *The Economist* 148 (1945): 76.

Day, Clive: "Keynes' Economic Consequences of the Peace." *American Economic Review* 10 (1920): 299–312.

De Vegh, J. "Imports and Income in the U.S. and Canada." *Review of Economics and Statistics* 23 (1941): 130–46.

Dillard, D. "Keynes and Proudhon." *The Journal of Economic History* 2 (1942): 63–76.

The Economist. "Protection and Britain's Future." *The Economist* 111, no. 4538 (August 16, 1930): 307–8.

———. "Second Thoughts on Protection." *The Economist* 112, no. 4563 (February 7, 1931): 279.

———. "The Inconsequences of Mr. Keynes." *The Economist* 112, no. 4568 (March 14, 1931): 549–50.

———. "Mr. Keynes and the Tariff." *The Economist* 112, no. 4571 (April 4, 1931): 722.

———. "Tariffs, Wages and Exports." *The Economist* 112, no. 4572 (April 11, 1931): 771–72.

———. "The Election and Fiscal Policy." *The Economist* 113, no. 4597 (October 10, 1931): 645–46.

———. "Sanity versus Tariffs." *The Economist* 113, no. 4599 (October 17, 1931): 696–97.

———. "Stark and Unashamed." *The Economist* 114, no. 4615 (February 6, 1932): 293–94.

———. "Mr. Keynes' Programme." *The Economist* 116, no. 4673 (March 18, 1933): 568–69.

———. "World Economic Conference." *The Economist* 116, no. 4685 (June 10, 1933): 1–11.

———. "The Gospel of Self-Sufficiency." *The Economist* 117, no. 4691 (July 22, 1933): 171–72.

———. "Mr. Keynes and Exchange Stabilisation." *The Economist* 121, no. 4807 (October 12, 1935): 700.

———. "Mr. Keynes on Money." *The Economist* 122, no. 4827 (February 29, 1936): 471–72.

———. "Full Employment." *The Economist* 123, no. 4832 (April 4, 1936): 5–6.

———. "Five Years off Gold." *The Economist* 124, no. 4586 (September 19, 1936): 503–4.

———. "A Chance for Statesmanship," *The Economist* 125, no. 4859 (October 10, 1936): 49–50.

———. "Mr. Keynes on British Policy." *The Economist* 126, no. 4873 (January 16, 1937): 108.

———. "An Anti-Tariff Move." *The Economist* 126, no. 4876 (February 6, 1937): 285–86.

———. "Is it Inflation?" *The Economist* 126, no. 4881 (March 13, 1937): 578–79.

———. "The Terms of Trade." *The Economist* 130, no. 4928 (February 5, 1938): 310–11.

———. "The Freedom to Trade." *The Economist* 141, no. 5113 (August 23, 1941): 220–22.

———. "The Principles of Trade." *The Economist* 141, no. 5124 (November 8, 1941): 553–54.

———. "The Problem of Stabilisation." *The Economist* 145, no. 5220 (September 11, 1943): 374.

———. "The Principles of Trade." *The Economist* 146, no. 5236 (January 1, 1944): 4–5.

———. "Balance of Payments." *The Economist* 146, no. 5237 (January 8, 1944): 32–34.

———. "Trade and Employment." *The Economist* 146, no. 5238 (January 15, 1944): 64–65.

———. "The Multilateral Approach." *The Economist* 146, no. 5239 (January 22, 1944): 94–96.

———. "Planned Expansion." *The Economist* 146, no. 5240 (January 29, 1944): 136–37.

———. "The Regional Solution." *The Economist* 146, no. 5241 (February 5, 1944): 169–70.

———. "Prices and Markets." *The Economist* 146, no. 5242 (February 12, 1944): 204–5.

———. "The New Liberalism." *The Economist* 146, no. 5243 (February 19, 1944): 232–33.

———. "The Joint Currency Scheme." *The Economist* 146, no. 5253 (April 29, 1944): 560–61.

———. "Trade and Employment." *The Economist* 146, no. 5257 (May 27, 1944): 701–2.

———. "Keynes on Gold and Sterling." *The Economist* 147, no. 5264 (July 15, 1944): 89.

———. "John Maynard Keynes." *The Economist* 150, no. 5357 (April 27, 1946): 657–58.

———. "The Law and the Prophet." *The Economist* 155, no. 5492 (November 27, 1948): 879.

Egle, W. "The Spreading of the Gold Points as a Means of Controlling the Movement of Foreign Short Term Balances." *The Journal of Political Economy* 47 (1939): 857–66.

Einaudi, Luigi: "Il Mio Piano Non E'Quello di Keynes." *La Riforma Sociale* 44 (1933): 129–42.

Einzig, P. "Gold Points and Central Banks." *The Economic Journal* 39 (1929): 379–87.

———. "Some New Features of Gold Movements." *The Economic Journal* 40 (1930): 56–63.

———. "International Monetary Fund—Is It a Gold Standard?" *The Banker* 71 (1944): 112–17.

———. "Economic Peace in our Time?" *The Banker* 77 (1946): 13–17.

———. "Lord Keynes—An Appreciation." *The Banker* 78 (1946): 80–81.

Elliott, G. A. "The Significance of the General Theory of Employment, Interest and Money." *The Canadian Journal of Economics and Political Science* 13 (1947): 372–78.

Ellis, H. S. "Notes on Recent Business Cycle Literature." *The Review of Economic Statistics* 20 (1938): 111–19.

Fellner, W., and H. Somers. "Alternative Monetary Approaches to Interest Theory." *The Review of Economic Statistics* 23 (1941): 43–48.

Gilbert, J. C. "The Present Position of the Theory of International Trade." *The Review of Economic Studies* 3 (1935): 18–34.

Grether, E. T. "The Means to Prosperity—A Review." *American Economic Review* 23 (1933): 347–49.

Haberler, G. "Currency Depreciation and the International Monetary Fund." *The Review of Economic Statistics* 26 (1944): 178–81.

———. "The Choice of Exchange Rates after the War." *American Economic Review* 35 (1945): 308–18.

———. "The Relevance of the Classical Theory under Modem Conditions." *American Economic Review* 49 (1954): 543–51.

Halm, G. N. "The International Monetary Fund." *The Review of Economic Statistics* 26 (1944): 170–74.

Hansen, A. H. "Mr. Keynes on Underemployment Equilibrium." *The Journal of Political Economy* 44 (1936): 667–86.

———. "A Brief Note on Fundamental Disequilibrium." *The Review of Economic Statistics* 26 (1944): 182–84.

———. "Dr. Burns on Keynesian Economics." *The Review of Economic Statistics* 29 (1947): 247–51.

Harris, S. E. "The Contributions of Bretton Woods and Some Unsolved Problems." *The Review of Economic Statistics* 26 (1944): 175–77.

Hawtrey, R. G. "Review of a Tract on Monetary Reform." *The Economic Journal* 34 (1924): 227–35.

Henderson, H. D. "The Case Against Returning to Gold." *Lloyd's Bank Limited Monthly Review* 6 (1935): 338–45.

Hicks, J. R. "Mr. Keynes' Theory of Employment." *The Economic Journal* 46 (1936): 238–53.

Hinshaw, R. "American Prosperity and the British Balance of Payments Problem." *The Review of Economic Statistics* 27 (1945): 1–9.

———. "Foreign Investment and American Employment." *American Economic Review* 36 (1946): 661–71.

Hirschman, A. O. "Devaluation and the Trade Balance." *Review of Economics and Statistics* 31 (1949): 50–53.

Hobson, J. A. "A World Economy." *The New Statesman and Nation* 1 (1931): 274–75.

Holden, G. R. "Mr. Keynes' Consumption Function and the Time Preference Postulate." *The Quarterly Journal of Economics* 52 (1938): 281–96.

———. "Mr. Keynes' Consumption Function: Rejoinder." *The Quarterly Journal of Economics* 52 (1938): 708.

Hoover, G. "Keynes and the Economic System." *The Journal of Political Economy* 56 (1948): 392–402.

Jastram, R, W., and E. S. Shaw. "Mr. Clark's Statistical Determination of the Multiplier." *The Economic Journal* 49 (1939): 358–65.

Johnson, A. "Keynes on Monetary Reform." *The New Republic* 37 (1924): 288.

Jones, Homer: "The Optimum Rate of Investment, the Savings Institutions and the Banks." *American Economic Review* 38 (1948): 321–39.

Kahn, R. F. "The Relation of Home Investment to Unemployment." *The Economic Journal* 41 (1931): 173–98.

Kaldor, N. "Stability and Full Employment." *The Economic Journal* 48 (1938): 642–58.

Kalecki, M. "Multilateralism and Full Employment." *The Canadian Journal of Economics and Political Science* 12 (1946): 322–27.

Klein, L. R. "Theories of Effective Demand Employment." *The Journal of Political Economy* 55 (1947): 108–31.

Knight, F. H. "Unemployment: And Mr. Keynes' Revolution in Economic Theory." *The Canadian Journal of Economics and Political Science* 3 (1937): 100–123.

Kurihara, K. "Foreign Investment and Full Employment." *The Journal of Political Economy* 55 (1947): 459–64.

Lachmann, L. M. "Notes on the Proposals for International Currency Stabilization." *The Review of Economic Statistics* 26 (1944): 184–91.

Lary, H. L. "The Domestic Effects of Foreign Investment." *American Economic Review* 36 (1946): 672–86.

Leontief, W. "The Fundamental Assumption of Mr. Keynes' Monetary Theory." *The Quarterly Journal of Economics* 51 (1936): 192–97.

Lerner, A. "Alternative Formulations of the Theory of Interest." *The Economic Journal* 48 (1938): 211–30.

———. "Saving Equals Investment." *The Quarterly Journal of Economics* 52 (1938): 297–309.

Lovasy, G. "International Trade under Imperfect Competition." *The Quarterly Journal of Economics* 55 (1941): 667–83.

Lutz, F. "The Outcome of the Saving-Investment Discussion." *The Quarterly Journal of Economics* 55 (1938): 588–614.

———. "Saving and Investment: Final Comment." *The Quarterly Journal of Economics* 53 (1939): 627–31.

Machlup, F. "Period Analysis and Multiplier Theory." *The Quarterly Journal of Economics* 54 (1939): 1–27.

———. "The Theory of Foreign Exchanges." *Economica* 6 (1939): 375–97; and *Economica* 7 (1940): 23–49.

Mackintosh, W. A. "Keynes as a Public Servant." *The Canadian Journal of Economics and Political Science* 13 (1947): 379–83.

Maffry, A. "Foreign Trade in the Post-War Economy." *The Survey of Current Business* (November 1944): 5–14

Marsh, D. B. "The Scope of the Theory of International Trade under Monopolistic Competition." *The Quarterly Journal of Economics* 56 (1942): 475–86.

Meek, Ronald L. "The Place of Keynes in the History of Economic Thought." *The Modern Quarterly* 6 (1950–1951): 34–51.

Metzler, L. "Underemployment Equilibrium in International Trade." *Econometrica* 10 (1942): 97–112.

The Midland Bank. "The Pound and the Dollar." *Monthly Review* (December 1938–January 1939): 1–3.

Mikesell, R. F. "The Role of the International Monetary Agreements in a World of Planned Economies." *The Journal of Political Economy* 55 (1947): 497–512.

Mitchell, A. A. "A Retrospect of Free Trade Doctrine: A Comment." *The Economic Journal* 35 (1925): 214–20.

Neisser, H. "Secondary Employment: Some Comments on R. F. Kahn's Formula." *The Review of Economic Statistics* 18 (1936): 24–30.

The New Republic. "Laissez-Faire vs. Nation Building." *The New Republic* 37 (1923): 84–85.

The New Statesman and Nation. "A Revenue Tariff—Correspondence." *The New Statesman and Nation* 1 (1943): 103–5.

Nicholson, J. S. "The Report on Indian Finance and Currency in Relation to the Gold Exchange Standard." *The Economic Journal* 24 (1914): 236–47.

O'Neil, H. C. "Men of Today." *Today and Tomorrow* 1 (1931): 130–35.

Paish, F. W. "Banking Policy and the Balance of International Payments." *Economica* 3 (1936): 404–22.

———. "The British Exchange Equalisation Fund." *Economica* 3 (1936): 78–83.

Pigou, A. C. "Mr. J, M. Keynes' General Theory of Employment, Interest and Money." *Economica* 3 (1936): 115–32.

Plumptre, A. F. W. "The Distribution of Outlay and the 'Multiplier' in the British Dominions." *Canadian Journal of Economics Political Science* 5 (1939): 363–72.

———. "Keynes in Cambridge." *The Canadian Journal of Economics and Political Science* 13 (1947): 366–71.

Polak, J. J. "Exchange Depreciation and International Monetary Stability." *The Review of Economic Statistics* 29 (1947): 173–82.

Reddaway, W. B. "The General Theory of Employment, Interest and Money." *The Economic Record* 12 (1936): 28–36.

———. "Special Obstacles to Full Employment in a Wealthy Community." *The Economic Journal* 47 (1937): 297–307.

Rist, C. "Keynes: The Means to Prosperity." *The Economic Journal* 43 (1933): 269–71.

Robbins, L. "A Reply to Mr. Keynes." *The New Statesman and Nation* 1 (1931): 98–100.

———. "The Problem of Stabilization." *Lloyd's Bank Limited Monthly Review* 6 (1935): 207–18.

Robertson, D. H. "Keynes: Economic Consequences of the Peace" *The Economic Journal* 30 (1920): 77–84.

———. "Mr. Keynes' Theory of Money." *The Economic Journal* 41 (1931): 395–411.

———. "Some Notes on Mr. Keynes' General Theory of Employment." *The Quarterly Journal of Economics* 51 (1936): 168–91.

———. "Changes in International Demand and the Terms of Trade." *The Quarterly Journal of Economics* 52 (1938): 539–40.

———. "The Future of International Trade." *The Economic Journal* 48 (1938): 1–14.

———. "Mr. Keynes and Finance." *The Economic Journal* 48 (1938): 314–20.

———. "Mr. Clark and the Foreign Trade Multiplier." *The Economic Journal* 49 (1939): 354–56.

———. "The Post-War Monetary Plans." *The Economic Journal* 53 (1943): 352–60.

Robinson, Austin. "John M. Keynes." *The Economic Journal* 107 (1947): 1–68.

Robinson, J. "The Theory of Money and the Analysis of Output." *The Review of Economic Studies* 1 (1933): 22–26.

———. "Official Papers. The U.S. in the World Economy." *The Economic* Journal 54 (1944): 430–37.

Roos, Charles F. "The Demand for Investment Goods." *American Economic Review* 38 (1948): 311–20.

Rueff, J. "The Fallacies of Lord Keynes' General Theory." *Quarterly Journal of Economics* 61 (1947): 343–67.

Salant, W. S. "The Domestic Effects of Capital Export under the Point IV Program." *American Economic Review* 40 (1950): 495–510.

Samuel, A. M. "Has Foreign Investment Paid?" *The Economic Journal* 40 (1930): 64–68.

Samuelson, P. A. "Interactions between the Multiplier Analysis and the Principle of Acceleration." *The Review of Economic Statistics* 21 (1939): 75–78.

Schumpeter, J. A. "Keynes: Essays in Biography." Review. *The Economic Journal* 43 (1933): 652–57.

Shaw, E. S. "A Note on the Multiplier." *The Review of Economic Studies* 3 (1936): 60–64.

Singer, Kurt: "Recollections of Keynes." *The Australian Quarterly* 21 (1949): 49–59.

Smith, J. C. "Economic Nationalism and International Trade." *The Economic Journal* 45 (1935): 619–49.

Smithies, A. "Full Employment in a Free Society." *American Economic Review* 35 (1945): 355–67.

———. "The Multiplier." *American Economic Review* 38 (1948): 299–305.

———. "Reflections on the Work and Influence of John M. Keynes." *The Quarterly Journal of Economics* 65 (1951): 578–601.

Somers, H. M. "Monetary Policy and the Theory of Interest." *The Quarterly Journal of Economics* 55 (1941): 488–507.

Soule, C. "Mr. Keynes' Recipe for Stabilization." *The Week* 66 (1931): 360–61

Stamp, J. "Mr. Keynes' Treatise on Money." *The Economic Journal* 41 (1931): 241–49.
———. "The Report of the Macmillan Committee." *The Economic Journal* 41 (1931): 424–35.
Swan, T. W. "Economic Interpretation of J. M. Keynes." *The Australian Quarterly* 11 (1939): 62–70.
Tarshis, L. "An Exposition of Keynesian Economics." *American Economic Review* 38 (1948): 261–90.
Taussig, F. W. "Great Britain's Trade Terms After 1900." *The Economic Journal* 35 (1925): 1–10.
———. "Employment and the National Dividend." *The Quarterly Journal of Economics* 51 (1936): 198–03.
Timlin, M. "John M. Keynes." *The Canadian Journal of Economics and Political Science* 13 (1947): 363–65.
Viner, J. "Mr. Keynes on the Causes of Unemployment—A Review." *The Quarterly Journal of Economics* 51 (1936): 147–67.
———. "International Finance in the Postwar World." *The Journal of Political Economy* 55 (1947): 97–107.
Von Hayek, F. A. "The Pure Theory of Money: Rejoinder." *Economica* 11 (1931): 398–403.
———. "Reflections on the Pure Theory of Money." *Economica* 11 (1931): 270–95.
———. "Reflections on the Pure Theory of Money of Mr. John M. Keynes—Part II." *Economica* 12 (1932): 22–44.
Warming, J. "International Difficulties Arising out of the Financing of Public Works during Depression." *The Economic Journal* 42 (1932): 211–24.
The Week. "On Keynes' Revenue Tariff." *The Week* 66 (1931): 190–91.
Whale, P. B. "International Trade in the Absence of an International Standard." *Economica* 3 (1936): 24–38.
Williams, J. H. "International Monetary Plans." *Foreign Affairs* 23 (1944): 38–56.
———. "An Appraisal of Keynesian Economics." *American Economic Review* 38, no. 2 (1948): 373–90.
Winston, R. P. "Does Trade 'Follow the Dollar'." *American Economic Review* 17 (1927): 458–77.
Wright, D. M. "The Future of Keynesian Economics." *American Economic Review* 35 (1945): 284–307.

GENERAL WORKS

Abbati, Alfred H. *Lord Keynes' Central Thesis and the Concept of Unclaimed Wealth.* Cardiff, William Lewis, 1947.
American Economic Association. *Readings in the Theory of International Trade,* edited by H. S. Ellis and W. Metzler. Philadelphia: Blakiston, 1949.
Angell, J. W. *Theory of International Prices.* Cambridge, Harvard University Press, 1926.
———. *Investment and Business Cycles.* New York: McGraw-Hill, 1941.
Balogh, T. "The International Aspects of Full Employment." *The Economics of Full Employment—Six Studies in Applied Economics.* Oxford: Basil Blackwell, 1945.
———. *Studies in Financial Organization,* Cambridge: Cambridge University Press, 1947.
———. *Dollar Crisis, Causes and Cure.* Oxford: Basil Blackwell, 1949.
Banerji, B. *A Guide to the Study of Keynesian Economics.* Calcutta: N. N. Dey, 1951.
Bell, J. F. *A History of Economic Thought.* New York: Ronald Press, 1953.
Beveridge, W. H. *Causes and Cures of Unemployment,* London: Longmans, Green, 1931.
———. *Full Employment in a Free Society.* London: George Allen and Unwin, 1944.
Beveridge, W. H., et al. *Tariffs: The Case Examined.* London: Longmans, Green, 1932.
Bidwell, Percy W. *A Commercial Policy for the United Nations.* New York: The Committee on International Economic Policy, 1945.
Bloomfield, A. I. "Foreign Exchange Rate Theory and Policy." In *The New Economics,* edited by S. Harris. New York: A. A. Knopf, 1947, 293–314.

Brenier, Henri. *The Revision of the Treaty of Versailles*. Marseilles: Comite' de Relations Internationales, 1922.

British Treasury. *Proposals for an International Clearing Union*, Cmd. 6437. London: H. M. Stationery Office, 1943. Reprinted in *The New Economics*, edited by S. Harris. New York: A. A. Knopf, 1947, 342–58.

Buchanan, N. S. *International Investment and Domestic Welfare*. New York: Henry Holt, 1945.

Buchanan, N. S., and F. A. Lutz. *Rebuilding the World Economy*. New York: The Twentieth Century Fund, 1947.

Burns, Emile. *Mr. Keynes Answered*. London: Lawrence and Wishart, 1940.

Butlin, S. J. *John M. Keynes* Sydney: The Economic Society of Australia and New Zealand, 1946.

Cassel, G. *Money and Foreign Exchange after 1914*. London: Constable, 1922.

———. *Postwar Monetary Stabilization*. New York: Colombia University Press, 1928.

———. *The Crisis in the World's Monetary System*, 2nd edition. London: Oxford University Press, 1932.

———. *The Downfall of the Gold Standard*. London: Oxford University Press, 1936.

Chang, Tse Chun. *Cyclical Movements in the Balance of Payments*. Cambridge: Cambridge University Press, 1951.

Clark, C. *Conditions of Economic Progress*. London: Macmillan, 1940.

———. "Principles of Public Finance and Taxation." The Third Arthur C. Moore Research Lecture. Brisbane: Federal Institute of Accountants, 1950.

Clark, C., and J. G. Crawford. *The National Income of Australia*. London: Angus and Robertson, 1938.

Clarks, C. *The Control of Investment*. London: The New Fabian Research Bureau, 1933.

———. *National Income and Outlay*. London: Macmillan, 1937.

Committee on Finance and Industry (Macmillan). *Report of the Committee on Finance and Industry*. Cmd. 3897. London: H. M. Stationery Office, 1931.

Committee on International Economic Policy. *World Trade and Employment*. New York: The Committee on International Economic Policy, 1944.

Committee on International Policy of the National Planning Association. *The States of Bretton Woods*. Washington, D.C.: National Planning Association, 1945.

Condliffe, J. B. *The Foreign Economic Policy of the U.S.* Memorandum No. 11. New Haven, CT: Yale Institute of International Studies, 1944.

———. *Exchange Stabilization*. New York: The Committee on International Economic Policy, 1945.

Corbett, P. E. *The Dumbarton Oaks Plan*. Memorandum No. 13. New Haven, CT: Yale Institute of International Studies, 1944.

Cortney, Philip: *The Economic Munich*. New York: Philosophical Library, 1949.

Crawford, F. W. *International, Monetary Developments between the First and Second World Wars*. Washington, D.C.: Finance Dept., Chamber of Commerce of the U.S., 1944.

———. *Proposed United Nations Bank for Reconstruction and Development*. Washington, D.C.: Finance Dept., Chamber of Commerce of the U.S., 1944.

———. *World Currency Stabilization Proposals*. Washington, D.C.: Finance Dept., Chamber of Commerce of the U.S., 1944.

———. *The Bretton Woods Proposals*. Washington D.C.: Finance Dept., Chamber of The U.S., 1945.

———. *Financial Agreement with the U.S.* Washington, D.C.: Finance Dept., Chamber of Commerce of the U.S., 1946

Crossland, C. A. R. *Britain's Economic Problem*. London: Jonathon Cape, 1953.

Currie, L. "Some Theoretical and Practical Implications of J. M. Keynes' General Theory." In *The Economic Doctrines of John M. Keynes*. New York: national Industrial Conference Board, 1938, 15–27.

Daniels, G. W., and H. Campion. "The Relative Importance of British Export Trade." Special Memorandum no. 41. The Executive Committee of the London and Cambridge Economic Service, August, 1935.

Dillard, D. *The Economics of John Maynard Keynes*. New York: Prentice-Hall, 1948.

Eaton, John. *Marx Against Keynes*. London: Lawrence and Wishart, 1951.

Edie, L. S. "The Future of the Gold Standard." *Gold and Monetary Stabilization* (Harris Foundation Lectures). Chicago: University of Chicago Press, 1932.

————. "The Practical Importance of Keynes' Doctrine." In *The Economic Doctrines of John M. Keynes*. New York: National Industrial Conference Board, 1938, 73–78.

Einzig, P. *The Tragedy of the Pound*. London: Kegan Paul, French, Trubner, 1932.

————. *The Comedy of the Pound*. London: Kegan Paul, French, Trubner, 1933.

————. *The Future of Gold*. London: Macmillan, 1934.

Ellis, H. S. "Bilateralism and the Future of International Trade." *Essays in International Finance*, no. 5. Princeton: International Finance Section, Princeton University, 1945.

————. *A Survey of Contemporary Economics*. Philadelphia: Blakiston, 1948.

Ellsworth, P. T. *International Economics*. New York: Macmillan, 1938.

————. *The International Economy*. New York: Macmillan, 1950.

Enke, S., and V. Salera. *International Economics*, 2nd edition. New York: Prentice-Hall, 1951.

Federal Reserve Board. *Prices, Wages and Employment*. Postwar Studies no. 4. Washington, D.C.: U.S. Federal Reserve Board, 1945.

Feis, H. *The Changing Pattern of International Economic Affairs*. New York: Harper Bros, 1940.

Findlay, R. M. *Britain Under Protection*. London: George Allen Unwin, 1934.

Gayer, A. D. *Monetary Policy and Economic Stabilization*. London: A. and C. Black, 1935.

————. *Public Works in Prosperity and Depression*. New York: N. B. E. R., 1935.

————. *The Lessons of Monetary Experience*. New York: Farrar and Rinehart, 1937.

Giuffre', A. *Studi Keynesiani*. Milano: Instituto di Economica e Finanza della Facotta' Giuridica di Roma, 1953.

Graham, F. D. "Fundamentals of International Monetary Policy." In *Essays in International Finance* no. 2. Princeton: International Finance Section, Princeton University, Autumn 1943.

Greidanus, Tjardus. *The Development of Keynes' Economic Theories*. London: P. S. King and Son, 1939.

Gulick, R. L. *Imports—The Gain from Trade*. New York: The Committee on International Economic Policy, 1946.

Haberler, G. "Money and the Business Cycle." In *Gold and Monetary Stabilization* (Harris Foundation Lectures). Chicago: University of Chicago Press, 1932.

————. *Theory of International Trade*. London: William Hodge, 1936.

————. *Prosperity and Depression*, 3rd edition. Geneva: League of Nations, 1941.

————. *Quantitative Trade Controls—Their Causes and Nature*. Geneva, League of Nations, 1943.

Hajela, Prayag Das. *Keynes' General Theory and Theories of Trade Cycle and Foreign Exchange*. Allahabad: Pothishala, 1952.

Halm, G. N. *Monetary Theory*, 2nd edition. Philadelphia: Blackiston, 1946.

Hansen, A. H. *Full Recovery or Stagnation?* New York: W. W. Norton, 1938.

————. *After the War—Full Employment*. Washington, D.C.: National Resources Planning Board, 1942.

————. *International Monetary and Financial Programs*. New York: Council on Foreign Relations, 1944.

————. *America's Role in the World Economy*. New York: W. W. Norton, 1945.

————. *Economic Policy and Full Employment*. New York: McGraw-Hill, 1947.

————. *A Guide to Keynes*. New York: McGraw-Hill, 1953.

Hansen, A. H., and R. V. Clemence. *Readings in Business Cycles and National Income*. New York: W. W. Norton, 1953.

Harris, S. E. *Monetary Problems of the British Empire*. New York: Macmillan, 1931.

————. *Postwar Economic Problems*. New York: McGraw-Hill, 1943.

————. *Economic Reconstruction*. New York: McGraw-Hill, 1945.

————. "International Economics: Introduction." In *The New Economics*, edited by S. Harris. New York: A. A. Knopf, 1947, 245–63.

————, ed. *The New Economics*. New York: A. A. Knopf, 1947.

———. *John M. Keynes, Economist and Policy Maker*. New York: Charles Scribner's Sons, 1955.

Harrod, R. F. *The Trade Cycle*. Oxford: Oxford University Press, 1936.

———. *International Economics*, 2nd edition. London: Cambridge University Press, 1939.

———. *Towards a Dynamic Economics*. London: Macmillan, 1949.

———. *The Life of John Maynard Keynes*. London: Macmillan, 1951.

———. *Economic Essays*. London: Macmillan, 1952.

Hart, A. G. *Money. Debt and Economic Activity*, 2nd edition. New York: Prentice-Hall, 1953.

Hawtrey, R. G. *Monetary Reconstruction*. New York: Longmans, Green, 1923.

———. *Art of Central Banking*. London: Longmans, Green, 1932.

———. *Capital and Employment*. London: Longmans, Green, 1937.

———. *The Gold Standard in Theory and Practice*. London: Longmans, Green, 1939.

———. *Bretton Woods for Better or Worse*. London: Longmans, Green, 1946.

———. *The Balance of Payments and the Standard of Living*. London: Royal Institute of International Affairs, Oxford University Press, 1950.

———. *Currency and Credit*, 4th edition. London: Longmans, Green, 1950.

Heilperin, M. A. *International Monetary Organization*. Geneva: International Institute of Intellectual Cooperation, League of Nations, 1939.

———. *International Monetary Economics*. London: Longmans Green, 1939.

———. *International Monetary Reconstruction: The Bretton Woods Agreements*. New York: American Enterprise Association, 1945.

———. *The Trade of Nations*, 2nd edition. New York: Alfred A. Knopf, 1952.

Hinshaw, R. "Keynesian Commercial Policy." In *The New Economics*, edited by S. Harris. New York: A. A. Knopf, 1947, 315–522.

Hobson, J. A. *International Trade*. London: Methuen, 1904.

———. *The Economics of Unemployment*. London: George Allen and Unwin, 1922.

Hoover, C. B. *International Trade and Domestic Employment*. New York: McGraw-Hill, 1945.

Hoselitz, B. F. *British, Trade Policy and the U.S.* Memorandum no. 5. New Haven, CT: Yale University Institute of International Studies, 1943.

Hutt, W. H. *The Theory of Idle Resources*. London: Jonathon Cape, 1939.

Institute of Statistics, Oxford University. *The Economics of Full Employment—Six Studies in Applied Economics*. Oxford: Basil Blackwell, 1945.

International Monetary Fund. *Balance of Payments Manual*. Washington, D.C.: International Monetary Fund, 1950.

———. *International Financial News Survey*. Washington. D.C. Volume 5, nos. 1–50 (July 1952–June 1953); volume 6, nos. 1–50 (July 1953–June 1954).

Irving Trust Co. *International Financial Stabilization—A Symposium*. New York: Irving Trust Company, 1944.

James, Cyril P. "Some Practical Effects of the Doctrines Suggested by Mr. John M. Keynes Prior to 1930." *The Economic Doctrines of John M. Keynes*. New York: National Industrial Conference Board, 1938, 1–11.

Jenks, L. H. *The Migration of British Capital to 1875*. New York: A. A. Knopf, 1927.

Kahn, Alfred E. *Great Britain in the World Economy*. New York: Columbia University Press, 1946.

Kindleberger, C. *International Economics*. Homesward: Richard D. Irwin, 1953.

Klein, L. R. *The Keynesian Revolution*. New York: Macmillan, 1947.

Kriz, M. A. "Postwar International Lending." *Essays in International Finance* no. 8. Princeton: International Finance Section, Princeton University, Spring 1947.

Lehmann, Fritz. "The Role, of the Multiplier and the Interest Rate in Keynes General Theory." In *The Economic Doctrines of John M Keynes*. New York: National Industrial Conference Board, 1938, 52–72.

Loftua, P. C. *A Main Cause of Unemployment*. London: Sir Isaac Pitman and Sons, 1932.

———. *Money and National Reconstruction*. London: Economic Reform Club and Institute, 1941.

Lutz, F. "International Monetary Mechanisms—The Keynes and White Proposals." *Essays in International Finance* no. 1. Princeton: International Finance Section, Princeton University, July 1943.

Machlup, F. *International Trade and the Foreign Trade Multiplier*. Philadelphia: Blakiston, 1943.

Macmillan, H. *The Next Step*. London: E. T. Heron, 1933.

———. *Reconstruction*. London: Macmillan, 1933.

Mandelbaum, K. "A Experiment in Full Employment Controls in the German Economy, 1933–1938." *The Economics of Full Employment—Six Studies in Applied Economics*. Oxford: Basil Blackwell, 1945.

Mantoux, Paul. *The Carthaginian Peace*. New York: Charles Scribner's Sons, 1952.

Martin, P. W. *An International Monetary Agreement*. London: The New Fabian Research Bureau, 1933.

Meade, J. E. *Public Works in their International Aspect*. London: The New Fabian Research Bureau, 1933.

———. *An Introduction to Economic Analysis and Policy*, 2nd edition. London: Oxford University Press, 1937.

———. *A Geometry of International Trade*. London: George Allen and Unwin, 1951.

Metzler, L. A. "The Theory of International Trade." In *A Survey of Contemporary Economics*, edited by H. S. Ellis. Philadelphia: Blakiston, 1948, 210–54.

Metzler, L., et al. *Income, Employment and Public Policy*. New York: W. W. Norton, 1948.

Metzler, L., R. Triffin, and G. Haberler. *International Monetary Policies*. Postwar Economic Studies no. 7. Washington, D.C.: Board of Governors, Federal Reserve System, 1947.

Mikesell, R. F. *Foreign Exchange in the Postwar World*. New York: The Twentieth Century Fund, 1954.

Miller, David H. "The Economic Consequences of the Peace." Address delivered to the League of Nations Association, New York, 1920.

Mosak, J. L. *General Equilibrium Theory in International Trade*. Bloomington: Cowles Commission for Research in Economics, 1944.

Musgrave, R. A. "Fiscal Policy, Stability and Full Employment." In *Public Finance and Full Employment* (Postwar Economic Studies no. 3). Washington, D.C.: Board of Governors of the Federal Reserve System, 1945, 1–21.

National Planning Associations. *Britain's Trade in the Postwar World*. Washington, D.C.: National Planning Association, 1941.

Neisser, H. *Some International Aspects of the Business Cycle*. Philadelphia: University of Pennsylvania Press, 1936.

Nicol, Finlay. *Prosperity By All Means*. Edinburgh: The Scots Free Press, 1933.

Nurkse, R. "Conditions of International Monetary Equilibrium." In *Essays in International Finance* no. 4. Princeton: International Finance Section, Princeton University, 1945.

———. "Domestic and International Equilibrium." In *The New Economics*, edited by S. Harris. New York: A. A. Knopf, 1947, 264–92.

Ohlin, B. *Interregional and International Trade*. Cambridge: Harvard University Press, 1933.

———. *The Problem of Employment Stabilization*. New York: Columbia University Press, 1949.

Pierson, J. H. G. *Full Employment*. New Haven, CT: Yale University Press 1941.

———. *Full Employment and Free Enterprise*. Washington, D.C.: Public Affairs Press, 1947.

Pigou, A. C. *Economic Science in Relation to Practice*. London: Macmillan, 1908.

———. *Memorials of Alfred Marshall*. London: Macmillan, 1925.

———. *Economics in Practice*. London: Macmillan, 1935.

———. *Employment and Equilibrium*. London: Macmillan, 1949.

Pigou, A. C., and C. Clark. "The Economic Position of Great Britain." Special Memorandum no. 43. London: London and Cambridge Economic Service, April 1936.

Polanyl, Michael. *Full Employment and Free Trade*, 2nd edition. Cambridge: Cambridge University Press, 1948.

Political and Economic Planning. *Britain and World Trade*. London: Political and Economic Planning, 1947.

Research Committee of the C. E. D. *The Bretton Woods Proposals*. New York: Committee for Economic Development, 1944.

———. *International Trade, Foreign Investment and Domestic Employment*. New York: Committee for Economic Development, 1945.

Robertson, D. H. *Essays in Monetary Theory*. Westminster: P. S. King and Son, 1940.

Robinson, J. *Essays in the Theory of Employment*. London: Macmillan, 1937.

———. *Introduction to the Theory of Employment*. London: Macmillan, 1937.

———. "Proposals for an International Clearing Union." In *The New Economics*, edited by S. Harris. New York: A. A. Knopf, 1947, 343–58.

Rostow, N. W. "Explanations of the Great Depression." In *British Economy of the Nineteenth Century*. London: Oxford University Press, 1948, 145–60.

Rowse, Alfred L. *Mr. Keynes and the Labour Movement*. London: Macmillan, 1936.

Salant, W. A. "Foreign Trade Policy in the Business Cycle." In *Public Policy*, volume 2. Cambridge: Harvard University Press, 1941.

Salter, A. "Foreign Investment." In *Essays in International Finance $12*. Princeton: International Finance Section, Princeton University, 1951.

Saulnier, Raymond J. *Contemporary Monetary Theory*. New York: Columbia University Press, 1938.

Schumpeter, J. A. *Ten Great Economists from Marx to Keynes*. New York: Oxford University Press, 1951.

Shackle, G. L. S. *Expectations. Investment and Income*. London: Oxford University Press, 1938.

Siegfried, A. *England's Crisis*. London: Jonathon Cape, 1933.

Staley, E. *World Economic Development—Effects on Advanced Industrial Countries*. Montreal: International Labour Office. 1944.

Stevens, R. *The New Economics and World Peace*. Philadelphia: The Pacifist Research Bureau, 1944.

Swanson, E. S., and E. P. Schmidt. *Economic Stagnation or Progress*. New York: McGraw-Hill, 1946.

Taussig, F. W. *Selected Readings in International Trade and Tariff Problems*. New York: Ginn, 1921.

———. *International Trade*. New York: Macmillan, 1927.

Taylor, A. E. *The 'Ten per Cent' Fallacy*. New York: The Committee on International Economic Policy, 1945.

Terborgh, G. *The Bogey of Economic Maturity*. Chicago: Machinery and Allied Products Institute, 1945.

Timlin, M. F. *Keynesian Economics*. Toronto: University of Toronto Press, 1942.

Tucker, R. S. "Mr. Keynes' Theories Considered in the Light of Experience." In *The Economic Doctrines of John M. Keynes*. New York: National Industrial Conference Board, 1938, 28–51.

U.S. Department of State. *Proposals for Expansion of World Trade and Employment*. Washington, D.C.: U.S. Government Printing Office, 1945.

———. *Articles of Agreement of the International Monetary Fund*. Washington, D.C.: U.S. Government Printing Office, 1946.

U.S. Department of the Treasury. *Financial Agreement Between the Government of the United States and the United Kingdom*. Washington, D.C.: U.S. Government Printing Office, 1946.

Viner, J. "International Aspects of the Gold Standard." In *Gold and Monetary Stabilization* (Harris Foundation Lectures). Chicago: University of Chicago Press, 1932.

———. *Studies in the Theory of International Trade*. New York: Harper and Brothers, 1937.

———. *Trade Relations between Free-Market and Controlled Economies*. Geneva: League of Nations, 1943.

———. *Two Plans for International Monetary Stabilization*. Memorandum no. 2. New Haven, CT: Yale Institute of International Studies, 1943.

———. *International Economics*. Glencoe: The Free Press, 1951.

Von Hayek, P. A. *Monetary Theory and the Trade Cycle*. London: Jonathon Cape, 1933.

———. *Monetary Nationalism and International Stability*. London: Longmans, Green, 1937.

Whale, P. B. *International Trade*. London: Thornton Butterworth, 1952.

Whidden, Howard P. *Preferences and Discriminations in International Trade*. New York: The Committee on International Economic Policy, 1945.

Whittlesey, C. R. *International Monetary Issues: The Art of Central Banking*. New York: McGraw-Hill, 1937.

Williams, J. H. "Monetary Stability and the Gold Standard." In *Gold and Monetary Stabilization* (Harris Foundation Lectures). Chicago: University of Chicago Press, 1932.

―――. *Postwar Monetary Plans*. Oxford: Basil Blackwell, 1949.

Wilson, J. S. G. *Lord Keynes and the Development of Modern Economic Theory*. Sydney: The Economic Society of Australia and New Zealand, 1946.

Wright, Q. *Unemployment as a World Problem*. Chicago: University of Chicago Press, 1931.

Index

About the Author

Joseph Cammarosano has combined two careers over this lifetime: one in public service and the other in higher education. A veteran of World War II, he has served as a U.S. Customs Inspector, as a fiscal economist in the U.S. Bureau of the Budget, and the NY State Department of Taxation and Finance. While teaching, he has served as a consultant to the U.S. Department of Commerce, the Department of Labor, and the Department of Health, Education, and Welfare as well as a number of state and local agencies, including membership on New York City's Independent Budget Committee. In academe, he has served as a professor of economics, vice president for finance, and executive vice president of Fordham University where he has spent more than fifty years. As a youth, he aspired to becoming a shortstop for the New York Yankees, but, unfortunately, had trouble with the curve ball. As a result, his baseball journey left him short of his destination, as the bus left him off, instead, at Fordham's Rose Hill Campus in the Bronx, just a short distance removed from Yankee Stadium.

CPSIA information can be obtained at www.ICGtesting.com
Printed in the USA
BVOW07*1040151213

338972BV00002B/2/P